About the author

David Leser was born in Montreal, Canada, in 1956 and raised in Sydney. He is a multi-award-winning journalist who has worked in Australia, North America, the Middle East, Europe and Asia for the past thirty-five years.

He began his career on the *Daily Telegraph* in 1979 and has since worked as a feature writer for the *Australian*, the *Sydney Morning Herald*, *HQ* magazine, the *Bulletin*, *Good Weekend*, the *Australian Women's Weekly*, Italian and German *Vanity Fair*, *Newsweek* and *The Daily Beast*. He has also worked as a correspondent in Washington, D.C., and Jerusalem.

David is the author of five books, including *Bronwyn Bishop: A Woman in Search of Power* (1994), *The Whites of Their Eyes* (1999), *Somebody Save Me* (2002), *Dames and Divas* (2006) and *A View from the Lake: The Egon Zehnder Story* (2014). He is also editor of *Paul Kelly: The Essays* (2013) and executive producer of the 2012 award-winning documentary *Paul Kelly: Stories of Me*.

He has two daughters, Jordan, a singer-songwriter, and Hannah, a photographer, and lives in Sydney.

TO BEGIN TO KNOW

Walking in the Shadows of My Father

DAVID LESER

ALLEN&UNWIN
SYDNEY·MELBOURNE·AUCKLAND·LONDON

Author's note

This is not an entirely original piece of work, unless plagiarising oneself constitutes a form of originality. A few of the passages that follow have been lifted from some of my previous feature articles and published anthologies. Apologies to the purists.

First published in 2014
Copyright © David Leser 2014

Allen & Unwin
83 Alexander Street
Crows Nest NSW 2065
Australia
Phone: (61 2) 8425 0100
Email: info@allenandunwin.com
Web: www.allenandunwin.com

Cataloguing-in-Publication details are available
from the National Library of Australia
www.trove.nla.gov.au

ISBN 978 1 76011 033 8

Set in 12/16 pt Minion by Post Pre-press Group, Australia
Printed and bound in Australia by Griffin Press

10 9 8 7 6 5 4 3 2 1

To my beloved daughters, Jordan and Hannah

CONTENTS

THE DESERT PLACES

Soon you will have forgotten all things; soon all things will have forgotten you . . .

Marcus Aurelius

I began this book out of love and disappointment for my father. I had wanted him to write his own story because I thought that if he could enter into a new dialogue with himself, he'd not only get to make sense of his life in new ways, he might even provide inspiration to others.

Filled with my own presumptions, I felt that my father's later life might have been more gratifying, less disappointing to him, had he been less guarded, better able to investigate his inner needs. That was my wish for him, but not his own wish for himself.

As with many men of his generation, and particularly men whose sense of the world was shaped by the horrors of Nazi Germany, my father had no real desire to probe what Robert Frost referred to as the 'desert places', the dark psychological regions of his own heart. He was afraid, I think, of that interior country, as I suspect we all are.

My father, Bernard Leser, left Germany as a boy on the eve of World War II and then, twenty years later, in 1959, launched Australian *Vogue* magazine, no small accomplishment when you consider that, at the time, the most stylish thing in Australia was probably the continental supper.

From 1976, he then went on to run British Condé Nast Publications, putting him in charge of magazines like *Vogue*, *Brides* and *House and Garden*. During that same period, he bought *Tatler* and *World of Interiors*, and, forty years after he'd left Germany, set up German *Vogue*, before being invited in 1987 to become president of Condé Nast Publications Inc, the magazine empire that included in its stable *Vogue*, *House and Garden*, *Vanity Fair*, the *New Yorker*, *Mademoiselle*, *Glamour*, *GQ*, *Condé Nast Traveler*, *Architectural Digest* and *Self*.

This put him behind the wheel of a fabulous global corporation, in the next office along, at Condé Nast's New York headquarters, from the Sun King himself, S.I. (Si) Newhouse Jr, the secretive, enigmatic publishing billionaire who had amassed one of the largest private fortunes in the world.

My father became the regent in the Newhouse Kingdom at a time when its magazines were rewriting the rules of American journalism, establishing a new celebrity culture throughout the English-speaking world.

By any measure it was an extraordinary career, and testament to the powers of charm, chance and the uncanny ability some people have to reinvent themselves.

I wanted him to write his story because it was a good story, possibly a great story, and, besides which, I could see his purpose faltering. After all his years on the mountain top, it seemed, at least from where I was standing, that he had lost his footing, and his view. This book would be a new project, a new routine, a new reason to get out of bed in the morning I told myself, and him.

But he never began writing, nor looked like doing so. In his late seventies and into his eighties he was finding greater companionship with the books that other men had written, and this is where he's stayed, in a way, for the past decade or so, reliving his glory days with increasing wistfulness, buried inside another great man's biography, a double Scotch on the rocks often by his side.

So about ten years ago I offered to write his story for him, and although he deliberated on this for some time, it was an offer I believe he welcomed more than he cared to admit. He was proud of his achievements, proud of what he'd made of his life; and deep down I think he was both flattered and warmed by my gesture of filial devotion.

I began gingerly at first, and then with a certain gusto, wading into his years in Germany between the flames of two world wars, then into his early life in New Zealand. I stalled somewhere across the Tasman Sea, at the point in the narrative shortly before he arrived in Australia in 1947 with five pounds in his pocket. I could see the vast stretches I was going to have to cover if I was ever to do him justice—the sharp trajectory of a damaged life turned privileged and successful, sweeping across four continents, from Australia to Canada to London, back to Australia, over to London again, onto Europe and then New York, with a great flourishing of trumpets.

I baulked at the task. I couldn't help but wonder why, at age forty-six, after a lifetime spent trying to get out from under my father's considerable shadow, I would now deliberately place myself right back in it. Why would I spend years writing about my father's life, giving him all of my rapt attention, when I now had the opportunity—the duty even—to live my own? Wouldn't that be tantamount to dimming my own light in order to brighten his?

It all came to a head in London in 2005, when I met him for a few days on my way to Los Angeles to interview June Newton, the Australian-born widow of the late fashion photographer,

Helmut Newton. It was one of those moments of confluence that had often occurred between us since I'd first become a journalist, writing about a person my father happened to know. He and Helmut Newton had both ended up in Australia after fleeing Berlin on the eve of World War II. Newton had become one of the first photographers to work on Australian *Vogue*.

My father had also arrived in London from Sydney, but while I was jetlagged he embarked with vigour on a relentless social schedule—breakfasts, lunches, afternoon teas, pre-dinner cocktails, after-dinner nightcaps. The Garrick Club. Annabel's. Harry's Bar. Editors, publishers, old colleagues, new chums. My father was eighty. I was forty-nine. I could barely keep up.

One evening in his hotel room I told him I didn't think I could continue to write his life story. I was too weighed down by the demands of writing feature stories, trying to help raise two young daughters, dealing with sometimes crippling insomnia, grappling with the politics of a modern marriage.

I felt exhausted, besieged by doubts, undone by the thought of more travel. 'Dad, I just don't think I can do it,' I said. 'I don't have the time and I'm not sure now that I want to write about you.' And then, for the first time I could remember since I was a little boy, I began to cry in front of him.

I apologised for my failure, for having let him down. I told him I didn't feel worthy of the trust he had bestowed upon me, that I didn't think I was equipped for the task.

'It's alright,' he said, putting his hand on my shoulder, then hugging me. 'Just drop it. You've got enough on your plate.'

I did have enough on my plate, but the truth was I also had too many contradictory emotions swirling through me to write his story in a way my father would have wanted it written. I'd spent my working life looking for—and uncovering—other people's strengths and fragilities, whereas my father had spent most of his life promoting the former and concealing the latter. He had always possessed purpose and ambition. He had woken early and gone to bed late, often in a boozy haze of work pressure and conviviality, and in the hours between had presided over the most elite privately owned magazine publishing company on earth. This had given him access and status beyond the reach of most ordinary mortals. It had put him in regular contact with the most talked about magazine editors and newspaper proprietors in the world; placed him at dinner tables and cocktail parties with kings, queens and fashion empresses; provided him with hotel suites and first-class travel; surrounded him with the best and brightest, and also, of course, a coterie of flatterers and lickspittles. The list of eminent people he knew was endless and endlessly fascinating.

Bernard Leser had been 'the Man from Condé Nast', who'd naturally come to see his own identity as being inseparable from the company he served. 'We at Condé Nast have always . . .' he would often declaim, as though the world really was an Edwardian play of *Upstairs Downstairs* dimensions.

My father had a more than healthy ego, but people loved him. They loved his magnetism and enthusiasm, his boundless energy. ('He invented the thirty-six-hour day,' one of his Australian colleagues once remarked.) They loved his tenacity, his panache, his salesmanship and his ability to motivate. Above all, they loved his kindness, the way he thought about people, put them together, sent them encouraging notes, boosted their faith in themselves, mentored them for bigger and better things. This was his lifeblood—human relations, the personal touch—and these instincts flowed through him like a mighty river, propelling him around the globe, feeding his sense of self, filling him with confidence and good humour, giving him a sense that life really was a party with his name on every list. Or, at least, the important ones.

By 2002, however, eight years after handing over the reins in New York, he'd begun to show signs of depression. We were all concerned for him. Many of his friends had died; people had stopped calling for advice; his body was slowing down; and, increasingly, he was self-medicating with alcohol. His conversation was invariably laced with references to Condé Nast and all the things he had achieved in the top position; the important people he'd known, the careers he'd helped launch, all the individuals he'd motivated, the culture of excellence he'd nurtured, and, by contrast, the corrosion of character he could now see insinuating itself into the modern workplace.

He was right about much of this, but I wanted him to move forward with the satisfaction of having had a remarkable career; to harness those successes as a springboard for other explorations, rather than continuing to excavate the past.

He didn't seem able to do that, or to want to do that. Perhaps no one ever told him it would be wise to try, although I'm sure I hinted at it on more than one occasion. Every new meeting, every discussion, was an opportunity to replay old achievements, to inform whomever he was talking to of the position he'd once held. He'd been a global leader in his field and, by golly, he'd done some leading and inspiring in his time. This was all true, of course, but to me it sounded so limiting—*and yes, often so tedious*—because he was more, much more, than just the summation of his working life.

My father has always wanted recognition (and who can blame him for that?) and so I thought that by writing a book about him I might spare him what writer Richard Freadman called 'the indignity of oblivion'; all those years of clambering, striving, flourishing, trying to make a difference, to leave a mark. And for what? Just to vanish?

It was so that my father wouldn't vanish that I took up the task of writing about him. But inevitably I began observing him like an interview subject, drafting questions for him, inspecting his wardrobe and his bathroom cabinets with the eye of a chronicler—or a burglar, as Janet Malcolm might suggest—rather than as the loving son I wanted to be.

'My goodness,' I'd think as I rifled through the 1001 Estée Lauder creams and Chanel colognes that lined the shelves of his bathroom cabinet, 'imagine how this will look in print.' I'd trawl through the work correspondence, the letters from friends and admirers, the old photographs, and I'd be forever thinking about how to make my father's life live on the page.

In doing so I lost the joy of just being with him, of being with him for its own sake—because he was the man who'd brought me into the world and because we loved each other and there'd been years, way too many years, when we'd not been able to do just this: sit with each other in the quiet.

My father had become a book project instead of a man. A book with chapters and headlines and breakout quotes. A book that attempted to be fair and balanced and of interest to people who might not necessarily have a skerrick of curiosity about him, or even know who he was, much less care.

I spent countless hours poring over my father's life and when that all proved too much—which it did—I turned to my mother's life, believing that because I'd spent way too long in the thrall of my father, I needed to balance the ledger. After my mother, I turned to her mother, my grandmother, and then to my grandmother's mother, until I ended up lost in the woods of Latvia where many of our relatives perished.

And it occurred to me, in the midst of these preoccupations, that the one person I was avoiding writing about was myself.

By this stage, I'd made my living for nearly twenty-five years writing about other people. Politicians, businessmen, bankers, media figures, lawyers, judges, artists, writers, poets, musicians, dancers, actors, theatre directors. I'd spent days and nights chronicling their exploits, winkling their stories out of them, listening to their confessions—if and when they came; getting around them, behind them, across them, trying to challenge them, but also understand and honour them, to bring their lives to the page in ways that might not do them too much rough justice. Unless, of course, they deserved it—which, on more than a few occasions, they did.

Now I'd reached a point of wanting to try to write a different story, one that went to the core of a different kind of conversation—the kind you have when the ground shifts and you shine the searchlight on yourself. I wanted to write my own story—about family and the way grim memories can be passed down through the ages to seep into the very tissue of your being; about marriage—*my marriage*; about ambition and ego—*my ambition and ego*—and how it might be possible to live independently of more shallow definitions of success.

Most journalists shy away from a pursuit like this, and rightly so. We pride ourselves on our non-alignment, our so-called objectivity, our capacity to set agendas, challenge authority, break new ground. The stories that matter are the stories of the day or the week—nation- or earth-defining stories on climate change or government corruption or the latest collapse in Middle Eastern negotiations. Or in these dumbing-down days of the early twenty-first century, stories of Angelina and Brad's marriage and Britney's stay in rehab and Mel's drunken, anti-Semitic rants and Lindsay's anorexia and, of course, Michael's brilliant and grotesque Peter Pan rise and fall.

We don't put *ourselves* on the line, certainly not in this way. Who would listen? Who would care? And to what purpose? To lay ourselves bare for all to see—to speak to all the rumblings and contradictions of the human heart that might invite the mirth and hilarity, if not outright scorn, of colleagues and friends?

This is no ordinary time. We know this in the same way an elephant knows a distant bull roar, or a bird takes flight long before the earth has begun to tremble. We are tuned to a band-width, a frequency, and it is in this heaving sea of atomic energy that we sense the threat. We might not be able to articulate it, but we know it in the most visceral parts of ourselves. This has been a time of great shifts, when the world's economy has unravelled and the old kings of capitalism have been dethroned and millions of Americans have begun living in their cars and tents; a time when European cities have begun to smoulder all over again in their discontent, with up to 120 million people now facing poverty and ruin, and when Pacific islands have sunk further and the Arctic ice caps melted faster than we ever feared possible.

And the shifts aren't just global. The year I resumed writing this book—after five years of indecision—I lost my job and my elder daughter left home, taking with her all the sweet melodies of her song-writing that had once floated from her bedroom.

It was the year when I started taking books of poetry and spirituality to bed with me instead of newspapers and magazines, looking for the sacred words that might explain the silent convers-ings of the heart.

It was the year I think I began to understand the pain of my parents' lives and the ways in which the sorrows of the old world shadowed them across the seas and down through the genera-tions, to me and my children.

It was the year that one work project after another fell over and I ended up feeling as uncertain and directionless as I'd ever felt; the year I began sleeping during the day and taking the phone off the hook and taking long, aimless walks along the beach, hoping that no one would recognise me or, heaven forbid, ask me what I did for a living.

It was the year I realised that all the old ways of doing things no longer worked, not for me, not for my marriage, not for my community, not for this country, not for the planet. It was the year I stopped seeing the world mostly through my head and began trying to process it through my heart.

This was the year—how could it have taken this long?—that I truly began listening to birdsong: the ribald laughter of kooka-burras, the fluting warble of magpies, the strangled cry of the currawong—at all times of the day, but particularly in that sad half-light of dusk.

I can think of plenty of other journalists in Australia who have had far more distinguished careers than mine; who have braved more war zones, won more awards, covered more political and economic cycles, and generally kept more abreast of the temper of the times than I've ever managed to do.

What this book is about is finding a way to use the personal as a vehicle for exploring bigger themes. The personal just happens to be mine. For all my working life it's been others—mostly people on the public stage, but not always—whose lives have influenced, inspired, united, divided and demanded our attention, however fleeting. The best of them were those whose lives offered up to us something deeper about the human condition, who took us to places of courage, ambition, guile, vanity, generosity, love, cruelty and a whole lot more.

Journalism has never just been about fact-gathering and storytelling. It has been about the exploration and celebration of ideas. At its best, according to the late, great American scribe David Halberstam, it is an 'expression of restraint and judgement on a community'. Its practitioners, if they behave and think well, can be the 'spiritual monitors of a community', where trust and loyalty are built in equal measure.

This might seem laughable today, given the bad odour in which journalists are often held by the public, not to mention the end of the business model that once funded print journalism and the noble enterprise that is investigative reporting. But there are any number of Australian journalists I know who hold—and deserve—this esteemed place in our society. They are smart and passionate, but also dispassionate when necessary, and they are brave and resilient too. They retain a sense of idealism, but they are also freethinkers, open to new ideas, allergic to the latest trend or to any notion of running with the pack.

There are others, though, who remain deeply cynical and angry with the world, as if all their years of reporting on other people's weaknesses, failings and peccadilloes have confirmed their darkest suspicions of the human endeavour. They have spent so much time as prisoners to the deadline, locked in the castle of political and economic decision-making, playing the role of king-maker or executioner, that their character, like those whom they report on, has become progressively undermined.

Every story is written through hidden filters, shaped by the culture of the newspaper or magazine that employs you, shaped by the impulses of the proprietor or editor who can hire or fire you, shaped by your own life experiences—by the things you have witnessed or not witnessed; by the information that has been revealed to you or not revealed; and by the motives of those revealing or not revealing.

I don't see how a journalist can write about another person's life unless he or she can come to grips with this, unless they understand the complexity of the human condition and how deeply conflicted and flawed we all are.

There are, of course, many people who, in the face of terror or terrible deeds, see the lines becoming clearer. They see themselves as having arrived at a point on the map closer to the truth.

They know the right way to respond. They recognise who thinks and acts like themselves, who is on their side and who isn't. They can say with absolute clarity and conviction where the moral and ethical boundaries should be laid.

I wish sometimes that this clarity and conviction were still with me; that the ability to know things with certainty had not been usurped by the torturous self-examinations that now seem to accompany almost every act of writing. And yet I know these torturous examinations help me to understand not just what others long for, but what I long for in myself—which is why, I suppose, this is the story of my own longing. A longing to understand my history, but a longing to escape it. A longing for freedom, but a longing for true commitment. A longing for the wisdom of the ages, but a longing—still adolescent to its core—to inhabit the land of the young. A longing for music. A longing for a true relationship with silence. A longing for home. A longing for places that don't look at all like home. A longing to keep my daughters close. A longing to let them go so that they might hazard themselves in the world as they're meant to do. A longing to be good. A longing to be a little bad. A longing to honour my father who, like Hamlet contemplating the exhumed skull of Yorrick, 'hath borne me on his back a thousand times'. A longing to abandon this father ship in order to steer my own sometimes wayward course. A longing for some kind of compact between all these blessed contradictions.

1

A FATEFUL MEETING

M y family has many stories and a few of them are dramatic in the way that many stories from many families are dramatic.

We make of these stories what we will. Often we bury them in our secret graves, we glide over them, or we rehearse them endlessly until we become one with them, because without these stories we might not know who we are.

The story that has long held the greatest power for me is the one about my paternal grandfather, Kurt Leser, a German Jew whose life was saved by a Nazi on the eve of World War II.

My grandfather had fought in the Battle of Verdun in 1916, the longest and costliest battle of the Great War, and although he was on the losing side, he was awarded the Iron Cross First Class for saving another man's life in the trenches. He was then offered an officer's commission if he agreed to convert to Christianity. He refused this commission, not because he was a devout or even practising Jew—he hardly ever went to synagogue in his life—but because he felt it would have been an act of hypocrisy to convert.

On my father's side our family could trace its German Jewish heritage as far back as the Thirty Years War of 1618–1648 and the Treaty of Westphalia that followed. As far as my grandfather was concerned, his German pedigree was as good as any Lutheran, Presbyterian or Catholic German's. He was either officer material or he wasn't, and seeing as he was born a Jew, he'd die one too.

By 1938, the head of the notorious Brownshirts, or SA (Sturmabteilung), for the region surrounding Sondershausen, was the same man whose life my grandfather had saved at the Battle of Verdun.

In early November he called my grandfather at home and said: 'Kurt, I need to see you.'

'Where?' my grandfather replied.

'At our usual place in the park.'

This was the city park in Sondershausen, and in 1985 my father took me there to show me where these two old World War I comrades—one a Jew, the other a Nazi—had had their fateful meeting.

My father and I sat on a park bench looking through the birch trees to the lake where children were playing with their toy boats. Nearby were a restaurant and the remnants of a small amphitheatre where locals had gone to hear Brahms and Beethoven concerts on weekends. It was a peaceful and civilised setting.

My father held my hand as he recounted the story that his own father had told him when he was a teenager.

'Kurt,' the SA chief said, 'you saved my life twenty-two years ago; I'm saving yours now. You must leave Germany as soon as possible—in the next few days.'

'But what about my son Bernd and my *Hausdame*, Ernie?' my grandfather asked.

'Don't worry about them. I'll make sure they're okay.'

Within two days my grandfather had packed his bags, never to return to Germany. Almost immediately, the country was plunged into an orgy of violence that would become known as Kristallnacht, the Night of Broken Glass. From 9 to 10 November, all over Germany, synagogues were set ablaze, tombstones desecrated, and Jewish homes and businesses looted. In cities, towns and villages, Jews were set upon by prowling Aryan thugs. Some families lost everything that night. Some never saw their loved ones again.

The event that triggered this night of destruction had occurred in Paris two days earlier, following the deportation of eighteen thousand Jews from the Reich, most of them to Poland. Among those transported were seventeen-year-old Herschel Grynszpan's mother and father who, without warning, had been ordered from their home and shipped by cattle car to the Polish border. Their son decided to take revenge on the Germans. On the morning of 7 November 1938 he walked into the German embassy in Paris and fired five shots at close range at the country's Third Secretary, Ernst vom Rath. Three of the shots missed their target; two of them lodged in the diplomat's stomach. Two days later, vom Rath was dead.

Hitler's minister of propaganda, Joseph Goebbels, wasted little time, his newspaper *Der Angriff* announcing: 'From this vile deed arises the imperative demand for immediate action against the Jews, with the most severe consequences.'

My grandfather's friend obviously knew what these consequences were going to be. He would be leading the charge. Yet he decided, at huge risk to himself, to repay the gift of life to a Jew.

My father was the only child of six marriages. Both his father Kurt and his mother Ellen had married twice after their divorce from each other in 1929, but none of these subsequent marriages would produce another son or daughter. Six marriages across four countries and only my father to show for it. He used to joke that his parents and step-parents took one look at him and decided the risks of another child were far too great.

By contrast, my father's great-grandmother, Seraphine Leser, had borne fifteen children, but some time in the late 1880s she had got out of bed in Sondershausen, walked to her fourth-floor window and thrown herself out. Pregnant with her sixteenth child, this long-suffering wife of Moses Leser had decided she could take no more. Fifteen children perhaps, but sixteen—that was beyond all endurance.

My father was born in Berlin on 15 March 1925 at a hospital in the fashionable western part of the city. His arrival coincided with that giddy, golden period that flickered briefly into life during the days of the Weimar Republic. Bertolt Brecht had just emerged as a powerful new presence in German theatre; Fritz Lang was establishing himself as a pre-eminent filmmaker; Christopher Isherwood was laying the foundations for *Cabaret*; the Bauhaus architectural movement was beginning to flourish. And my father was entering a world that had gone mad and would soon erupt again, but, for the moment, was offering its citizens a few years of almost hallucinatory respite.

With the currency scrapped, people no longer had to cart wheel-barrows full of deutschmarks to the bakery just to buy a loaf of bread. There were still beggars everywhere and the wave of suicides that had gripped Germany at the height of the economic collapse had only just begun to subside. But poverty was receding, if only for the briefest of periods before the Great Depression. For the first time in years it was possible to imagine a future, despite the fact that a former Austrian house painter and part-time tramp by the name of Adolf Hitler had just been released from eighteen months in prison, the ink from his hateful tract, *Mein Kampf*, barely dry on his hands.

❧

It says something about a child's ignorance of his parents' lives that it wasn't until I was in my forties that I began to fully appreciate what it must have meant to be born a Jew in Germany in the mid-1920s and to have spent one's childhood under the heel of the jackboot. Or what it must have been like to have become aware, as did my father, that his country not only no longer wanted him but, worse, wanted him dead.

Like every other Jewish child of my generation I'd grown up with the knowledge that something monstrous and unique had happened to our parents' generation and that we, their children, had somehow been miraculously spared. But having said that, I'd never truly taken the imaginative leap into the depths of evil. I'd never truly conceived of a childhood set to never-ending martial music and drums, and goosestepping SS parades. Nor had I ever tried to conjure up the terror that mass hysteria creates, or the loneliness that being a pariah instils in the marrow of your bones. I'd never known, never smelt, this kind of fear and, to be sure, my father had never talked much about it.

Although good with words, my father, like most men of his generation—particularly German men, perhaps—was never much given to expressions of emotion, especially emotion that had long ago been buried. You had to prise things out of him or, better still, sit patiently in the troubled waters of his silence until ripples broke the surface. At least that's what it often felt like. Even then, he would articulate his thoughts only with the kind of formal precision you might expect from a history professor declaiming on the sweep of Prussian history. Consciously constructed rather than coming to you in an artless, natural way.

German men, we are told, prefer to suffer in silence, and in this way, I suppose, my father was a lot like his own father. Kurt Leser was a man of supreme elegance and personal magnetism, a man who could disarm a room full of people instantly, including every woman in it—but a man who, I've come to see, carried around inside himself all the trace elements of war, persecution and exile.

At the end of World War I he had returned to a shattered nation. On the Continent eight million men had been killed in the fighting, seven million had been left permanently disabled, and another fifteen million seriously wounded. Throughout Europe another five million people had succumbed to disease and famine—and that was before the influenza epidemic of 1918–1919 carried off millions more. In total, some sixty million people had died—and that's excluding those in Russia. Of this unprecedented squandering of humanity, the noted historian Paul Kennedy wrote in *The Rise and Fall of the Great Powers*: 'There is no known way of measuring the personal anguish and the psychological shocks involved in such a human catastrophe, but it was easy to see why the participants—statesmen as well as peasants—were so deeply affected by it all.'

My recollections of my grandfather are scant but I remember him for his handsome face, aquiline nose and brushed-back silver hair, and for the way his shoulders used to hunch forward when he walked, as if he was carrying some monumental load that I could never see. He used to smile at me and wiggle his ears whenever I asked him to, his face as still as granite.

I suppose my grandfather was a sad and remote figure, but perhaps it was just the pain he was in. I had no idea—until my father told me years later—that one side of his body and his upper legs were still full of shrapnel. He could barely move without wincing, yet he never complained.

Straight after the Great War, my grandfather went to work in Berlin for his great-uncle, Eduard Leser, who was then running a company called Meyerhofter, a successful textile business turning out high-quality silks and woollen fabrics for the European market. Eduard Leser was known as the Silk King of Germany and he owned a big mansion on Lake Wannsee, where my father used to holiday occasionally as a small boy, not far from the conference room in which Reinhard Heydrich and his fellow criminals from the Third Reich would later devise their 'Final Solution' for European Jewry.

A few years later my grandfather took up with another uncle, Egon Leser, also in the textile business, and was put in charge of a company called Eduard Gers, which manufactured wool for hand-knitting. Egon Leser had made a fortune prospecting for gold in South Africa before returning to Germany prior to the war. A shrewd businessman, he'd somehow managed to protect his savings at a time when the majority of Germans were losing their livelihoods virtually overnight.

Egon Leser lived in Dresden but his factories were based in Berlin and Sondershausen, a salt-mining town 180 kilometres south-west of Berlin, near the historic cultural centre of Weimar. Egon hated Sondershausen with a passion. He hated its smallness, its provincialism, its isolation from the commercial centres of Europe, but he needed someone there to run what had become a vital part of his operations. The company had thousands of home workers scattered throughout the town and surrounding villages, people who would be paid to knit garments according to the company's specifications, before being on-sold to retail stores throughout Germany. My grandfather was good at sketching garments and, more importantly, he was trustworthy and eager to get ahead. When his uncle invited him to become a partner in his business, he jumped at the chance.

It was 1927 and Germany was enjoying a renaissance under the most liberal regime in all of Europe. Although the Weimar Republic was destined to fail spectacularly, these were the years when anything seemed possible, particularly in Berlin, then a rival to Paris as the most exciting city on earth. The Great Depression was still two years away, and the Nazi Party still a rump organisation of country yokels and gangsters.

My grandfather was looking to the future. Three years earlier he had married my grandmother, Ellen Weiss, in a synagogue in Berlin, and the following year, 1925, Ellen had given birth to my father. After the devastation and deprivations of war, Kurt Leser was anxious to establish a life for himself and his family—except that his marriage to Ellen was never going to work.

My paternal grandmother was a woman of beauty and considerable style, a product of middle-class Berlin society with an entirely different temperament to my grandfather's. She was serious-minded, wedded to the traditions of Judaism but also a woman of high culture. Her home was a salon of sorts, where she and her friends would gather to sing and play piano. My father remembers her as good-natured, even-tempered and gregarious.

Kurt was more humorous, but also more reserved. He revelled in his solitude—partly, I suspect, because of the constant pain from his war injuries. Books were his friends and he could converse widely on the subjects that interested him, mainly politics and history. My father would become more and more like him as he aged.

And there was something else. As my grandfather was to later tell my father, he was never in love with my grandmother but, rather, her younger sister Gerda. This union could never be realised, however, because Ellen and Gerda's parents insisted their elder daughter marry first, in accordance with Jewish custom.

I suppose my grandfather thought he could make things right. He was wrong, and his mistake would prove costly to them both, but even more so to my father who would spend his formative years—from the age of three to fourteen—in a motherless home.

In 1928, my grandmother became the centre of a village scandal after it was discovered she'd been having an affair with a Czech actor. My grandfather had also had affairs—numerous affairs, apparently—but this was Germany in the early part of the twentieth century and there was no question that if either of them was to do the leaving it would be the errant wife, not the husband.

Over the years I have given a lot of thought to how the gaping hole left by his mother must have shaped my father's life. I can picture their three-storey house on Von Hindenburg Strasse, and the garden full of apple trees and chirping birds, the surface comforts that were theirs—the car and driver for my grandfather, as well as the governess, housekeeper and cook—but also the glaring absence of a mother whom my father would only see in Berlin twice a year.

When I asked him one day to describe his earliest memory he referred immediately to this period—how when he was nearly three and a half years old his mother had left Sondershausen. 'I remember her packing her cases and I remember the tearful goodbye and that was it,' he said.

She didn't tell my father why she was leaving; only that she had to go and that it was best if his father, my grandfather, looked after him. She cried as she packed her bags and later, too, when she boarded the train for Berlin. There was no conversation about this between my father and his.

For the next two years my father never saw his mother, although she regularly sent him letters. By the time he was six or seven, however, he was taking a train to Berlin alone to see her.

He was not yet eight years old when President Von Hindenburg—the man who'd given our family's street its name—summoned Adolf Hitler to the Chancellery and bestowed on him the title of Chancellor of the Reich. It was 30 January 1933 and a political earthquake had just convulsed a nation of sixty-six million people. Almost immediately Hitler was issuing daily tirades against Jews, and mobs were now being given carte blanche to break into Jewish homes at night.

Almost from day one no Jewish musician was allowed to perform in Germany, nor were Jewish poets allowed to have their work recited. In the city of Breslau, Jewish lawyers were forbidden to appear in court; in Potsdam, Jewish judges were summarily dismissed; and in Thuringia itself—the state in which my father and grandfather lived—an organisation called the Association of Jewish Citizens was banned because it had dared to criticise the National Socialist government.

By April 1933 all Jewish businesses were boycotted, concentration camps institutionalised and a wide-ranging education campaign unleashed against Jewish citizens.

'A whole nation,' wrote Sebastian Haffner in his devastating memoir, *Defying Hitler*, 'was turned into a pack of hunting hounds.' As early as March 1933,

to fear for the life of a Jewish (person) was not unreasonable—even if the fear turned out to be groundless.

Every day one looked around and someone else had gone and left no trace. At some point in the summer the newspapers carried a list of thirty or forty names of famous scientists or writers; they had been proscribed, declared to be traitors to the people and deprived of their citizenship.

More unnerving was the disappearance of a number of quite harmless people . . . the radio announcer whose voice one had heard every day . . . the familiar actors and actresses who had been a feature of our lives disappeared from one day to the next . . . Brilliant young Hans Otto, who had been the rising star of the previous season, lay crumpled in the yard of an SS barracks. He had thrown himself out of a fourth-floor window in a moment when the guards had been distracted. A famous cartoonist, whose harmless drawings had brought laughter to the whole of Berlin every week, committed suicide, as did the master of ceremonies of a well-known cabaret.

There was also the burning of books in April and the disappearance of contemporary German literature from bookshops and libraries. Certain newspapers and journals simply vanished, while those that kept going—many distinguished broadsheets with strong democratic traditions—were reduced to crude mouthpieces for the Nazi propaganda machine.

And yet, as Haffner also observed: 'It [was] typical of the early years of the Nazi regime that the whole façade of everyday life remained virtually unchanged. The cinemas, theatres and cafés were full. Couples danced in the open air and in dance halls. People strolled down the streets.'

To my father, a small asthmatic boy of eight, the appointment of Hitler as chancellor hardly seemed a shattering event, especially when compared to the divorce of his parents. My grandfather still went to work each day and came home each night for dinner. He still employed more than a thousand home workers and maintained a lifestyle that was the envy of most Germans. And his son, awkward and bespectacled though he was, continued to ride his bicycle to school and play with his friends as though nothing had happened.

But the signs were increasingly ominous. My father's school principal began wearing a swastika on his lapel, even though he was no Nazi supporter, and by 1935 the Nuremberg Laws had, almost overnight, stripped Jews of their citizenship rights, as well as their right to marry or have sexual relations with German nationals. My grandfather's family lawyer was forced to close his practice.

Did my grandfather meet quietly with other Jewish men in

Sondershausen to discuss this? Did he start salting away money for what was surely coming?

Apparently he did. My grandfather knew a man in Prague, a friend of Jan Masaryk, the Czech foreign minister, who agreed to help him transfer his money from Prague to London. Every time my grandfather went to Prague—and that was twice a year, to visit one of the spas in the Bohemian countryside—he would carry with him wads of cash for this courageous Czech man to then cable to London. This was the money that would eventually give my family its new beginning on the other side of the world.

In 1935 my grandfather was still clinging stubbornly to the belief that the nightmare would pass. Like so many other Jews, he couldn't imagine the unimaginable. He couldn't believe that the birthplace of Bach, Beethoven, Goethe, Schiller and Einstein, his very own birthplace, had—in the words of William L. Shirer, author of *The Rise and Fall of the Third Reich*—'turned down a dark and savage road from which there was to be no return'.

My grandfather had his mind on other matters. He'd fallen in love with Lilly Katz, a woman from the nearby town of Wildungen, and in 1934 he'd married her. 'I adored her,' my father told me. 'She was a lovely person, very soft and very intelligent. She was lovely to be with and she was lovely to me. Very warm and affectionate. She took me to the cinema and out for cake. It wasn't for long but I remember it well.'

Soon after the marriage, Lilly was diagnosed with throat cancer. By 1936 she was dead, depriving my father of his second mother in eight years.

～

In the summer of 1936, the year of the Berlin Olympics, my father took the nearly two-hour train trip to visit his mother in the German capital. I have often tried to picture the scene that would have greeted this eleven-year-old Jewish boy. All the towns and villages ablaze with flags and swastikas. The stirring sounds of military music, and the sight of saluting Nazi processions.

Berlin had been awarded the Games five years earlier—before the IOC could grasp what Germany was about to become—and Hitler was keen to exploit the moment. Here was the Third Reich's opportunity to showcase before the family of nations the superiority of the master race, its chance to promote the ideology and efficiency of National Socialism. Gone for the moment were the anti-Semitic posters and signs saying JEWS NOT WELCOME. Instead, there was the pretence of civility and a whole new Olympic village thrown into the bargain.

My father could barely contain his excitement when he learnt his father had obtained tickets for the two of them to see the great black American athlete, Jesse Owens, run the 100-yard final. Owens was then the most famous athlete in the world, the fastest man alive over 100 and 200 yards, as he was to prove again that Berlin summer by winning four gold medals.

My father would often recall the heart-stopping moment when Hitler refused to shake Owens' hand after the black American had blitzed the field in the 100-yard final.

'There would have been 100,000 people in the stadium,' he told me. 'It was tense, exciting and one could see Hitler and Goering and all the major figures in their deluxe seats. And all the Brownshirts and the SS in their black uniforms and thousands of swastikas everywhere.

'The winners went up to receive their medals from the president of the IOC and they were then ushered towards the bigwigs of the German government. I remember Goering shaking Jesse Owens' hand but Hitler turned his back. I was perplexed by this but overtaken by the excitement of his win. That's what everybody was talking about.'

Later Hitler would tell one of his subordinates, 'The Americans should be ashamed of themselves letting Negroes win their medals for them. Do you really think that I will allow myself to be photographed shaking hands with a Negro?'

❧

My father began attending secondary school at the end of the 1936 summer holidays. It was an unhappy experience. As one of only a few Jewish children still left in the school, he was regularly teased and shunned by most of his peers.

In all the conversations I have had with him over the years about this period of his life, I think this is where I have felt his hurt most deeply. He explained this best to me one day while on holiday in north Queensland, sitting under a tropical sky.

'Let's say from August 1936 things became unpleasant. For instance, during recess and lunch breaks, no one would play with me. I would be very much on my own. In fact, I used to go home for lunch and then come back again. I was rather isolated and I couldn't be part of the soccer team or any of the sporting teams; also I wasn't part of the Hitler Youth movement to which all German boys and girls belonged, and I was very sorry about that because it seemed a lot of fun. They went out camping and barbecued sausages at night. I knew that my father was a highly decorated army veteran so I couldn't understand why we were treated differently. It was all very puzzling, and I felt very lonely.'

Did people call him names? I asked.

'Yes, yes, yes, they called me stinking Jew and this and that and the other. They called me names but there was no physical violence.'

The other children weren't allowed to play with my father. Only Gerhard Braun, now his oldest friend, dared to defy this decree, stealing away to Von Hindenburg Strasse after school to spend time with him in secret, occasionally bringing other friends with him. My father never forgot his kindness.

By early 1937 my grandfather had been advised by the principal that it was no longer possible for my father to remain at school. Jews were no longer welcome. In the winter of 1937, my father was sent to a Jewish boarding school in Coburg, 150 kilometres south of Sondershausen in the state of Bavaria. For many children this would have seemed like one more loss; for my father it was a welcome relief. For the first time in years he would have friends. He would identify with other children in similar predicaments. He would be shielded from the growing menace that was swirling around the Jewish population although, here too, there was only so much protection the boarding school could offer.

Scorched into my father's memory is the time a gang of young Nazi hoods set upon him and his friends as they were riding their bikes in the forest outside Coburg. It was the first and only time my father was ever in a brawl, and by his own sunny account he acquitted himself well.

'They saw us and said, "You must be filthy Jews from Internat Hirsch." And they attacked us. I think there were about fourteen of us and about thirty of them.

'I was one of the youngest and smallest in our group but we had some pretty big people on our side, including our leader, who was big and blond and looked like a Nazi himself. He said to them, "I'll show you what we are," and he turned to us and said, "Let's give them hell." And we beat them and we were very happy. We made mincemeat of them and they turned around and shot off.'

In April 1938 my father had his bar mitzvah at a synagogue in Berlin. The general mood in the city was one of terrible foreboding. A month earlier—on 14 March, the day before my father's thirteenth birthday—Hitler had made his triumphal march into Austria, annexing the country of his birth. Austrian Jews were now emigrating en masse if they could afford to, encouraged by the new Office for Jewish Emigration, headed by Adolf Eichmann. Others were choosing a more drastic course. Within one month, 500 Jews had committed suicide, including a family of six who reportedly shot themselves in a Viennese neighbourhood rather than face further torments at the hands of SS henchmen.

In Germany, Jewish people were now the forbidden caste. At the very time my father was smoking his first cigarette on his Aunt Alma's verandah, having just fulfilled his bar mitzvah obligations, thousands of his fellow Jews were being arrested and shipped off to concentration camps. All over the country Nazi stormtroopers were hanging posters with obscene depictions of Jews being tortured and maimed. Cafés and cinemas were subject to frequent raids, Jewish shop windows repeatedly smashed. No one was safe.

And yet for my father there was one small comfort to be had during that cold spring of 1938: his bar mitzvah had brought his parents together under the same roof for the first time in ten years. Appreciating how difficult it would be for his sister Alma and her family to travel to Sondershausen, not to mention the rabbi officiating at the service, my grandfather had agreed to have the bar mitzvah in Berlin. It would be the last time Kurt and Ellen ever saw each other.

Seven months later my grandfather left Germany without telling my father. There was no way he could. The following year, my father said goodbye to his mother at the Zoo train station in

Berlin, a tearful, gut-wrenching farewell before she departed for Bolivia, the only country that would agree to take her. He had no idea whether he would see her again.

'It was very emotional,' he told me one day. 'Very sad.'

A few days after my grandfather left Germany, Jews were summarily evicted from orphanages, hospitals and old people's homes and, by 12 November, all Jewish children were barred from attending school, my father among them. On the night of Kristallnacht, German authorities closed down my father's Jewish boarding school and ordered all the students paraded through the streets of Coburg. He was thirteen at the time and remembers the night as if it were yesterday:

'The Gauletier, the chief of the local SS, came round and gave orders for the school to be closed and for all the boys over the age of sixteen to be sent to Dachau concentration camp. At that time Dachau was not an extermination camp, it was a very basic, primitive camp. ["Empty huts in a gravel pit," wrote one survivor.] But because I was under sixteen and so was my cousin Gerhard, we were frogmarched from school through the town, between jeering hordes of Nazis who were throwing stones and spitting at us.

'We were then put into a gymnasium which was part of a youth hostel and made to sit there on bare boards for two nights. We were just given dry bread and water and then after two nights and one day we were all allowed to go back to our respective cities, towns, homes.'

Kristallnacht was, of course, to mark the point of no return in Germany's modern history. It was at this juncture that it became horrifyingly clear to the Jewish population that something unique and evil was at work. The Germany they had known had been extinguished, and not since medieval times was such barbarism given free rein.

I write this now more for my daughters and those of their generation than for readers acquainted with this gruesome chapter of history. Before I started to do so I'd thought I'd known my own family's history. I thought I had understood the horror which had lodged itself deep inside the collective Jewish soul.

I'd noticed—and absorbed—the collective summoning at the Pesach table of all the critical moments in Jewish history: the bondage of Egypt, the destruction of Judah, the Maccabean fight for survival, the crematoria of Europe. I'd duly noted my maternal grandmother's icy reproof when I had bought my first car, a Volkswagen beetle.

I thought I'd understood what it meant to be Jewish. I was hopelessly wrong. I don't think words could ever come close to describing what was beginning to happen to a defenceless people nearly eighty years ago. I don't think the moral imagination could ever truly apprehend that. Not unless you were there, and even then it seemed inconceivable.

From the night of 9 November 1938 onwards, German Jews were forced to pay for the destruction that had been heaped upon them, as well as pay an extra collective fine of one billion marks. They were to be removed entirely from the German economy, their businesses, properties, artworks and jewellery transferred into Aryan hands. They were to be banned from shopping, eating in restaurants, owning cars or pets, and visiting public libraries, cinemas and swimming pools. They were to be compelled towards the ghetto and beyond.

As Field Marshal Hermann Goering was to tell a cabinet meeting at the time, 'I would not like to be a Jew in Germany.'

At the age of thirteen my father had become an outcast, a terrible burden for any child to bear and one which he found almost impossible to talk about in the years to come, unless urged and prodded in that direction.

When he returned home to Sondershausen on 12 November, after the closing of his school, his father was already in America, trying to arrange visas for his now terrified family, including my father, my grandfather's sister Alma, Alma's son Gerhard, and my father's great-aunt Sophie. There was also Ernie, the woman my grandfather had appointed to work for him a year earlier and to whom he would soon propose marriage. Ernie Cheikowsky—the third Mrs Kurt Leser—would prove crucial to my father's survival.

My father told me, 'She was the one who organised our departure and our immigration and the moving of our furniture and all the documentation. She was the one who negotiated with the SA.' And by SA, he meant my grandfather's friend.

My father had no idea that his own father had decided to leave Germany for good until he returned from Coburg. He had seen him a couple of weeks earlier—when my grandfather had visited him at school, just before the country had erupted into anti-Jewish violence. There had been no hint of his intentions. 'He told me he was going to America and England; that he was going to be very active in working out where we were going because we were going to leave Germany. He didn't tell me he wasn't coming back.'

It is difficult for me to reconcile myself to my grandfather's decision. No doubt he was convinced that unless he left Germany immediately, no one would get out, and that this was his—and his family's—only possible choice. But to leave his only son behind, knowing he would never return, and to have no guarantee—except the word of the SA chief—that he could secure safe passage for him, is a decision I'm not sure I would have taken. Less Sophie's choice, more Giant Leap of Faith.

For the next six months—between November 1938 and April 1939—my father lived at home in the care of a woman he barely knew. Like all other Jewish children he was now barred from attending school. He seldom went out because in the streets Jews were hunted down, abused and beaten. It was not uncommon to see bonfires blazing in neighbourhoods where they lived, their prayer books, Torah scrolls and philosophical texts hurled onto the funeral pyres.

As many as 150,000 German and Austrian Jews had already fled. Thousands more had been evicted, Aryanised or sent to concentration camps. My grandfather, having prevaricated, delayed and probably justified to himself countless times between 1933 and 1938 why he should stay put, was now desperately seeking visas from three countries. His choices—in order of preference—were America, Australia and New Zealand, but America had already begun tightening its rules of admission in response to the increasing number of refugees. Australia, too, had left little doubt as to its thinking with respect to the Jewish plight. 'It will no doubt be appreciated,' Australian delegate T.W. White told an international conference on refugees in Switzerland in July 1938, 'that as we have no racial problem we are not desirous of importing one.'

It was New Zealand that finally came to the rescue, a case— if ever there was one—of geography coming to the rescue of history. In the late 1800s my father's great-aunt Sophie (or Issy as she was known) had married Hermann Braun, a brilliant businessman by all accounts, and a man with an unquenchable pioneering spirit. In 1868 Braun had set sail for the South Pacific from Sondershausen and ended up founding a company in Auckland called Brown and Barratt, which was to become one of New Zealand's leading importers and wholesalers of high-quality groceries, spirits and wines. (A passionate Anglophile all his life, Hermann had changed his name from Braun to Brown shortly after stepping onto New Zealand soil.)

In the late 1890s, following the death of his first wife, Brown had married Issy Leser, one of the fifteen children born to the unfortunate Seraphine Leser and, soon after, he had been appointed honorary German consul to Auckland by Kaiser Wilhelm II and Chancellor von Bismarck.

Brown had held that position until he'd decided to return to Germany in 1911, but so deeply affected was he by his South Pacific experience that he'd renamed his Victorian-style manor in Sondershausen Villa Zealandia, furnishing one of the rooms with Maori art and weapons of war. (All this was confiscated by the Nazis in 1938 and, despite efforts on the part of our family, it was never returned by the Communist East German government.)

Hermann Brown died in Sondershausen in 1918 with seven-eighths of his fortune appropriated by the New Zealand government. Under the *Enemy Alien Act* of 1914 it seized the money and put the remaining one-eighth in trust for my family. This would later prove crucial to their survival.

Without knowing it, Hermann Brown had taken a branch of the Leser family tree and transplanted it to New Zealand, setting in motion a relationship with that country that would continue well into the twenty-first century.

In the late 1890s, Brown had encouraged two of his brothers-in-law, Max and Gustav Leser, to emigrate to New Zealand, in order to capitalise on the gains he'd already made. These two brothers of Aunt Issy's had established a trading post in the country's North Island, where they'd sold food, blankets and whisky to the Maori. They'd made a small fortune, enough to enable them to act as guarantors for my grandfather and father on the eve of World War II.

Gustav Leser even went to Wellington to argue for my father and grandfather's admission, an act of decency that almost certainly saved my father's life. The equation was simple: without permits from New Zealand, none of the family would have been allowed to leave Berlin, given that both Australia and America had already turned them down.

On 4 April 1939, five months before the outbreak of World War II, my father, together with his aunt, cousin, great-aunt and Ernie, flew from Germany via Amsterdam to England, where they boarded a ship for Auckland. They flew from Tempelhof, the same airport that would soon launch a thousand Luftwaffe bombing missions over Europe.

2

LITTLE BIGHORN

I remember at the age of four or five hearing a calamitous sound coming from the bathroom, strangling the morning stillness with its desperate, primal fury. It was my father dry-retching over the basin—AAAREGHCHU, AAREGHCHU—the noise reverberating through the bathroom wall into my bedroom.

Some people wake to Mozart or pneumatic drills or the gossip and tweeting of birds. I used to wake to the sound of my father heaving from stress. For up to ten minutes I would listen to these convulsions, until suddenly the noise would stop and I would get up, slightly shaken, bathed in my own sweat.

'Are you okay, Daddy?'

'Sure,' he would reply, in tones so reassuring I found myself wondering if I'd actually imagined it all.

Most mornings were like this—his loud disturbances, my anxious inquiries and then the gentle assurances that all was well with the world. That's when I started to equate success with tension. It seemed to me you couldn't have one without the other. You couldn't possibly rise to the top of your profession—in his case magazine publishing—unless you were having a bilious attack each morning.

My father was urbane and full of unquenchable ambition, but with all the repressed unhappiness of his unmentioned past. I must have intuited this from the time I was young because I used to write him letters when he was away on work trips, hoping, perhaps, that my words would touch the sides of a sadness I didn't quite understand.

My darling Daddy,

I miss you terribly and I'm longing to see you again. A lot has happened while you've been away. First of all I got into the football team which I hope you are very happy with. Secondly I went to Richard Hossel's party and we saw at the pictures The Murderous Row which was very sexy.

Please do me a favour and don't bust yourself all the time and have a bit of a good time. After all you're not in Hong Kong all the time. We have been having a few tests at school in which some quite good and some quite bad [sic]. Thank you very much for your lovely postcard which I thought was lovely.

You don't know how much I miss you and I hope you miss me to [sic]. Please come back safe, happy and well.

All my love
Your loving son,
David

What strikes me most about this letter now—apart from its unabashed tenderness—is how, even then, at the age of eleven, I was worried about the stress my father was carrying. *Please do me a favour and don't bust yourself all the time.* It's a big thing for a young boy to ask of his father. Perhaps I was just mimicking my mother, who was forever imploring him to slow down, go out less, say no more often. But he couldn't. He'd been programmed to keep moving from the time he fled Germany.

For years my father would never admit he was born in Germany, that he could speak German almost as well as English. It reminded him too much of his own pain and torment. He was not the little boy whose mother had left the family home in 1928, or the young Jew marched through the streets of Coburg while Nazis jeered and spat and pelted stones at him, shouting, *Juden heraus, Juden heraus* (Jews out, Jews out). He was not the teenager who'd been forced out of his country, arriving in New Zealand in 1939 with little English, no friends and precious few memories worth preserving.

Forty years later, my father would return to launch German *Vogue* magazine. For a year prior to its launch in September 1979 he travelled the length and breadth of West Germany, meeting with the heads of department stores and people in the advertising, fashion and cosmetics industries.

Throughout his travels he found himself willing to speak his native tongue again, but never explaining how it was that he spoke German so well. 'I felt much more secure as time elapsed,' he told me once, 'but also at that point I kind of got a kick out of being Jewish and starting an enterprise on behalf of a leading company in its field. I also liked working with a younger generation who hadn't been tarred by Hitler. I might have occasionally reflected on what their father or grandfather would have been doing during the war years, but as soon as I did that I put it out of my mind as totally irrelevant. I ceased being anti-German once I got to know another generation.'

Whenever a colleague asked him why he spoke German with such fluency, he responded: 'I was brought up in Auckland, New Zealand, by a German-born grandmother. She ran a bilingual household and insisted I learn German and speak it like a native.' It was a tall tale that soothed my father's troubled soul.

Besides which, the course of his life had taken him literally millions of (frequent flyer) miles from his boyhood in Germany so that, until well into his seventies, all he'd ever really known was a long string of successes.

As a young boy, and in my early adulthood, I felt uncomfortable about the privileges that had come from these successes, especially when I compared our lifestyle to that of most of my friends. We had housekeepers who made our beds and cooked our meals. We took holidays in Fiji and Perisher Valley. We had famous people for dinner. We had book-lined walls and original artworks, and a Blüthner grand piano dominating the living room, which overlooked Shell Cove in Neutral Bay. This was where my mother accompanied her friend Anna Tiessen, wife of the general manager of Lufthansa Airlines, as she trilled Schubert and Schumann lieder in the late afternoon on my return from school.

During those afternoons I would play a lot on my own. My favourite place to play was a giant camphor laurel outside my bedroom, where I had a makeshift cubby-house in the fork of the tree. From this private universe I fought a number of historic battles, all around me the smell of grapeshot, the whoosh of arrows, and the screams of anguish from the dead and dying.

I spent months of my childhood playing Cowboys and Indians from this well-camouflaged position—one afternoon shooting up an entire Indian reservation; the next day, having grown tired of another Cheyenne defeat, switching sides to Crazy Horse.

I don't think my parents or sister had any idea that I was fighting the Battle of the Little Bighorn from the tree next to my verandah, let alone contributing to General Custer's final ignominy. But what I realise now is that I took far greater delight in joining the Indians than being on the side of the cavalry. The Indians were the underdogs and I happened to like underdogs. Jews were underdogs, even though to my childish eyes they were often successful ones—people like my father who left our house each day in a beautiful tailored suit, driving a gleaming Jaguar.

I liked killing cowboys from my treehouse because it seemed to satisfy all these ill-defined impulses to go down fighting with the also-rans. I would be a better person for killing cowboys instead of Indians. Later in life I'd be a better boss's son if I was on the workers' side. And, naturally, I'd be a better Jew if I could one day make friends with the Arab.

By the age of thirty-four my father had already worked in four countries—New Zealand, Australia, Canada and England. He'd arrived in New Zealand on 2 June 1939, after a six-week voyage aboard the P&O *Strathmore* with my grandfather and family and, thanks to Ernie's negotiations with the head of the SA in Sondershausen, they'd travelled first class with all their furniture, paintings and crystal.

From the moment my father saw the sparkling blue waters and wooded reserves of Auckland Harbour, he knew he'd reached his Arcadia. Beyond the curve of the bays was a country still emerging into nationhood, still reeling from the catastrophe of World War I, still coming to grips with those parts of its British heritage it wanted to retain.

After my father stepped off the *Strathmore*, he began to reinvent himself. He was Bernie Leser now, an adopted New Zealand son, not Bernd Leser, the German boy from Sondershausen. He would speak English, not German, and he would admit to no aspect of his German-ness. In New Zealand he would make friends rather than be rejected and shunned. He would learn to sail on Auckland Harbour instead of going on his own to the North Sea to overcome his childhood asthma. He would join the Zionist youth movement and go on Jewish camps instead of cowering in the corner of the playground.

At fifteen years and nine months my father left school and began his working life as a clothes cutter for an outfit called Stylish Clothing Company. It was there he learnt how to grade and mark the patterns on the cloth and how to use a piece of apparel machinery called the Hoffman press. The job didn't suit him. He had no eye for it, and so he tried becoming a clothes designer. When that didn't work out either, he got a job as a time-and-motion man in a clothing factory. That had matched his temperament better—standing on the factory floor with a stop-watch, recording each operation, always searching for maximum efficiencies from his workers.

My father's real talent, though, proved to be in sales and marketing, and in the ten-year period before starting *Vogue Australia* he built an impressive résumé in women's fashion, swimwear and shoes, beginning with a five-year stint working for Hek Marler.

Sidney Ernest Marler (better known as Hek) was one of the great trans-Tasman business figures of his day, head of H.M. Marler, the leading importer of shoes into Australia and New Zealand, and co-owner of the clothes and shoe company California Productions Limited.

At the age of twenty-two, eager to expand his horizons beyond New Zealand, my father arrived in Sydney from Auckland and began working in a clothing factory. Shortly afterwards, he was hired by John Rankin, the managing director of David Jones, to work in their shoe department. It was through Rankin that my father met Marler and, six months later, he was working for Marler in Bathurst, New South Wales, inside an old munitions factory that had been converted for the production of apparel and shoes. Marler appointed my father his 'productions investigation officer'.

Over the next five years, Hek Marler would prove one of the most important figures in my father's life, a man whose vision was nothing less than a global market in which ideas, people and products were unconstrained by geography. It was Marler who taught my father how to manage and give people confidence, how to correct and criticise without destroying self-esteem. Marler opened doors for my father and encouraged him to believe that anything was possible. He was, in fact, the first person to recognise my father's considerable talents and energy. He also taught my father how to drink properly—gin martinis before dinner, dry sherry with soup, white wine with fish, red wine with meat, followed by port with dessert.

At twenty-four my father was already travelling to the United States on behalf of California Productions (Australia and New Zealand), meeting the people who ran Cole of California, then the leading swimwear designers in the world. Cole of California had been founded in 1925 by actor Fred Cole, and the company's greatest asset at that time was the beautiful swimming star-turned-actress Esther Williams, who was to help revolutionise women's swimwear. ('It took the space industry 10 years to put a man on the moon,' Fred Cole's designer daughter Anne Cole once said. 'It took the swimwear industry 100 years to move from the ankle to the crotch.')

Esther Williams turned my father's head during those early days, dancing with him one memorable night at the famous but now defunct Romanoff's restaurant in Beverly Hills, and later posing with him for a photograph in her swimsuit, a photograph that would forever take pride of place in our living room.

In 1952, Marler was keen to establish Horrockses Fashions under licence in Canada, Horrockses then being the oldest—and probably finest—manufacturer of cotton fabrics in England, their ready-to-wear dresses coveted not just by the general public, but by the royal family itself, including Her Majesty the Queen.

Not long after my father married my mother Barbara in Sydney, Hek Marler appointed my father vice-president of H.M. Marler (Canada) Ltd and Horrockses Fashions (Canada) Ltd, and charged him with setting up an office in Montreal from scratch. This was where he worked for the next four years, and where both my sister Deborah and I were born—me at the Jewish General Hospital in January 1956 during a blizzard. Seven days later I was circumcised, an act of such bloodcurdling precision that it caused my father to faint for the first and last time in his life.

Four years after moving to Canada, Bernie Leser was offered another job, this time in London, heading up the marketing division of Everglaze and Ban-Lon, a textile company operating on behalf of Joseph Bancroft & Sons in Wilmington, Delaware, which specialised in easy-to-wash-and-wear cotton fabrics.

By this time my father knew his way around clothes, fabric and shoes the way some men know their way around lathes and saws. He could tell you how to keep fabrics in fine condition. He could talk about bulking and crimping processes and how they should be applied to nylon filament. He could wax lyrical on the subject of wools, cashmeres and synthetic yarns and the non-porousness of nylons, particularly in hot climates.

We lived in London from 1956 to 1959 as my father travelled throughout England and Scotland marketing and promoting the trade names of Everglaze and Ban-Lon to weavers, spinners, knitters, garment manufacturers and retail stores. They were good years, and my parents lived well, renting homes in suburbs like Hampstead and Swiss Cottage, where a hooting owl used to terrify my sister and me from the tree outside our bedroom. Our parents were often away, leaving us in the care of nannies, and when they were home they were often entertaining, so much so that at the age of two I managed to discover the pleasures—and hazards—of a dry martini.

My father had learnt that the best way to make a jug of martini was to apply the formula of eight nips of gin to every one of vermouth and to stir it over ice in a martini shaker. One day, at a luncheon party for eight, he finished pouring a third round of martinis just as my mother called everyone to the table to eat. It was the second time she'd announced that lunch was ready, so in their haste the guests abandoned their drinks in the living room. That left six martinis essentially untouched.

I'm told it was the housekeeper who first saw a two-year-old boy lurching around the house and decided to tell my parents that their son might well be drunk. Apparently I slept for the next twenty-four hours, the only indication of my excesses being the dark circles under my eyes the following day.

In late 1958, two and a half years after arriving in London, my father received a phone call from Reggie Williams, the managing director of British Condé Nast Publications. Williams was a brusque Englishman with a short fuse, a former deputy military attaché to Washington during Lord Halifax's term as British foreign secretary. He wanted to see my father that day.

'I had to ask him three times what Condé Nast was,' my father told me, 'because I'd never heard of it.'

The two of them met for a ploughman's lunch at a pub near Wigmore Street and Williams explained that while Condé Nast already published three *Vogue* Australia supplements each year inside British *Vogue*, the company now wanted to start a stand-alone magazine for the Australian market. There was already a person selling advertising space on commission in Sydney, as well as an editorial representative, Rosemary Squire, looking at Australian fashion and commissioning photographs.

What they needed was someone to actually run the business and print the magazine in Australia, initially as a division of the British company, and then—if that proved successful—as a subsidiary of the American-owned parent company. 'Are you interested?' he asked my father.

'I said to Williams, "Look, I know nothing about publishing. I've bought advertising and I know a lot about marketing and promotion and I think I can lead a team, but I have no knowledge or experience with anything to do with publishing, advertising and printing."

'"Well, you could learn that," Williams replied.'

That was in November. A few weeks later, Williams formally offered my father the job of launching Australian *Vogue*. He wanted him to begin in February the following year, but my father said this was too soon; he'd promised the Everglaze people that he would give them six months' notice before taking another job.

'Is that in writing?' Williams asked.

'No, Mr Williams, it isn't,' my father replied.

'Well, then, there is no contract,' Williams pointed out.

'But I gave my word,' my father countered.

'What if I said to you that I can't wait six months and that I've got two other candidates who I think could do the job as well as you and that you might be at risk of losing this?' Williams asked. 'What would you say to me?'

'Well, Mr Williams,' my father responded, 'I would be very unhappy, but I can't walk out on these people. They have been totally fair with me. I have no choice.'

Williams was trying it on. He wanted to gauge my father's sense of loyalty, and whether he was a man who would cave under pressure. Luckily he was not, and luckily again, Everglaze agreed to let him go three and a half months early. They'd known for some time of his desire to return to Australia and they were happy to find a compromise.

In early 1959, my father flew to New York to undergo six weeks' training at Condé Nast 's Madison Avenue headquarters while my mother, sister and I made the voyage to Australia on the Dutch liner *Wilhelm Ruys*, sailing through the Suez Canal to Colombo, Singapore and on to Sydney. This would become my first Proustian memory: the taste of Carnation milk and chocolate sprinkles on white bread, and the smell of lavender in the toilets.

By the time my father started Australian *Vogue* on 1 March 1959, he was a young man with a fierce determination to establish *Vogue* as the premier glossy magazine in the country, particularly in the face of all the naysayers—of which there were many—who said it couldn't be done, that the country didn't need a magazine like *Vogue*; that, indeed, the magazine was too snooty and highbrow for an egalitarian society like Australia's.

My father wanted to prove them wrong. 'I truly believed that Condé Nast had a future in Australia and that Australia would become increasingly sophisticated,' he told me. 'I had a vision of everything to do with quality in Australia growing as Australians travelled more and became more exposed to Europe. I felt that, together with immigration, this was going to deepen and broaden our culture, especially as a new generation came through.'

To realise his vision my father had to educate advertisers on why they needed to place their business with an upmarket magazine like *Vogue* instead of mass-market publications like the *Australian Women's Weekly*, *Woman's Day* or *New Idea*. For that to happen he had to entertain them. Often. Which was why there were always so many martini-soaked lunches and dinners for friends and colleagues from the fashion, cosmetics and advertising world held in our family home.

As a child I remember Rosemary Cooper, the first editor of Australian *Vogue*, coming to dinner wearing her gloves and trademark pillbox hat, and Sheila Scotter, her successor, assuming a regular spot at our table. Sheila Scotter was always so impeccably spoken and immaculately groomed, so handsome in her well-tailored black and white outfits and her silver hair, which had earned her the moniker 'Silver Duchess', that she would put a knot in my stomach just by looking at me.

Scotter was in many ways an early version of Anna Wintour, the despotic style queen of American *Vogue* fame. A daughter of the Raj, born in Calcutta and educated in England, she'd arrived in Australia in 1949 and begun working as a high fashion buyer for the Myer Emporium before taking a job at Everglaze, the same company my father had worked for in London.

Brilliant, provocative and tyrannical, she had cultivated powerful friends in Australia, like Harold Holt, Frank Packer and Reg Ansett, and she was absolutely fearless in promoting both them and herself.

My father appointed her in 1962 as the third editor of Australian *Vogue*—Joan Chesney Frost had been the second editor for a brief period—and for the first five years their relationship flourished, along with rising circulation figures and advertising revenue. By 1967, however, the year of *Vogue Living*'s launch, the figures for *Vogue* were starting to tell a different story, along with the story that Sheila Scotter was telling about herself.

'She was increasingly taking the view that *she* was *Vogue*,' my father explained, 'and that my role was a relatively unimportant one. And she began playing politics by going to my masters in New York.

'I had a very simple philosophy—then and now—in business: if you run a business, you really have to satisfy three parties. First, you have to satisfy your customers, which, in our case, were our readers and advertisers. Second, you have to satisfy your share-holders, your owners. And third, you have to satisfy—and have a good relationship with—your colleagues and staff.

'Sheila was totally ego-driven. She loved building editorial features around her friends. She loved putting her friends in the social pages. And she was a tremendous bully who ran the magazine through fear. She was good to people who were sycophants, who told her what she wanted to hear, but she was very bad with people who opposed her point of view. And they usually didn't last.'

By 1970 my father and Scotter were barely on speaking terms and the following year he finally called her to his office and told her he was letting her go.

'You can't do that,' she said. 'You have no authority to fire me.'

'I believe I have,' my father replied, 'but I think in your own interests it would be better for you to resign.'

'I will *never* resign,' she retorted. 'You are going to have to fire me.'

'May I suggest,' my father said, 'that you take legal advice before you go down that road.'

She did, and from none other than Tony Larkins, Frank Packer's legal counsel. The following morning at 7 am she called my father. 'I've changed my mind,' she said. 'I'm resigning.'

Sheila Scotter never forgave my father for dismissing her, and I became aware of this at a *Vogue* party in 1999, twenty-eight years later, when I overheard her talking loudly to a group of people while my father was making a speech to mark forty years of Australian *Vogue*. 'He never gives anyone credit for his success,' she complained. 'It's always about him.'

All my life I'd heard my father speak warmly of the people who'd shown faith in him, who'd opened the right doors for him, who'd brought their creative talents to bear on the work he'd done. He knew his limitations and he credited a legion of people with making him look better, Sheila Scotter among them.

When Scotter kept criticising him as he spoke, I had a brain snap. She had no idea who I was because it had been nearly three decades since we'd last seen each other. I'd changed far more than she had. 'You are way out of line, Sheila Scotter,' I said to her. 'I think it's time to shut up.'

She looked at me with horror. 'I don't even know who you are,' she replied incredulously.

'I'm David Leser,' I responded, 'and you are way out of line.'

She was suitably mortified, as were those around us.

Curiously, a year earlier, Scotter's book, *Sheila Scotter: Snaps, Secrets and Stories From My Life*, had been published by Random House and she had invited my father to the launch. Just as curiously, my father had accepted the invitation—until he read a story by Daphne Guinness in the *Sydney Morning Herald* outlining some of Scotter's claims, including that it was *her*, not *him*, who had made *Vogue* and that he never acknowledged what others had done for him throughout his career.

My father had fired off a letter to Scotter.

In more than thirty-eight years with Condé Nast, I have always held to the conviction that our editors are our most important assets. When we satisfy the market, i.e. readers and advertisers—and in that order—the editors deserve the lion's share of the credit.

When, on the other hand, our magazines become weaker and diminish, the editors have to take responsibility as well. I suggest you ask your immediate successors, Eve [Harman] or June McCallum, or for that matter Beatrix Miller in London or Anna Wintour and Tina Brown in New York, whether or not they felt supported by me over the last thirty years plus.

You have so much talent, so much ability, that it is precisely this attitude which has caused your career to come adrift over and over again. And that's sad. As far as your respect for me is concerned, I frankly could not care less.

I do want to say, however, that I still think that appointing you as editor was one of the best decisions I ever made but so, equally, was my unhappy decision to let you go. I fully understand that even after all these years you still bear me ill will because of that. To be asked to leave can never be anything other than hurtful to the person at the receiving end. But I assure you, it wasn't easy for me either. In fact, I hated it.

My father then took aim at what he regarded as the most egregious claim in Daphne Guiness's story—that Scotter saw Condé Nast as being run by a 'Jewish mafia'.

To link the word mafia with Condé Nast is about as ridiculous, untruthful, unrealistic and unfair as it could be, and the way the term is used by you could almost be considered defamatory. But don't worry. I have no intention of pursuing this through legal channels. Life is too short.

More importantly, to link mafia with the word Jewish conveys beyond a shadow of doubt that you are an anti-Semite. As it happens, even though my Jewish friends would hardly consider me a good Jew, certainly not a very observing one, I am rather proud of my historical and cultural heritage. I could have done a lot worse.

In using this term you insult not only me but indeed every Jew, whether known to you or not, including Daniel Salem [then head of international operations for Condé Nast], Alex Liberman [former editorial director of Condé Nast] and, indeed, our [half-Jewish] friend Bails [Sidney Baillieu Myer, son of the founder of the Myer Emporium].

There is, of course, another way of looking at it, and that is that the term Jewish mafia used in such a derogatory fashion by you is really a terrible indictment on you, and underlines your miserable prejudices and intolerance.

I find your reference offensive and unacceptable and that is why I shall not attend the Random House function, nor any other function at any time which is arranged for the purpose of honouring you.

And yet my father changed his mind and went to the launch—and was received warmly by Scotter—because, as he told me years later, he was still grateful for all she'd done for *Vogue*. Despite everything she'd said about him—and he'd said about her—he still wanted to pay his respects.

Not so Sir Frank Packer's widow, Lady (Florence) Packer. Although Lady Packer had ended up launching Scotter's book, she did so without having read it first. It was only after the launch that she found out that her late husband had been one of Scotter's regular breakfast companions. Lady Packer never spoke to Scotter again.

Another regular at our house during those early *Vogue* days was Norma Mary Marshall, my father's assistant, who would later go on to become the magazine's advertising manager. I was besotted with Norma Mary. To me, she had the hair of an angel and the most wonderful cleavage I'd ever seen. I was five years old when I first invited her into my bed. 'Would you like to get in and have a cuddle?' I suggested when she'd come to my room to kiss me goodnight. 'That's a sweet offer,' she replied. 'Perhaps not tonight.'

Seven years later Veruschka von Lehndorff, the German-born supermodel, arrived for supper with her Italian photographer boyfriend, Franco Rubartelli, and again it was love at first sight. She was the most attractive, elusive creature I'd ever seen. I knew nothing, of course, about how she'd come to be a supermodel; nothing about her Prussian count father who'd been executed in

Germany in 1944 for his role in the plot to kill Hitler; nothing about her mother, who'd been imprisoned by the Gestapo, nor anything about the fact that Veruschka herself, along with her sister, had been interned in a POW camp for the remainder of the war.

All I could see through the Turkish-bath lens of my pubescent fantasies was a future linked to this six-foot-tall Aryan beauty. Would she leave Rubartelli for me? If she did, what would I do then? And how would we dance, given she was more than six feet tall and I wasn't quite five foot four?

On another occasion, I found myself sitting opposite Dame Margot Fonteyn. England's finest prima ballerina had come to dinner at our home with her wheelchair-bound husband, the former Panamanian politician and ambassador Roberto Arias. I was thirteen and, once again, hopelessly unaware of the company I was in. This ignorance extended, naturally, to ballet, but also to politics and how it was that Mr Arias had come to be paralysed from the waist down. Perhaps my parents had told me that he'd been suspected of organising a coup against the government of Panama, and that five years earlier he'd been shot in the back by a former political ally. I doubt it.

What I know now, though, is that at the time of the assassination attempt, Dame Margot had been planning to leave him but, instead, had chosen to devote her life to tending his needs, forcing herself to dance until she was sixty—and bankrupting herself in order to pay for his medical bills. And this despite all the grief he'd apparently caused her with his long absences and serial adultery.

Again, I was aware of none of this while watching Dame Margot spoon-feed the paraplegic Roberto Arias the herrings my mother had prepared for them. All I sensed was that the world, my world, was full of interesting people—in particular interesting, glamorous women—and that I was drinking in something important about them from my parents.

❧

I was also imbibing something about being Jewish—this inchoate sense of being special, marked, chosen, of having a different language, a different set of dates and rituals and customs, of belonging to a dark history and contested geography that few others in my own shallow-rooted country could claim to possess, unless, of course, they were the indigenous Australians that we never thought much about.

As a young Jewish boy growing up in Australia, I sometimes felt as though I'd entered the picnic grounds through the wrong gate. It felt like I'd come out of the pine forest, covered in damp and nettles, while everyone else had been leaning against the palm trees, gazing out at the Pacific breakers. Often I had this feeling of immense gloom and foreboding. Gloom over what had happened in the Shoah, of things so calamitous they could never be accounted for, let alone properly explained. And foreboding—a deep, abiding sense that something awful might still occur if we weren't careful, if we didn't stick together, if we didn't remain forever strong. And if we didn't refrain from taking unnecessary risks.

No, David, you cannot have a bicycle. We should survive the Holocaust so that you can kill yourself on a bicycle?

Perhaps my mother, Barbara, never actually uttered these words, but it seemed as though she was always thinking them. The air I breathed was charged with anxiety and, at times, a feeling of unutterable sadness. We'd come from somewhere else, somewhere European but also pre-European; God-granted but God-forsaken; civilised but brutish and wretched. Everyone who was Jewish had suffered and knew other Jews who had also suffered and there were a few million of us who had suffered—although millions less than there used to be—and you couldn't possibly be part of this community, this people, this nation, this universe of suffering, unless you took all this to heart and made it your own, even if you didn't understand it. It was like having bars of misery playing through your bones, with their own distinct notes and lamentations.

When I was in synagogue as a young boy I would look at all the men and their sons and wonder whether they, too, were carrying the same enormous weight of sadness. I felt sure they were because, otherwise, why was there so much keening, so much mournful prayer, so much hand-wringing going on behind those big old green iron gates of the Great Synagogue in Elizabeth Street, Sydney?

Of course there was conviviality and warm embrace too, small talk and gossip and introduction to sons and nephews and 'How's your business doing?'. There was all of that, but it was washed through with sombre tones of awe and repentance and a deep remembrance of terrible things. The sun would be blazing outside, and the rest of the country would be heading to the beach, preparing picnics, placing bets, putting out the washing, donning their cricket whites, embracing the Australian way of life, yet here we were—the chosen ones—indoors, genuflecting to an invisible, omnipresent God with His clear moral laws, listening to our rabbi chanting holy words in a language that one day I would have to chant in myself. And even though I understood not a word of it, I knew from an early age what the stories were about: all the years of wandering and persecution and arrest and forced conversion and upturned gravestones and pogroms and exile and the profound sense of struggle and hopelessness and loneliness that had gripped us, this tribe of mine. Stories of Creation—Adam and Eve, Noah and the Flood, the Tower of Babel. Stories of the

Exodus. Stories of Moses and the Burning Bush and the laws he brought down from Mount Sinai. Stories of parting waters and the Promised Land. Stories of prophets, priests and kings. Stories of expulsion and return. Stories of wisdom and courage. And how blessed was I to belong to such a people, with all this suffering but with all its civility and humanity and enlightenment, too, and its dreams of restoration and redemption.

There was only one redemption in all of this for me, however, and it lay not in any afterlife but immediately above me in the upstairs gallery of the synagogue. Every Saturday morning all the dark-eyed daughters of the faith would be sitting with their mothers and grandmothers, looking down on us boys with blushing cheeks and furtive gazes, and it was then that I, twelve years old and fast approaching puberty, would thank the Almighty Lord for having saved my family from the ovens, for having allowed me to be born so that I might share one day soon—God willing, perhaps even at Marty Rosenberg's party next Saturday night—the ambrosial delights of Margot or Virginia or Donna or Karen or Debbie or Vivian or Marilyn or Lesley or Sandy or either of the two Susies. These synagogue maidens were the girls of my generation from good Jewish families who would one day marry the boys from good Jewish families, but who, at this deliciously uncertain point in our history—the late sixties to be precise—were still very much up for grabs for a kiss or fondle or something higher, lower and deeper.

'Did you go upstairs outside with her?' a friend asked me at a party one night, giving me a conspiratorial wink. I was thirteen at the time.

'Sure,' I said, not knowing what he meant, especially given that the house was only single storey and there were no balconies.

'What was it like?' he said.

'Great,' I replied.

'What about downstairs inside? Did you go there?'

'Look, we've been down there most of the night,' I said, revealing my astonishing ignorance of the codes of teenage petting. It was then he explained that 'upstairs outside' was the term for fondling the breast from outside the clothes, and that 'downstairs inside' . . . Well, you'd have to have been Joshua entering the Land of Canaan to have spent even a minute in that place, and I was not him, although I most definitely had aspirations in that direction.

On the weekends I would spend most of my Sundays in the Eastern Suburbs with other Jewish kids, vying for the favour of one of these girls, hoping to see what was underneath their bikinis once we'd managed to get them from Bondi Beach to somewhere less public. We would congregate on the stairs outside the main pavilion at Bondi—a place dubbed Little Jerusalem because of the number of (mostly on heat) Jewish kids who hung out there.

Afterwards, if you were lucky, you would find yourself in Lesley's treehouse or Marilyn's father's toolshed or, as I was on one occasion, hiding in Karen's wardrobe when her parents came home. I'd been on the bed with Karen and was just finding my way across her Land of Milk and Honey when her father, the president of the Great Synagogue, called out to see if his daughter was home. She was very much at home, but I was a long way from mine, so I hid in her wardrobe for two hours, submerged in her shoes and dresses, trying not to breathe, praying to a merciful God not to be discovered, and for my tumescent excitement to subside.

Most of those girls were in the Great Synagogue on that day in February 1969 when I was bar mitzvahed, a quivering wreck of a boy-man trying to sing in a foreign language with a voice still cracking into the downward registers of adulthood.

I remember that day for a number of reasons, chief among them being the terror of singing in front of a packed synagogue, and the panic that overwhelmed me when I suddenly lost my place halfway through the service. The portion of the Torah that I was chanting was purportedly the longest one of the year, some fifty-one verses from the Book of Judges, detailing the heroics of the prophetess Deborah. In the middle of one of these verses, I looked up and saw a friend pulling faces at me. When I looked back down at the page I had absolutely no idea where I was, or what I was supposed to be singing. I froze in front of a full congregation, until my teacher, Rabbi Israel Porush, the man responsible for guiding and moulding the reconstruction of Judaism in Australia following World War II, walked over to me, singing the words I'd forgotten, and pointing to the correct place on the page.

I received thirteen Seiko watches that day and delivered a speech to more than 100 people in which I thanked the rabbi and my family for everything they'd ever done for me. Then the music started up and I danced, first with my mother, and then with my tall Aunty Rozzie, who crushed me to her bosom as we waltzed around the dining room.

That was the last time I saw my grandfather, Kurt Leser. He was sitting at the lunch table in his silk gabardine suit, still an elegant figure at seventy-two but stooped and grey and terribly withdrawn. I learnt later that he'd been so ill he nearly hadn't made the trip from New Zealand. He died four months later.

My father was such a somebody, a *big somebody*, that as a child I felt I had to be a somebody too. Otherwise I would just end up as an anybody or, worse still, the son of a somebody who himself had turned out to be a nobody. It wasn't a conscious thought but it was there, ticking away in the background, creating its own irresistible storyline, fuelling me with a large ambition.

I was desperate to win my father's approval and I can see now that it's one of the main reasons I became a journalist. I wanted to stand up to him, to counter his arguments, to challenge all his airs of authority, formality and high certitude. My father held strong opinions on a lot of things: on subjects like history and politics, and also on people of importance, people of 'excellence'. And he argued about all these things with such conviction that you needed good ideas and choice words to match him, otherwise you could be ground to dust.

Sometimes I felt my mother had been ground to that place a long time before, not just by my father, but also by her mother Hansey, grandmother Ettie and adopted Aunty Poppie—three Jewish empresses with a propensity to scold and dictate to a little Jewish girl the tenets of proper behaviour. That was always a theme in my family—proper behaviour—and it came down from both sides of the line. The combination of my father's German-ness—with all its strictures around punctuality, courtesy and dress code—together with the style dictates of *Vogue*, meant that proper behaviour assumed a supreme role in our moral universe. I think my mother suffered under the weight of this although, God knows, her own lineage boasted matriarchs as stubborn and judgemental as Old Testament High Priestesses. (Ettie, my Latvian great-grandmother, for example, never approved of my German grandfather Kurt and stepmother Ernie because they didn't speak Yiddish.) And even though my mother's parents were highly cultured, she had, in many ways, the sensibilities of a country girl, raised in Bowral in the Southern Highlands of New South Wales, where she loved nothing better than to collect pine cones and pick fruit, play piano, listen to music—her beloved Chopin and Beethoven—talk to friends, read by the fire.

Her father had died when she was four, leaving her to a grieving, self-absorbed mother and a brilliant, caustic stepfather, Sam Simblist QC, who married my grandmother six years later.

Sam Simblist knew the law better than most, but his heart was hidden behind his decrees and sarcasms and any father-love he might have had was reserved for his natural daughter, Diane, my mother's half-sister.

After growing up without a father, and under the tyranny of her mother, grandmother and aunt's severe strictures, my mother was beset by deep insecurities. When she married my father in 1952, their life together suddenly catapulted her into a glamorous, international world for which she was not entirely prepared. But my father gave my mother confidence. He made her believe in herself, up to a point. He took her on a magic-carpet ride around the world, introduced her to people and places she might never have been exposed to otherwise. 'I couldn't have achieved what I achieved if it hadn't been for Mum,' he told me once. 'Asking her to marry me was probably the most important decision I ever made.'

As my father lost his foothold later in life, my mother would come to dominate him in ways she never had before. 'Have you taken your pills, Bern? Why not? I put them out for you. And don't tell me you're having another drink? For goodness' sake, can't you see what it's doing to you? You'll just have to stop or I'll hide the bottle. Now do you want some dinner? No? You can't just exist on liverwurst and bread.'

Such a shifting of the earth's axis. When I was younger it was always my father who dominated the room. I'm sure that's why my sister, Deborah, developed such a lifelong antipathy to political and business discussions, and why my brother Daniel often felt awkward at the dinner table. Our father often held court on Condé Nast-related issues (as well as Churchill, Hitler and Roosevelt) and there was nowhere to go except to become sullen and withdrawn (my brother), feign ignorance or change the subject (my mother and sister) or respond with verbal volleys of one's own—as I eventually did.

The way to engage with my father, I realised, was through the power of words. My father had obviously grown up speaking German but had learnt to speak English as a teenager without a trace of the Saxon man on his tongue. Perhaps that's why words were so crucial to him—a love of language to be sure, a vehicle for conveying ideas certainly, but also, in a very real sense, a means of concealing who he was, concealing his origins. He spoke as though he'd never set foot in Germany. In fact, he spoke not unlike his hero, Winston Churchill.

At fourteen my father had set about wiping his native land from the map of his mind, snuffing out the language, erasing the memories, severing all links to the country that had rejected him. My grandfather had done the same, although his act of reinvention was never as successful or urgent. He'd been broken by two world wars and his injuries, both physical and emotional, persisted throughout his life. Over a lifetime my father became a phenomenal success story, but also one of the proudest and most protected men I have ever known; protected, I suspect, even from himself, although as I write that I think: *who am I to judge?*

Throughout my teenage years and young adulthood I railed against many of my father's values. They were, in large part, the values of the ruling class and, in my father's case, values all too often worn with a sense of self-importance I found discomforting. How else to say this? My father, for all his progressive political views on many things, for all his love of family and friends, for all his charm, courtesy and goodness of heart, was an unashamed snob and elitist. This often made him more remote to me than he might otherwise have been.

As my father's ascent within Condé Nast gathered pace throughout the late seventies, eighties and early nineties, so too did many of the trappings of wealth and power. I recoiled from the chauffeurs and upper-class gentlemen's clubs in England after he went there in 1976 to run Condé Nast's British operations. I chafed at the black-tie dinners and *Vogue* party chatter. I shuddered over the obsession with how things looked, rather than how things were or might be. I didn't like my father's stiff punctuality, which he no doubt inherited from his German forebears. I didn't like his obsession with etiquette and manners, with what was considered 'the right way of doing things'.

My father was formal and proper and buttoned up and so, naturally, inevitably, I rebelled. In my late teens and early twenties I became a hippie and grew my hair long. I wore tattered jeans, smoked dope, played guitar and listened to protest songs, most of which were aimed squarely at the heart of men like my father. I adopted socialist views and argued relentlessly with him about the role of unions, the greatness of Whitlam (now there was an argument to be had after Whitlam's dismissal), the shrill conservatism of Murdoch (and what a hypocrite I would soon turn out to be), the desirability of women without makeup (and how that cocked a snook at the *Vogue* cover girl!) . . . all these things forever simmering away in the background, creating what I sometimes felt was low-lying mutual indignation. Mutual indignation tempered, of course, with great love.

As a student at Sydney Grammar School I was often placed on detention, or caned for impertinence, mostly for challenging my teachers. After I finished school, I came to relish this challenging of authority, and anyone in a position of power seemed to me like fair game. What a benevolent sign from the universe it would turn out to be, then, that I would eventually get paid to be impertinent, to ask questions others feared asking, to catch people off guard, to size them up, pull them down, turn them around and show them to the world in new, often less flattering colours. My father might have been content dog paddling in the shallows of the fashion world, but I was never happier than diving down into the murky depths of the human condition.

Any good psychologist—or blind prophet—could have told you I was making ready to star in my own little Sophoclean play, one that would see me try to kill (metaphorically speaking) my father through the printed word. I would prove and best him at my chosen profession. I would target people in power so as to test the theory of clay feet, his and everyone else's. I would profile people who my father and mother actually knew and liked, and then write devastating critiques of them. I would expose people's puffed-up pretensions and examine their contradictions. I would lay bare their falsehoods, boosting myself by bringing others down. I would be sent on choice assignments, win accolades for my fearless reporting and sometimes lyrical prose, and I would inhabit my job every bit as much as my father had, without recognising any of this for a second.

What I wilfully chose to ignore during these callow years, however, was that my father was actually the standard-bearer for much of what I would come to regard as good and noble in journalism and politics. He admired Rupert Murdoch's extraordinary success but he abhorred the way he used his newspapers and editors to advance his own ideological agendas. He believed fervently in the separation of church and state, and the right of editors and journalists to report and interpret the news as they saw fit.

He raised eyebrows among his Liberal Party friends by casting his ballot for Whitlam in 1972. He voted for Hawke three times, Keating once, Beazley once, Rudd once, Gillard once, while never resiling from his historical support for Menzies, Holt, Gorton, Fraser and Howard, nor his admiration for Margaret Thatcher and his undying reverence for Winston Churchill.

His creed was generosity of spirit and largeness of heart. He believed that those who held to a strong ideology often severed themselves from their own humanity. He recoiled from the zealous and dogmatic. His library was filled with books on history, politics, philosophy, biography and the constant, relentless probings of the Fourth Estate.

At heart, he was a Jewish libertarian and later, during the late eighties and early nineties in New York, together with Si Newhouse and Alex Liberman, the Russian-born painter, sculptor and editorial director of Condé Nast, my father would be part of the Jewish triumvirate—*not mafia!*—that ran America's richest media empire, and employed the best editors, publishers, art directors, photographers and writers in the world.

He would regularly send me articles from the *New Yorker*, *Vanity Fair* and the *Spectator*, marking out great passages of writing, pointing to the spirited position of the writers, extolling the virtues of a free press and—by implication—planting in me the strong self-belief that I might even belong in their company. 'See attached,' he would write. 'This is what you're capable of. With all my love, Your Dad.'

It has taken me the better part of fifty years to come to terms with all this, to wrestle with all these conflicting emotions, and to understand just how and why words would become so important to me as a way of dealing with them. Words, if used well, could crack the armour, challenge the construct, command the attention of people—particularly my father, whose attention span could sometimes be alarmingly short. They could wrestle with paradoxes, prise open the heart, create some soft meadow through which two people might wander, particularly a father and son. They could also fill the unbearable silences into which we would fall when discussions weren't being conducted on agreeable terms.

Looking back now, this is why in 1979, after having spent a year writing woeful advertisements for car upholstery, after having wandered around India, Nepal and the Greek islands, after having done three weeks of commerce at university before changing to an arts degree, I became a reporter on Rupert Murdoch's Sydney *Daily Telegraph*.

3

'THIS IS NOT THE FUCKING *JERUSALEM POST*'

Jobs on newspapers don't just fall out of the sky. Long before the decline of the printed word on paper and the rise of social media, a position on a newspaper was hard to get, so hard you needed to have grafted your way up from the inside, first as a copyboy, then as a young cadet, to secure your place as a journalist. Or, alternatively, you needed to have been given a parachute which could miraculously drop you into a newsroom without any of the requisite skills.

That was the way I landed in 1979, with a graceless thump, right in the middle of one of the toughest, most competitive newspaper offices in Australia. 'What can you write about?' the *Telegraph*'s chief of staff, Cliff Neville, asked me when we were introduced on my first morning as a young journalist.

I'd just completed my arts degree in English literature and Middle Eastern politics so I said, 'Well, I think I know a fair bit about the Arab–Israeli conflict and patron–client relations in the Middle East.'

Before I give you Cliff Neville's devastating riposte, let me just provide the back story . . .

Two years earlier, at the age of twenty-one, I landed in Israel for the first time, a few weeks before the Egyptian president Anwar Sadat crossed the Suez Canal on his historic mission of peace.

I spent some time on a kibbutz so when I arrived in Tel Aviv on 19 November 1977 I hadn't read a newspaper or heard a radio report for a month. I was shocked by the preternatural calm that had fallen over Israel's largest city. No tramp of feet, no swelling crowds, no car horns; just a suspended hush, as if war or plague had suddenly been declared and a people ordered indoors.

The nation was, in fact, indoors, as I discovered when I walked into a café on Dizengoff Street. A crowd had gathered around a television set and there on the screen was Anwar El Sadat, walking down the stairs of his presidential plane and being greeted by the Israeli prime minister, Menachem Begin, President Ephraim Katzir and a twenty-one-gun salute. Anwar Sadat—the same man who, four years earlier, had nearly defeated the Jewish state in a surprise attack by Egyptian forces on Yom Kippur, the holiest day of the Jewish calendar. I couldn't believe what I was seeing.

'What's happening?' I asked the man next to me.

'You don't know?' he replied, looking at me with a mixture of condescension and pity. 'Sadat is here.'

'In Israel?'

'Yes, in Israel. Where have you been?'

'On a kibbutz.'

'Well, he's here. Look. At Ben Gurion Airport.'

'What's he here for?'

'You don't know?'

'No.'

'He's here to talk to us, to talk to the Jews. He wants to kill us, now he wants to talk. So let's talk.'

Sadat had declared his intention ten days earlier of visiting Jerusalem and it had sparked demonstrations across the globe, not to mention angry denunciations throughout the Arab world, which still refused to recognise Israel's right to exist. The Soviet bloc was also incensed, countries like Hungary, East Germany, Yugoslavia and Albania warning they would attack Egypt if it attempted to make peace with the Jewish state.

Sadat addressed the Israeli parliament, the Knesset, the next morning, in a speech broadcast to hundreds of millions of people. I watched in disbelief and awe:

Ladies and gentlemen, there are moments in the lives of nations and people where it is incumbent upon those known for their wisdom and clarity of vision to survey the problem, with all its complexities and vain memories, in a bold drive towards new horizons.

Those who, like us, are shouldering the same responsibilities entrusted to us are the first who should have the courage to make determining decisions that are consonant with the magnitude of the circumstances. We must all rise above all obsolete theories of superiority, and the most important thing is to never forget that infallibility is the prerogative of God alone.

If I said that I wanted to avert from all the Arab people the horrors of shocking and destructive wars, I must sincerely declare before you that I have the same feelings and bear the same responsibility towards all and every man on earth, and certainly towards the Israeli people.

Any life that is lost is a human life, be it that of an Arab or Israeli. A wife who becomes a widow is a human entitled to a happy family life, whether she be an Arab or an Israeli.

Innocent children who are deprived of the care and compassion of their parents are ours. They are ours, be they living on Arab or Israeli land . . .

Allow me to address my call from this rostrum to the people of Israel. I pledge myself with true and sincere words to every man, woman and child in Israel. I tell them from the Egyptian people who bless this sacred mission of peace everywhere . . . Introduce to the entire world the image of the new man in this area so that he might set an example for the man of our age, the man of peace everywhere. Ring the bells for your sons. Tell them that those wars were the last wars and the end of sorrows. Tell them we are entering upon a new beginning, a new life, a love of life, prosperity, freedom and peace.

You, sorrowing mother, widowed wife, you, the son who lost a brother or a father, all the victims of war, fill the air and space with the recitals of peace, fill bosoms and hearts with the aspirations of peace . . .

Anwar Sadat said many other things that historic day, words that to my impressionable ears seemed holy, and were to inform my thinking on the Middle East forever. He talked about how a people's happiness could never be built on the misery of others. He said he was now welcoming the Jews to live among the Arabs in security and safety, but that no durable peace could ever be reached without a just solution to the Palestinian problem. He admitted that, yes, the Arabs had refused to meet or exchange even the most cursory greetings with Israelis for thirty years but that now, as the leader of the Arab world, he was extending the olive branch to Israel in a partnership based on peace and justice.

He said the psychological wall of separation that had been built by Israel over the years—a separation based on its legitimate fears and its assumed superiority over Arab forces—had been decisively destroyed by Egypt's stunning advances during the 1973 Yom Kippur war.

He said no peace could ever be achieved by the occupation of Arab land and that if Israelis were to ever know true peace, they would need, once and for all, to withdraw from the Occupied

Territories and Arab (East) Jerusalem. By doing so, Israel would have all its security concerns guaranteed by the two Superpowers, guarantees which would be accepted by the Arab world.

'You should clearly understand the lesson of confrontation between you and us,' Sadat continued.

> Expansion does not pay. To speak frankly, our land does not yield itself to bargaining, it is not even open to argument. We cannot accept any attempt to take away or cede one inch of it, nor can we accept the principle of debating or bargaining over it. I sincerely tell you also that before us today lies the appropriate chance for peace. If we are really serious in our endeavour for peace, it is a chance that may never come again. It is a chance that if lost or wasted, the resulting slaughter would bear the curse of humanity and of history.

I have been contemplating those words for more than thirty-five years now, but back in 1979, on my first day at the *Daily Telegraph*, my pretensions of Middle Eastern expertise were lost on Cliff Neville. In fact, what followed was a dreadful silence and then Neville's withering reply: 'Mate, this is the *Daily Telegraph*, not the fucking *Jerusalem Post*.'

'Right.' I blushed. 'Well, I've also studied Proust, Flaubert and Thomas Mann.'

'Is that right?' he said, hissing like a bearded cobra. 'I guess that's going to come in very handy when you're doing the weather reports and police rounds, isn't it? Tell me, mate, do you know how to type yet? What's your shorthand like?'

'I don't do shorthand,' I replied. 'And my typing's not so great either.'

Cliff Neville looked at me as if I'd just pissed on his shoes. I was there against his own best instincts. He was under instructions from the editor, Adrian Begg, to give me a desk and something to do. Adrian Begg was under instructions from management to do the same. The instructions had come from none other than Rupert Murdoch.

Although not yet the leviathan figure he would one day become, even in 1979 Rupert Murdoch was not a figure to be messed with. In 1953 he'd taken charge of News Ltd following the death of his father, Sir Keith Murdoch, and through the 1950s and early '60s had begun to expand his empire to include television licences. In 1964 he'd become a major player on the Australian political scene by launching the *Australian*, the first national newspaper in the country. Four years later he'd created waves in England by purchasing the racy but now defunct, scandal-spreading and scandal-plagued *News of the World*. It was the first of many audacious acquisitions that would earn him the sobriquet of the 'Dirty Digger'. During the 1970s his ambitions began to soar. He bought the *Daily Telegraph* and *Sunday Telegraph* newspapers in Sydney, then a publishing company in San Antonio, Texas, followed by the *New York Post* and then the New York Magazine Company, publisher of *New York* and *Village Voice*.

By the time I was finishing off my last university essays on Marcel Proust and the Arab–Israeli Six-Day War, he was well on the way to becoming the newspaper prince of the world. And here's the thing: he owed my father a favour.

In 1977, shortly after taking over as managing director of British Condé Nast, my father had given Murdoch's daughter, Prudence MacLeod, a job on British *Vogue*. It was a lifeline, a confidence boost, to Murdoch's eldest child—at that time a talented but unhappy woman—and my father thought it only fair and reasonable to ask Murdoch to return the favour. And so the *Daily Telegraph* was to become my baptism by the banks of the River Jordan, except there was not a sprinkler of consecrated water or a spruiker of good Christian virtue within sight. There was, however, Norm Lipson.

Norm Lipson was a short, tough, angry working-class Jew with an extraordinary propensity to pick fights—with his colleagues, his interviewees and, it seemed, with anyone who happened to glance at him the wrong way. Up until that point, I'd never met a person like him.

On my first day in the newsroom, he walked up to my desk with a menacing glint in his eyes. 'How ya goin'? Norm Lipson.'

'Good thanks,' I replied.

'You're the new fourth-year cadet, are you?'

'Yes, I am.'

'Where've you come from?'

'Macquarie University.'

'Yeah? What were you doing there?'

'Bachelor of Arts degree—English and Middle Eastern politics.'

'Yeah, well, you know, mate . . . a good Arab's a dead Arab.'

I should have let that go through to the keeper but for some reason I decided to take issue with my new colleague.

'I don't know, Norm,' I said. 'Once you get to understand Arab society, Arab culture, the Arab street, it's a lot more complex than that. If you look at the history of colonialism in the region . . .' I prattled on like this for a few more seconds until I noticed that Norm's pupils had narrowed into black pinheads and his body had become taut.

'Mate, you're a fucking gig, do you know that?' (I didn't actually know that because I wasn't quite sure what a gig was, although I found out later it was something close to a bloody fool.) 'Do you want to step outside while we sort this one out?'

'Look, not really, Norm. This is my first day here and I don't really want to fight you.'

'Well, you're a fucking idiot, aren't you?'

'I don't know, Norm. Maybe I am. Maybe all Arabs are fucked. I just didn't think they were as fucked as you claim, but maybe you're on to something.'

'Alright,' he said. 'But think about what I've told you—because you're a Jew yourself, is that right? You're a fucking Red Sea pedestrian like me?'

'A Red Sea pedestrian? Yes, Norm, I am.'

'Well, we've got to stick together, right?'

'Yes, we do, Norm.'

As I was to discover later, Norm was also a very good reporter and a man I would cautiously grow to like. He had contacts going all the way from the top of the political hierarchy to the bottom of the criminal pile—police commissioners, police informers, underworld figures, petty spivs, smooth-talking lawyers—and he could wheedle, tease, cajole and threaten information out of just about all of them, and then return to the newsroom to bash out a 600-word page-one story in thirty minutes flat.

In late December 1979, the Soviet Union invaded Afghanistan and I was assigned to accompany Norm to the Soviet consulate in Sydney, where members of the local Afghan community had gathered in protest. By the time we arrived in the early afternoon, the demonstration was already heating up.

I had begun to construct an opening paragraph in my mind—'A crowd of 300 anti-Soviet demonstrators gathered yesterday outside Sydney's Soviet consulate . . .'—when suddenly a wild scuffle erupted around me.

'Don't you fucking push me, you fucking Arab gig,' I heard Norm yelling at a group of demonstrators, while unleashing a volley of punches.

It didn't matter that Afghans weren't Arabs—never had been, never would be; what mattered was that here we were in the middle of a brawl with them. Even then I knew enough about reporting to know this wasn't meant to happen.

'Norm, it's okay, mate. They didn't mean to push you.'

'You fucking gig,' he said through a sea of arms. 'Don't you come into this country and start pushing me around, you fucking gig.'

The scuffle lasted a couple of minutes. Norm was pulled off the demonstrators. The police stepped in. We went back to reporting on the fury being directed at Moscow's representatives in Sydney by a group of Afghan Australians.

That was my introduction to news reporting.

It took me a while to learn where to pitch my tepee on this wild reservation. In those first few days I was shown to a desk next to veteran journalist Ronnie Gibson, a woman with an impressive cleavage and an apparent fondness for pig-shooting. She used to bang away at her typewriter with a cigarette dangling from her mouth and a smoke-cured squint in her eyes. She was not into small talk or niceties, at least not with me.

One day she saw me at my desk writing a story in longhand, and asked what I was doing. I told her I was writing a story. 'Well, why don't you learn to use a fucking typewriter?' she said.

So I did. I went to the Judy Suiter secretarial college in the evenings where, along with twenty young women, I discovered the practical pleasures of touch-typing and shorthand. Within twelve months I could type faster than any other reporter on the paper and I could take down 100 words a minute in Mercury shorthand, a bastardised version of shorthand that was to become my own secret script, illegible to anyone but myself.

These were handy skills for a newsroom, although there were times I would have preferred competency in martial arts. Not long after starting at the *Telegraph* another senior reporter, Dorian Wild, made his feelings known to me. I'd arrived at my desk to find all my files, notebooks and diaries scattered on the floor and Wild sitting in my chair.

'Excuse me, Dorian,' I said politely. 'I think you'll find this is my desk.'

'Fuck off, Leser,' he said. 'Find another desk.'

My response was not the kind you'd expect from someone who'd only been in the newsroom a few months. 'Listen here, you imperious prick,' I replied. 'Give me my desk back.'

Wild's response was elementally Australian. He stood up, pushed his chair back and decked me.

Dorian Wild doesn't know this but he taught me one of my first big lessons in journalism, and it didn't involve aiming a left hook at his ugly, pink, jutting jaw. It was more to do with ethics than pugilistics.

A few months after I started on the paper, Wild replaced Cliff Neville as chief of staff and, in that capacity, sent me to cover an event for the United Nations Media Peace Awards. The main award was being given to the then head of the Australian trade union movement, Bob Hawke, for a series of Boyer lectures he'd delivered earlier in the year on the theme of non-violent resolution of conflict. Hawke was the beer-swilling Rhodes Scholar who four years later would become Australia's Labor prime minister. My job was to interview him afterwards.

That's exactly what I did, except what I failed to do was far more important. Bob Hawke wasn't the only one receiving a peace prize that day. Monica Joyce was accepting one on behalf of her husband, ABC journalist Tony Joyce, a brave and eloquent man who'd been killed earlier in the year while covering civil unrest in Zambia.

During the ceremony, Tony and Monica's five-year-old son

Daniel was asked to come to the stage to collect his father's award, and I noticed that he was wearing the same black and gold Sydney Grammar uniform that I'd worn for twelve years. This was our point of contact, and following the ceremony, after my interview with Bob Hawke, I went up to little Daniel Joyce and asked him how he liked the school and what he thought of the school principal, Mr Billing. 'Good,' he answered in his sweet, high-pitched voice.

'Well, congratulations on your daddy's award,' I said, then returned to the newsroom to write my story on Hawke.

At 6 pm, after I'd filed my unremarkable piece, Dorian Wild came up to me and said, 'So what did the kid say?'

'What do you mean?' I replied.

'What did the kid say when you asked him how he felt when his old man was killed?'

'I didn't ask him that,' I said.

'Well, call him up,' Wild growled, 'and ask him what it was like when his old man was killed in Africa.'

'Dorian, I can't do that.'

'Why not?' he said.

'Because it's wrong. He's just a kid. He's only five years old.'

'Listen, Leser, if you don't do it you're out of a job,' came the brisk retort.

For the next two hours I pretended to make phone calls to little Daniel Joyce. I called friends and asked them if they'd mind staying on the line so that it looked like I was having a conversation.

The deadline came and went. I never spoke to Daniel Joyce but the next day's paper ran a page-three photo and a story about Daniel Joyce with my by-line attached. The headline read: BRAVE DANIEL, and it included information gleaned from I don't know where, certainly not from me and certainly not from 'Brave Daniel'.

⌣

One of my next assignments was in a place called Thirlmere, a small town south-west of Sydney where an eighteen-year-old woman had vanished from her home. Her near-naked and battered body had been found ten days later in an orchard thirty kilometres away.

I'd gone to the town with a senior reporter to try to gauge the reaction of the community to her murder. We did that by sitting in the pub and talking to locals; me earnestly taking notes as my colleague downed one schooner after another.

When we returned to the newsroom later that evening my drunken co-worker began tapping out the opening paragraph: 'Thirlmere was a town of tears and anger last night as residents mourned the death of Carol Ann Astley.'

After nine more scintillating paragraphs written at breakneck speed he then turned to me and asked, 'So what did the bloke you were speaking to in the pub say?'

I began rifling through my notes, but before I had a chance to select the most appropriate quotes my colleague was already putting down the thoughts of one distressed resident: 'I can't believe this has happened in this town . . .'

'Hey, you can't say that,' I protested.

'Who says I can't?' he said.

'How can you have her saying that? She didn't say it.'

'Yeah, but that's what she meant to say. Don't be a fuckwit, mate. We're just helping her to be more succinct.'

I worked on the *Daily Telegraph* for three years. During that time I learnt how to cover parliament, court cases, fires, murders, industrial disputes and general news. Once I even got to write a feature story about the Middle East. It was on the death of the King of Saudi Arabia and the question marks hanging over his successor.

The by-line above the story was by David Le Ser, probably an unconscious indicator of what the *Daily Telegraph* thought of my Middle Eastern posturings.

For a year I was the paper's religion and ethnic affairs reporter, the highlight of which was sitting through a private screening of Bob Guccione's controversial new movie, *Caligula*, with Fred Nile, the deeply conservative clergyman-turned-politician. The two of us had never met before, but we sat together for 156 excruciating minutes in a small theatre in George Street, watching a mad emperor's various acts of violence and sexual depravity on the screen.

I had only one wish that day—for Fred Nile to fulminate and thunder sufficiently that I would have myself a front-page scoop. For that to happen *Caligula* needed to be as graphic a depiction of imperial Rome's decadence as was possible. Thankfully, the filmmakers didn't disappoint. Caligula was the wild-eyed lunatic history had led us to believe, and he had a magnificent sexual appetite to match. There he was, fornicating with the virgin bride on the night of her marriage before fist-fucking the groom and then having the groom's penis chopped off for good measure. What a great way to meet the Reverend Fred Nile. I glanced at him numerous times during the movie as he shifted in his seat, muttering, 'Oh my God.' At one point he turned to me, completely ashen, and asked for a strong cup of tea. 'This is the most disgusting thing I've ever seen in my life,' he said.

The next day's paper walked off the stands.

I think one of my greatest achievements during those first years in journalism was not surviving the Afghan demonstration with Norm Lipson, nor picking myself off the floor after Dorian Wild had thumped me, nor even securing that front-page scoop on *Caligula* with the Reverend Fred Nile. It was avoiding being arrested by the New South Wales Police.

Neville Wran was premier at the time and in 1980, as a new member of the press gallery, I was invited to his end-of-year Christmas party at Parliament House in Sydney—a rowdy, jocular affair at which journalists and politicians swapped mostly apocryphal stories under the influence of too much alcohol. Halfway through the night, veteran radio reporter Sean Flannery asked me and a female colleague if we'd like to smoke a joint with him outside.

'It's fabulous stuff,' he assured us. 'Pure Lebanese blonde.'

I'd never been stoned in Parliament House before. This seemed like a good time.

After rolling up on his news bureau desk the three of us walked down two flights of stairs to a landing outside the parliament building, overlooking Macquarie Street. No sooner had we each taken a drag than a police car suddenly came towards us with its spotlight glaring and a voice booming through the megaphone. 'This is the police. Don't move.'

Natural prudence should have told us to stamp out the joint, pretend we'd been smoking a cigarette, then introduce ourselves as members of the press gallery enjoying a break from the premier's party. But prudence deserted us that evening as Sean Flannery yelled, 'Quick, run for it!'

I'd been covering state parliament for less than two months. I'd been a reporter for no more than a year. I had no political friends and certainly no police sources who would come to my aid. I was a panic-stricken cadet reporter way out of my depth. And as Sean Flannery bounded up the stairs two at a time, yelling, 'Fuuuuuck!' I was in hot pursuit—as were two police officers.

The police caught our female friend on the stairs but Sean and I made it to the second floor, where the media bureaus were positioned, one after the other down either side of the corridor. Sean reached the end of the corridor first and dived under a couch in the ABC newsroom. I kept running.

'Stop!' ordered the police officer. 'Stop or I'll shoot!'

DID HE SAY 'STOP OR I'LL SHOOT'?!

There was no way on God's earth I was stopping, so I dashed past the ABC office, rounded the corner, jumped an entire set of stairs, then a second set, to find myself one floor below in the tranquil confines of the Hansard reporters' room. I began leafing through the transcripts of that day's parliamentary proceedings as casually as I could, hoping desperately to look like a young man diligently doing his job. The fact that I was flushed scarlet and gasping for breath didn't exactly help my cause.

The tap on my right shoulder came a few seconds later.

'Come with me,' the officer said.

'What do you mean?' I replied. (It was more like 'What [pant] do [pant pant] you [pant] mean [pant pant]?')

'You were just outside on a landing with two other people.'

'I don't know what you're talking about,' I said.

'We've already got your friend in the back of our car so you'd better come with us.'

'I don't know what you're talking about,' I repeated.

'Don't bullshit me, mate. I saw you on the landing outside and you were the one I was chasing.'

'Listen, Officer, I'm just trying to get a bit of work done before I go back to the premier's Christmas party.' Pant. Pant pant. Pant.

'Come with me,' he replied.

I was under arrest. In a few hours I would lose my job and probably find myself a news item in the next day's opposition newspaper. I could see the headline in the *Sydney Morning Herald*: MURDOCH REPORTER ARRESTED IN STATE PARLIAMENT. At least it wasn't going to be: MURDOCH CADET SHOT BY POLICE!

As I was being marched back up the stairs and down the corridor to the waiting police car, Sean Flannery emerged from his hiding place with a look of casual insouciance on his face, his eyes bloodshot.

'Good evening, Officer,' he said. 'Sean Flannery, 2UE.' Sean had been a police reporter for probably twenty years before being sent to Macquarie Street to cover state politics. He knew most of the state's senior police officers and they all knew him, or had heard of him.

'Sean, how's it going?' the policeman replied.

'Not bad, not bad. What are you up to?'

The police officer pointed at me. 'This bloke was downstairs on the landing with two other people. We saw them smoking something. One of them's in the car already.'

'Oh, you mean Jane?' Sean said. 'I wouldn't worry about her. She's with me.' And then Sean whispered conspiratorially to the officer, 'Look, the thing is, she's married to . . . and she's having it on with . . . and her husband doesn't know.'

He had just named the well-known press secretary to a well-known federal Labor politician and an even better-known NSW Labor figure. 'Know what I mean?' Nod nod wink wink.

'Bloody hell, Sean, I don't need this kind of bullshit on Christmas,' the officer said, believing every word of Flannery's confection. Then the two of them were slapping each other on the back with blokey delight and the officer next to me was yelling out to his colleague to let our friend (whose name wasn't Jane) out of the police car. 'Hey, Bill . . . this is Sean Flannery. Remember him? 2UE. Yeah. Listen, mate, she's fine to go.'

And then: 'Have a great night, Sean.'

'Yeah, you too. Merry Christmas.'

Suddenly we were free. Stoned and free. Just like at Woodstock.

Sean Flannery died in November 2011 after a long battle with cancer, and I'm sorry I never took the opportunity to thank him for having saved my sick and sorry arse.

❧

In my third year on the *Daily Telegraph* I was invited to become the newspaper's Melbourne correspondent. I was twenty-six years old and I'd graduated from novice university cadet journalist and fugitive reporter to someone who could be trusted to run a one-man bureau in Australia's second largest city. It wasn't New York but it felt like a promotion, even though the paper's interest in Melbourne often reflected the smug indifference of a larger city for a smaller one.

It was in Melbourne that I encountered my first dead body. A helicopter carrying a television news crew had crashed in a paddock on the outskirts of the CBD and I'd raced from the office to find four bodies charred and, in some cases, still smoking amid the wreckage. The pilot had stumbled seventy metres with his clothes on fire before collapsing. I never found out whether he survived or not. It was a story with a twenty-four-hour life cycle and all I knew from that day on was that it would take a lot to get me inside a helicopter.

In 1982 Melbourne felt more like a large provincial town than Australia's second metropolis. I was the only reporter covering the city for the *Telegraph* but I shared a newsroom with a number of others. It was pretty obvious from the first day that some of them didn't like me.

'Here he comes,' one of them smirked as I walked into that sad little newsroom at the Warsaw end of La Trobe Street one morning. 'Here comes the Christ killer. Let's pin him up on the wall and do to him what he did to our Saviour.'

There was general guffawing as I stood there looking at them, shocked and red-faced. For years afterwards I replayed that moment, chastising myself for being just another Jewish lamb to the slaughter, but this journalist was a good five inches taller than me and I knew he was probably less the anti-Semite and more the alcohol-fuelled intellectual with a large but sozzled brain. He had a vast knowledge of history, politics and religion and he loved to spice his comments with mordant wit and religious metaphor.

Twenty years later I saw him at the Byron Bay Blues Festival and I pointed him out to my wife, Merran, as the man who'd once called me a Christ killer. Merran confronted him and he exploded, denying he'd ever said such a thing and accusing me of defamation. I think B.B. King was on stage at the time, belting out 'Sweet Little Angel' though, in the spirit of some of my earliest lessons as a reporter, I might be making that up.

4

AND THE BAND PLAYED ON

At the end of 1972, as Gough Whitlam was being sworn in as Labor prime minister, my father was putting together a consortium to buy the rights to publish *Vogue* and *Vogue Living* in Australia under licence from the American parent company.

These two men who, strangely enough, would become good acquaintances later in life, would become the two towering figures of my young teenage life—one a lofty idealist determined to put an end to the born-to-rule assumptions of the Tories; the other a publishing idealist determined to establish a new journal of style, taste and high society in his adopted land—possibly the most un-Australian thing a man could do in a former penal colony.

Thirteen years after Australian *Vogue* had been established, S.I. Newhouse agreed to my father's buy-out proposal and the new company—Bernard Leser Publications Pty Ltd—was launched in typically *Vogue* style.

On the last evening of Condé Nast Publications' existence in Australia, my father and his colleagues held a wake for the company with black candles, caviar and champagne. The following morning my father arrived at the office of Bernard Leser

Publications to find a large white satin ribbon and bow draped over the front door and a breakfast of champagne and smoked salmon prepared by his adoring staff.

'He was so lovely we used to call him Father Bear,' Norma Mary Marshall, the woman I'd tried to bed as a five-year-old, said many years later. 'We were like a family.'

So much so that each Friday at noon Norma Mary and my father and the rest of the female-dominated management team would shut themselves off in the beauty department and drink Bloody Marys mixed by the beauty editor, Joanne Fuller. It was a far cry from the metropolitan newsroom where journalists would often head to the pub for a liquid lunch, veteran reporter Jim Oram apparently distinguishing himself one day by pissing into his wine carafe in the middle of a meal.

For those first years in journalism I was never able to entirely vanquish the charge of nepotism. That was understandable then, and seems even more understandable now. Australians—with their felon origins, their bushranger folklore, their hell-raising, working-class impulses—weren't inclined to look favourably on acts of patronage, especially when bestowed on the son of a silver-tail magazine publisher.

Never mind that the newsroom, like the suburban dentist surgery, family business or cattle property, was often the training ground for the sons and daughters, nephews and nieces, distant cousins and bastard children of the reporter, dentist or farmer. That wasn't how Australians saw themselves. We saw ourselves as the classless, egalitarian society of our romantic myth-making. We were all as good, if not better, than our despised masters.

That being said, there was nothing remotely classless or egalitarian about Australian *Vogue*. This bible of fashion, this arbiter of all things chic and trendy, had, from its inception in 1959, been the glossy dream space in which Australian women could first enter the worlds of Paris, London, Milan and New York high society. Better still they could dress themselves just as the women of these glittering cities did.

This was the high society load I carried into the newsroom and it added considerably to the fear already roiling around inside me—fear of not knowing my city well enough and of not having developed sufficient contacts to inform my stories. Fear of getting scooped by the opposition. Fear of being underprepared for an interview. Fear of not asking the right questions. Fear of being overwhelmed by the demands of filing up to five stories a day. Fear of being too dim-witted, credulous or slow. And, of course, fear of being seen just as my father's son and dismissed accordingly.

This fear took up permanent occupancy inside my nervous system, but it was given a good run for its money by its more devious—and desirous—bastard child: ambition.

I had no real awareness of this at the time, but I can see now that I was a young man with the burning desire to prove I was more than just the privileged, first-born son of a Jewish glossy magazine king. The burning desire to prove that Rupert Murdoch had not been wrong to order one of his editors to give me a job. The burning desire to prove I could actually write.

I was completely driven by this need to make my mark, and in the spring of 1982, two possible ways of doing so presented themselves. One was to go to Kampala, the war-torn capital of Uganda, as Reuters' correspondent; the other was to go to New Orleans, the gastronomical and musical epicentre of the American Deep South.

Three years after starting at the *Daily Telegraph* in Sydney I was offered the job in Uganda by an Australian reporter looking for someone to replace him in his one-man Kampala bureau. I was seriously tempted. It had been three years since Idi Amin, the wife-eating butcher and president-for-life, had been ousted by his political nemesis, Milton Obote, and from the outside it seemed things could only improve. Idi Amin was in Saudi Arabia and, more importantly, no one on the streets of Kampala had any idea my father was the man who'd started Australian *Vogue*. This was reason enough, I figured, to get lost in Winston Churchill's 'Pearl of Africa'.

It would have been a disastrous move. The day after I was due to begin my new posting, Milton Obote expelled every foreign journalist from the country. The bloodletting commenced then with renewed vigour, away from the prying eyes of the press.

New Orleans was a far more civilised alternative. It was the House of the Rising Sun, the Big Easy and, unlike Kampala, it had restaurants and bars and pecan pies and Bourbon Street, where a young man could get lost, wasted, or both. It had Mardi Gras and the world-renowned Jazz and Heritage Festival and a French Quarter full of dilapidated charm fronting onto Huck Finn's Mississippi River, where the night always seemed to promise a hint of romance or magic.

Bob Dylan once described New Orleans as a 'very long poem', and it was. In the French Quarter nearly every doorway opened onto secret gardens of tropical lushness and in the Garden District you could take the Streetcar Named Desire along wide oak-lined boulevards of French, Greek and Italianate mansions belonging to old Southern families. There were jazz clubs and above-ground tombs ('cities of the dead') and venerable music institutions like Preservation Hall, where legends such as Louis Armstrong, Jelly Roll Morton and Sweet Emma Barrett had once performed.

The air was steamy and dreamy and the food was out of this world—oysters the size of clenched fists, hot steaming bowls of gumbo, and Cajun restaurants like Antoine's and Galatoire's where, in the case of the latter, patrons were forced to queue in the street for a table, even if they happened to be the president of France.

'I'm sorry, sir,' the maître d' had apparently told President Charles de Gaulle's aide-de-camp when he'd tried to book a table during a state visit to the Deep South. 'We don't take reservations for anyone. Monsieur de Gaulle will have to queue like everybody else.'

I liked the sound of a place that told presidents to wait in line for their shrimp remoulade. It appealed to the anti-authoritarian spirit that this son of Australian *Vogue* was desperate to cultivate.

I loved American popular culture—its music, writing, films, art and architecture; I just hated its foreign policy—in Panama, Guatemala, Nicaragua, El Salvador, Chile, Ecuador, Vietnam, Laos, Cambodia, the Middle East . . .

And here, now, was my father, by this time managing director of British Condé Nast, the Newhouse family-owned group that published *Vogue*, *Tatler* and *Brides* in the United Kingdom, asking me if I wanted to try out on one of the Newhouse newspapers in America.

Yes, I did, and no, I didn't. I didn't want to have to live up to my father's name all over again—and yet I knew I'd be crazy to let the opportunity slide. I also conned myself into believing that if someone at an American newspaper saw what I'd written in Sydney and Melbourne, I'd be given a trial period. Opportunism and self-delusion, therefore, took precedence over pride.

'Well, sure,' I said, 'but why would they give me a job?'

'They'd only give you a job after a suitable trial period on the paper,' my father replied. 'And then only if you're good enough.'

'What if I'm not good enough?' I asked.

'Then you won't last,' he said.

'Are you able to get me an introduction?'

'Of course.'

'Where do they have newspapers?'

'All over the country,' he said.

'Like where?'

'There are papers in Michigan, Massachusetts and Mississippi.'

'Is that all?'

'I think they've got papers in Alabama and certainly in New Jersey and New York.'

'Anywhere else?'

'They've also got a paper in New Orleans.'

'New Orleans?'

'Yes.'

New Orleans wasn't Newark, New Jersey, and it definitely wasn't Kalamazoo, Michigan, or Pascagoula, Mississippi.

'That's it,' I said. 'That's the place I want to go.'

It was as easy as that.

I arrived in New Orleans on a scorching afternoon in September 1982 to be met at the airport by the seventy-six-year-old billionaire chief executive of the only newspaper in town, the *Times-Picayune*.

I'd flown into a city I had scant knowledge of, with journalistic credentials limited to three years in a country no one cared about, coins in my pocket I couldn't count—owing to the fact I didn't yet know the difference between a dime and a nickel—and only one name in my contact book: Norman Newhouse.

Norman Newhouse was the youngest brother of the late Samuel I. Newhouse, founder of the Advance Publications Empire which owned and operated Condé Nast Publications. He was also uncle to Si and Donald Newhouse, Samuel's two sons who, upon their father's death in 1979, had acquired the riches of Solomon through magazines like *Vogue, House and Garden,*

Glamour, Brides, Mademoiselle and *GQ*, the Random House book-publishing group (in 1980), a large cable television operation and twenty-six newspapers throughout the country.

At the time of my arrival in the US, Condé Nast Publications was the biggest family-owned media empire in the English-speaking world, and Norman Newhouse was responsible for many of the papers in the South: the *Hunstville Times, Birmingham News* and *Mobile Press-Register* in Alabama; the *Mississippi Press* in Pascagoula, Mississippi; and, of course, the *Times-Picayune* in New Orleans, Louisiana. Despite his shyness and humility, Norman Newhouse was arguably the most powerful individual in the city and he was now standing beyond the customs lounge, all five foot five inches of him, wearing a blue seersucker suit and bow tie, with a sign bearing my name.

'Hello, Mr Newhouse,' I said, moving towards him. 'I'm David Leser.'

'Davey?' he replied with a broad grin and a decisive thrust of the hand. 'Davey Lessa?'

'Yes, that's me.'

'Welcome to N'Awlns,' he drawled.

'Thank you, sir. It's great to be here.'

'The car's just over here,' he said, leading me out of the terminal and into the blazing Delta heat.

'Is this your first time in N'Awlns?'

'Yes, sir. First time in America.'

'Well, I'll be.'

Norman Newhouse was five years old when he'd started selling newspapers on New Jersey street corners in 1911. He'd become a reporter on the *Staten Island Advance* after his brother bought the paper in 1922, and had gone on to become managing editor before transferring in 1937 to the *Long Island Press*. During World War II he'd been seconded to the United States Army Air

Corps as a writer and then sent to North Africa to take up the position of executive officer for the Office of Strategic Services, forerunner to the Central Intelligence Agency. He'd been one of the instrumental figures in setting up that first historic meeting between Winston Churchill and Yugoslavia's Marshal Tito in Naples in 1944. Now he was barrelling down the highway in his powder-blue Buick, perched on a couple of cushions so he could see better over the steering wheel, having invited me to stay in his two-storey, five-bedroom mansion on Arabella Street with his wife Alice and son Jonathan.

'Mr Newhouse, I'd like to thank you for giving me this trial period on your newspaper,' I said after a few minutes of companionable silence.

'Son,' he said, turning towards me with an impish grin, 'we *baleeev* in nepotism around here.'

Did he just say what I thought he said?

'Excuse me, sir?'

'I said we believe in nepotism around here, boy. Now look over there, that's the new Superdome—finished ten years ago—cost us a fortune; home to the Saints. Biggest domed structure in the world. And over here is . . .'

Norman Newhouse had just said in plain language what I'd known all along, but refused to admit to myself or anyone else. I was in this city because of patronage, not merit, even though I'd sent to the newspaper some—I see now in retrospect—fairly undistinguished samples of my work from Australia: page-one helicopter stories; feature articles on feral cats and Middle Eastern potentates. Who was I kidding? As if he or anyone else would have bothered to read them! This three-month trial period was a piece of high farce. I would have to be brain dead not to keep the job for the one-year period of my visa. As I was to learn, you didn't necessarily have to be good at your job to stay employed by the *Times-Picayune,* the name of which was derived from an old Spanish doubloon, but also meant trifling or irrelevant.

Podine Schoenberger, the medical/science reporter, had joined the paper some time around 1932 and fifty-odd years later, at the age of eighty-something, was still there, as capable of understanding the latest developments in quantum theory as I was of passing myself off as a Cajun fisherman.

Podine had poor circulation and was forever swathed in woollen suits and hats, even during the height of summer. She had no life outside the paper and had to be eased out of her job gently, around the time the AIDS virus came to town. It would have been way too much for her.

Mabel Simmons had also been there for the long haul. When I arrived she was in her nineties, a typist with big breasts and a predilection for sweetheart necklines. One morning she walked into the newsroom with a band-aid stuck to the exposed part of her bosom. She told us she'd been burnt while frying bacon in the nude. Even though she was surrounded by reporters, not one of us asked her for more information.

One day, a few months later, Mabel was discovered fast asleep at her computer terminal. A compositor downstairs had noticed a mile of zeds running through the computer system and contacted the newsroom. Mabel had drifted off with the last letter of the alphabet pinned under her left elbow: zzzzzzzzzzzzzzzzzzzzzzzz zzzzzzzzzzzzzzzzzzzzzzzzzzzzzzzzzzzzzzzzzzzzzzzzzzzzzzzzzzz.

And yet there were some first-class reporters on the paper as well, many of them Ivy League graduates bursting with energy, desperate to break new stories, expose corruption and put themselves—and their newspaper—on the map.

Dean Baquet was one of them. Son of a black New Orleans restaurateur, he was, at the time we met, a softly-spoken, chain-smoking sleuth who, through dint of shining intelligence and sheer hard work, had managed to ascend from his humble origins to a job at the *Picayune*, then, in later years, the *Chicago Tribune*, the *New York Times* and the *Los Angeles Times*. In 1988 he won the Pulitzer Prize for his investigations into Chicago City Hall corruption, before going on to become national editor of the *New York Times*. In 2005 he became the first African American to become managing editor of the *Los Angeles Times*, only to be sacked two years later for refusing to institute budget cuts that would have ripped the heart out of the newsroom. That was just like Dean. Back in the early 1980s I'd never met a man so deeply wedded to the craft and calling of journalism. Nothing was ever going to stop him from becoming one of America's finest reporters and—at the time of writing—he is managing editor of the *New York Times*, the first African American to be appointed to that position too.

Another gun scribe was Rick Raber, graduate of Princeton University, who had left an internship on the *Philadelphia Inquirer* to take up a reporting position on New Orleans' only newspaper. Rick was a dead ringer for Luke Skywalker from *Star Wars* and, with his Pacific-blue eyes and knock-'em-dead smile, he could melt a Southern belle from thirty paces. He was also a gifted wordsmith, the envy of every other writer on the newspaper, myself included.

When he wasn't at work Rick was usually in his French Quarter apartment with the phone off the hook, reading F. Scott Fitzgerald or Raymond Carver, and periodically taking aim at the giant cockroaches dive-bombing from the kitchen walls. Although sociable and often riotously funny, he was more at home with his books and writing. It was Rick who first introduced me to William Faulkner, Walker Percy and Robert Penn Warren, and who would later share with me his deep insights into the other giants of the American literary project—Ernest Hemingway, Fitzgerald, Philip

Roth, Norman Mailer, John Updike, John Cheever, Saul Bellow, Tom Wolfe and Truman Capote.

On Sunday afternoons I would often find him in a café near the Mississippi, thumbing through a dog-eared copy of *All the King's Horses* or *The Great Gatsby*, taking the cure from all those men of letters who'd come before him. Tennessee Williams once had an apartment around the corner from where we both lived; William Faulkner wrote *As I Lay Dying* in his garret just off Bourbon Street. To me, Rick Raber, in all his youthful, preppy, self-effacing ways, was the real deal.

John Pope was another who left a lasting impression, not just because he could write about almost anything with wit and elegance, but because he was fond of wearing bow ties and performing calisthenics at his desk while yodelling the words 'lawdy, lawdy, lawdy'. He was a singular character and the one who welcomed me most warmly into the newsroom—the main reason, I suspect, being that he was the only one on staff who had ever ventured as far as Australia. John Pope taught me a lot about the difference between American and Australian reporting in those days and it was no surprise twenty-three years later to learn that he'd been part of the team of *Picayune* journalists who'd won two Pulitzer Prizes for their reporting on Hurricane Katrina.

In September 1982, the very idea that the newsroom I had just entered would one day be evacuated, or that floodwaters would submerge eighty per cent of the entire city, was simply too fanciful for words. At that time I had my own terror to deal with and it had nothing to do with burst levees and Category 3 hurricanes. It was simply making myself understood in the canteen when I turned up to order my lunch.

'I'd like a chicken and salad sandwich to take away,' I said to the woman behind the counter.

'I'm sorry, honey, I don't get ya.'

'A chicken and salad sandwich to take away, please,' I said again.

'I'm sorry, dawlin, still don't get ya,' she said.

'I'd Like A Sandwich And I'd Like You To Put Chicken, Lettuce And Tomato On It,' I said slowly, with emphasis on the Tomato. 'And I'd Like To Take It Away From Here.'

'Ya mean cheekn dresta go?' she replied.

'Yes, I think that's what I mean.'

'Ya not from here, are ya, honey?' she said, and with that the line of journalists behind me erupted in laughter.

No, I wasn't from here. I was from way beyond the bayou. I was an impostor with a strange accent, a shock of curly black hair, decked out in yellow pants, black boots and a black leather tie— *what in God's name was I thinking?*—and living my own version of *Five Easy Pieces*, except that unlike Jack Nicholson I didn't trash the canteen; I just slunk away red-faced back to the newsroom to consider my predicament.

As far as I could tell, the questions my colleagues were asking themselves over their grits and eggs and fried chicken and dressed-up sandwiches to go were: Who is this guy? How did he get here? Can he write? And why is he wearing yellow pants and black cowboy boots?

The first two questions were easy enough to answer. I was the son of the man who headed British Condé Nast and I'd got here, just as Norman Newhouse had described that first morning, because of blatant nepotism.

The third question was the crucial one. I might have covered various beats for the Sydney *Daily Telegraph* and taken the odd Christian fundamentalist politician to films glorifying wild promiscuity, but whether that qualified me to cover a city renowned the world over for its music and food and wild hybrid culture remained to be seen.

In truth I didn't think I could do it. I thought I had made a gigantic mistake and it would be better to leave now and not subject myself, or the family name, to the ignominy that would surely follow. I could return to Israel, where I'd spent a few months prior to my arrival in New Orleans trying to briefly cover the Israeli invasion of Lebanon. And so one night, a few weeks after landing in New Orleans, I phoned my father in London to tell him of my decision.

'Dad, I don't think I can stay here,' I said. 'Everybody thinks I'm a member of the Newhouse family. Do you know what Norman Newhouse said to me in the car on the way from the airport? He said, "We believe in nepotism around here." Can you imagine what that feels like? Dad, it's just impossible. I feel like a freak every time I walk into the newsroom. People ask me how I got the job, which newspaper I've come from. They laugh at my accent. I want to leave.'

My father's silences could be excruciating. I could picture him there in his Chelsea apartment, mouth set hard against the dewy light of the Thames, Scotch in hand, a barge hooting from behind the willows, staring at the pile carpet.

'David, all I've done is open the door for you. If you're no good you won't last.' That was his constant refrain. Open doors lead to golden opportunities. Doors slam shut again if opportunities are squandered.

'But, Dad, there are thousands of college graduates who could have got this job if I hadn't taken it. You said I was on a three-month trial period. There isn't a trial period. They've given me the job because I'm your son.'

Long silence. And then: 'Is it only when I'm dead you'll feel okay about being my son?'

The suggestion was appalling but probably nothing less than I deserved. I'd let my father float the New Orleans option knowing full well the Newhouse family would never have given me the time of day without his connections. I'd allowed myself to believe I would be assessed on merit and given an appropriate trial period, even though I knew it didn't operate that way. Once you were in, you were family.

All I could say was: 'Oh Jesus, Dad, don't be like that. I love and respect you. You just don't understand what it's like being your son sometimes. There's a lot to live up to.'

There was no response on the end of the line.

◈

I stayed with the Newhouse family for a week before moving into my own apartment on St Philip Street in the famed French Quarter. It was an old slave quarter with a tropical garden and giant rats, which crawled from the banks of the Mississippi River three blocks away.

This was the year AIDS arrived and the panic was growing by the day—particularly in the gay community, where young men were beginning to report rare lung infections, malignancies of the skin and impaired immune systems.

For some reason, I was made the newspaper's first AIDS reporter, so that within a few months of arriving I was cruising the bars and bathhouses of the French Quarter trying to find out what on earth was happening.

'You wanna suck the head and squeeze the tip with me?' my muscular, moist-lipped landlord had asked me one night—and, no, he hadn't been referring to the local technique for eating crawfish.

I declined because I didn't have even the slightest homosexual leanings, and because I'd just been given some insight into the easy virtue of New Orleans gay life.

'You won't believe me if I tell you,' the doctor from Southern

Baptist Hospital had replied when I'd asked him to describe the sexual behaviour of the first AIDS victim he'd seen (at this time it was still called Gay Immune Deficiency Syndrome).

'Try me,' I said.

'Well, if I told you he was having one hundred and twenty sexual encounters a week, what would you say to that?'

'I'd say that's impossible.'

'Well, that was what he was doing.'

'That's nearly eighteen a day! How did he manage that?'

'He was on the receiving end.'

This took a few seconds to digest.

'Eighteen a day? Where was all this happening?'

'In the bathhouses and saunas.'

In those early days of homophobic-inspired AIDS hysteria I was floored—and, yes, a little disgusted too—by this level of carnality. I was also a little envious of all that defiant, transgressive sexual celebration. I figured that most heterosexual men would have gladly done the same thing had they (a) found enough women willing to go to bed with them, (b) had the stamina—and the control—to satisfy that many partners in one day, (c) been able to get away with it and (d) had the time.

I eventually decided that, rather than this being exclusively gay behaviour, it was actually more about men in general and their perennial desire to shag anything that moved.

I could relate. Sex had been on my mind for a long, long time.

Ever since I'd been rejected by my father's assistant at *Vogue* magazine at the age of five, I'd been determined to press on in search of divine convergence. My early home life had looked at times like a tear sheet from *Vogue*, with an assembly line of beautiful women regularly visiting for lunch, dinner or supper parties. At the age of five or six, I'd roll down the garden path so I could see under the dresses of the departing female guests.

It was too fantastic for words: garter belts, sheer stockings, soft pale thighs, panties—black and red and sheer—the hint of pubic hair. Enough to feed a boy's lurid imagination for years.

My younger brother, Daniel, would do a similar thing when he was a little boy. Between the ages of three and six he would often walk into my parents' dinner parties, scratching his willy and claiming an inability to sleep. He would then proceed to plant himself under the dining table and, for the next hour or two, amuse himself by taking off all the women's shoes while, presumably, sizing up their ankles and thighs. No one seemed to mind.

Our father adored women and the feeling was entirely reciprocated. As managing director of *Vogue* he not only employed and promoted them, he also cultivated their rich talents—despite what Sheila Scotter had to say about him. He listened to them. Advised them. Guided and motivated them. Earned their trust and respect. Became godfather to some of their children. Befriended them in ways that would leave their indelible mark not just on him, but on my brother and myself.

Women like the Hungarian-born clothes empress, Maria Finlay; former Miss Victoria and Qantas Ambassador, Pat Tudor; top fashion designers, Norma Tullo and Carla Zampatti; famed artist, Judy Cassab; high-profile PR consultant, Glen Marie Frost; British journalist, Erica Goatly; former *Vogue* beauty editor and Esteé Lauder publicity director, Mary Ellen Ayrton; Eve Harman, Sheila Scotter's replacement as editor of *Vogue*; her successor, Northern Irish-born June McCallum; her successor again, Pittsburgh-born beauty Nancy Pilcher. And lesser known—but equally talented— women like Carol Ashley-Wilson, Ann Coventry and Kate Smith. All these smart, elegant, gifted people who would fuel my love of— and desire for deep friendships with—extraordinary women.

Between the ages of five and fourteen I stole as many kisses and fondles as I could from the girls of my social group until suddenly, one miraculous God-flouting night, I was given permission to enter the Promised Land. I was fourteen years old and visiting my ex-girlfriend and her mother, Mrs G.

'Are you still awake, David?' Mrs G called from her bedroom.

'Hmm,' I mumbled, feigning sleep in the living room.

'Are you still awake?'

'Yes, sort of,' I half whispered, wanting her to think I was asleep. Crazy as it sounds, I was still wearing shorty pyjamas. They were my favourite. They had red trains on them.

'Come in here and keep me company,' she said.

'Sorry?' I replied, no longer remotely sleepy.

I'd had a strong sense this was going to be the night of a major train derailment after we'd gone to see *The Graduate* at the Rose Bay Wintergarden Theatre that evening. Mrs G could have taken her daughter and me to see *Gone With the Wind* or *The Dirty Dozen*, but she hadn't. She'd chosen that epoch-defining movie in which Dustin Hoffman's bumbling Benjamin Braddock is seduced by Anne Bancroft's older, sexually aggressive Mrs Robinson.

'Do you find me undesirable?' Mrs Robinson asks Benjamin.

'Oh no, Mrs Robinson,' Benjamin replies, 'I think, I think you're the most attractive of all my parents' friends.'

My parents barely knew Mrs G, but they were trusting—or clueless—enough to think that if I stayed the night at her house I would return home the same boy who had gone off to the movies the day before. They hadn't seen *The Graduate*.

'Come in here,' my Mrs Robinson called again from her bedroom. 'I want you to keep me company.'

By this time, my train was beginning to hoot and steam and move steadily up the tracks.

I got out of bed—actually a couch in the living room of her

small apartment—and moved cautiously towards her bedroom. My ex-girlfriend was asleep in the next room and her brother, two years younger, was shut away in a third bedroom down the hall. Mr G was no longer living with the family, so the coast was clear for me to step into the marital chamber and perch myself, shivering, on the end of Mrs G's bed.

She was dressed in a soft pink nightgown and was watching Cary Grant and Audrey Hepburn having a domestic argument in black and white. The film was *Charade*.

'You look cold. Get in here,' she said, patting the sheets next to her.

'I'll be okay,' I squeaked.

'Don't be silly, David—get in here and watch the movie with me.'

The train was now beginning to throb and career out of control.

'Isn't that better?' she said, putting her hand inside my pyjama pants.

Suddenly my trolley was leaping from the rail yard, searching for a tunnel through the shorts and into the waiting clutches of my veteran conductor. No kissing, no fondling, no lovemaking, just a passionless late-night shunting from Bewilderment Station to Mercy Street.

I decided not to stay and watch Cary Grant repair his relationship with Audrey Hepburn. After fifteen minutes I went back to the couch and tried to sleep. Within an hour my caboose had begun to rattle once more.

'I thought you'd be back,' she said, barely stirring, and this time pulling me on top of her. Within seconds I was plunging into what I thought was the deepest point of entry into her dark cave. I found myself abseiling down the walls. *Must be somewhere here*, I thought before she took me in her white witch's hand and guided me into the widest, warmest, wettest place I'd ever had the holy pleasure of finding myself in.

I came like a fire hose within twenty seconds . . . No, make that ten. But this time I had the good sense to take hold of the church bells under her nightgown and give them a mighty good tweaking.

They were fine breasts too, round and ample in my small hands, and I remember lying there on top of her in the hours before dawn, thinking: 'The guys at school are never going to believe this.'

She must have read my mind because she said to me, 'Now this is strictly between you and me, David—you know that, don't you?'

I nodded vigorously, having absolutely no intention of ever keeping my word.

As I was still good friends with Mrs G's daughter, I went back to their place on a regular basis for the next nine months. Once a fortnight, on average, I would take the school bus in the opposite direction to home and go and shag my ex-girlfriend's mother. Usually she'd have music on—the new Crosby, Stills and Nash album, David Bowie's *The Man Who Sold the World*—and there'd be incense burning as I walked into the kitchen for a glass of milk and an arrowroot biscuit.

'How was school?' she'd ask, but I knew she wasn't the slightest bit interested in what I'd learnt that day because, mid-stream, she'd wander off into the living room singing along with Stephen Stills' 'Wooden Ships'.

I'd follow her a few minutes later with a milk moustache and a violent heaving in my shorts to find her sitting on the couch with her dress hoisted up around her hips and her tanned legs opened wide, looking at me with the first pair of bedroom eyes I'd ever encountered.

'You took long enough,' she'd say with a dirty smirk, and I knew there wasn't going to be any maths homework that afternoon.

Sometimes we'd linger on the couch for fifteen minutes while she undid my school tie and shirt with quick, deft fingers. At other times I'd walk into her apartment to find her already in the bedroom. No glass of milk or arrowroot in sight. No unloosening of the school tie. Just a quick advance into her Red-Light District.

In the evening we'd have dinner—the mother, her children and me—and we'd watch television afterwards before cleaning our teeth and going to bed. (It was assumed I'd be staying the night on the couch.) In the morning, after late-night sex with Mrs G, and cornflakes and tea with her son and daughter, I'd take the bus to school.

One night, shortly before it all ended, my ex-girlfriend walked into her mother's bedroom and found us between the sheets. 'You slut, Mum,' she said, slamming the door.

Although I haven't seen Mrs G for forty-three years, I've often thought about her—not in the tormented way that Bernard Schlink's character, Michael Berg, obsessed about Hanna Schmitz in *The Reader*, but certainly with a sense of astonishment and disbelief. Why would she have wanted to deflower a boy in shorty pyjamas, and where did she go in subsequent years with all those unlawful desires?

During that first year in New Orleans I gave myself over to love, while at the same time trying to prove myself worthy of a place in the great enterprise that was American journalism. The two tended to go hand in hand. A young man with a press pass, a foreign accent and an apartment in the French Quarter was a man with considerable access. I would have been a fool not to have made full use of it.

The newspaper had decided—sensibly enough—to ease me into the city slowly, sending me off during my first week to cover a murder trial with their senior court reporter. I was given the task of adding colour to the court reporting, rather than covering the trial itself, just in case I failed to understand the finer points of Louisiana's French-drafted Napoleonic legal system.

Over the ensuing weeks and months the assignments became more regular. Before being given the AIDS beat, I was asked to write about city hall politics, education, race relations, popular culture and the local fallout from Nicaragua's Sandinista revolution. I ventured into black housing projects, white uptown mansions, courtrooms, police stations and jazz bars. I headed north-west along the petro-chemical corridor of Interstate 10 to Baton Rouge to report on the International Special Olympics and the workings of the state legislature where, fifty years earlier, Governor Huey Long had reigned over his citizenry before being mortally wounded in the State Capitol building, only to be replaced by his brother Earl who, for a while, governed the state from a mental hospital.

After Baton Rouge I spent a month in St Bernard Parish, south-east of New Orleans, writing about armed robberies, bashings and murders, and being treated like an exotic bird by the sheriff and his staff. 'Henree,' the secretary would twang each morning as I pushed through the white picket gate leading to Sheriff Henry's office, 'Aw-straylya's here.'

I'd never encountered a place like St Bernard Parish before. It might have been known for the famous Battle of New Orleans fought one hundred and seventy years earlier, but to me it was *Deliverance* country—a patchwork of swamps and bayous populated by hillbillies, oyster farmers and Spanish Cajuns who played zydeco and spoke an incomprehensible dialect. Twenty-two years later this whole parish would be wiped out by the fury of Hurricane Katrina and the seven-metre wall of water that smashed through the levees. There would not be a home left standing, but in 1983 it felt like the parish had been there forever, and would stay that way too.

I'm not sure at what point the editors of the newspaper decided they could trust me with important assignments, but it might have come after the Saturday-night murder of a young woman on her way to a friend's birthday party. The twenty-three-year-old fashion student, Patti Owens, had only been a few doors from her friend's apartment when two young men—and, yes, they happened to be black—drove by, one of them shooting her in the back.

When I got the call from the editor the next morning I was as hung-over as I'd ever been, thanks to an obscene number of frozen margaritas the night before. The editor wanted me to visit Patti Owens' parents and find out what I could about their dead daughter.

'She always had dreams,' her mother said, as she showed me through Patti's bedroom, pointing to the unfinished oil painting on the mantle.

I hated every minute I was there, but the story ran on the front page the following day.

When I left New Orleans after twelve months, I was seven kilograms heavier and twice the reporter I'd been on my arrival, thanks to editor Jim Amoss and his colleagues. I'd conquered some of my anxieties by writing my way into legitimacy and favour. I'd made half a dozen close friends, forged a lifelong connection to one of the most fascinating cities in the world (without ever discovering the joys of jazz!) and developed insights into the American psyche that would help balance all the left-wing assumptions I'd carried for years.

My visa was renewed for a year and I headed to Washington, D.C., to join the Newhouse News Service as correspondent for the Springfield *Daily News* in Massachusetts. I'd never been to Massachusetts before, let alone Springfield, but as with New Orleans this didn't seem to matter much. A vacancy had miraculously opened up in the Washington bureau, and on the basis of my experience in the Deep South—no, scrap that—on the basis of my father being who he was, the gates to the Newhouse kingdom were again flung open for me.

With exactly one year's reporting experience in the United States I now had the job of covering national politics for a newspaper I'd never read, reporting to editors I'd never met, writing for a city and state I'd never visited, and speaking to readers I had not the foggiest notion about.

If New Orleans had given me cold feet, this was far worse. As with New Orleans I didn't know anyone in the city, but in Washington, D.C., it took years to cultivate the kind of professional contacts that mattered. I had a few days to work out where Capitol Hill and the White House were, find out the names of the congressmen from Massachusetts, and get to work.

There was plenty to do. It was 1983 and Ronald Reagan had been orchestrating a covert war against Nicaragua's left-wing government, while also supporting right-wing death squads in neighbouring El Salvador. Acid rain was killing waterways all across America, including up to seventy per cent of the lakes, streams and reservoirs of Massachusetts. The economy was failing and American cities were in fast decay, with soup kitchen lines becoming an ever-present feature of daily life.

Many of Reagan's most vocal opponents were from Massachusetts—people like Paul Tsongas; Thomas (Tip) O'Neill, the Speaker of the House; Edward Kennedy, the state's senior senator; and Edward Boland, chairman of the House Intelligence Committee. It was my job to get to know these men and their staffers, and to get the drop on stories that might be relevant to the good citizens of Springfield, Massachusetts.

The word 'intimidated' doesn't even get close. One morning I actually found myself in a telephone booth on Capitol Hill with the entire American budget balanced on my knees. The 1984 US$925 billion financial plan for America had just been released and I was dictating a story to a typist in Springfield about the effect this budget was going to have on my 'home' state. It didn't help that I was on deadline and that the typist was having trouble understanding my accent. I was bathed in sweat, trying to decipher how millions of dollars worth of disbursements would affect a place I'd never visited. I had no idea what I was talking about, but the story, like practically every other one I wrote, made its way to page one by dint of the fact that I was based in the nation's capital.

During my year in Washington I lived in a basement apartment in Georgetown, the elite neighbourhood by the Potomac River where the then senator John F. Kennedy and his wife Jackie had resided, and where Ben Bradlee, editor of the *Washington Post*, and his top investigative reporter, Bob Woodward of Watergate fame, were still living.

I didn't meet either man, but I did end up interviewing Woodward by phone a couple of years later when a new book accused him of being the 'cat's paw' for a military spy operation inside the Nixon White House. His former naval role, the book alleged, was the key to Woodward's legendary Watergate investigation and the identity of 'Deep Throat'. Unwittingly I was doing the authors' bidding when I phoned the legendary reporter at home one evening.

'Bob Woodward?'

'Yes.'

'David Leser's my name. I'm from the *Sydney Morning Herald*'s colour magazine, *Good Weekend*.'

'How can I help you?'

'A book called *Silent Coup: The Removal of Richard Nixon*, by Len Colodny and Robert Gettlin, has been published. Have you heard of it?'

'Only vaguely.'

'That's surprising. It mentions you a lot.'

'Really?'

'Yes, it describes you as a communications liaison officer between the Pentagon and the White House prior to becoming a reporter.'

'Who did you say you were again?'

'David Leser.'

'Thank you for your call.' Click.

This is not an exact account of what was said but it's close. Bob Woodward was not amused, nor do I blame him. It was a fantastic case study of impudence (mine) masquerading as fearless interrogation. Without realising it I'd decided to target America's most famous reporter in the vain hope that some of his gold dust might drift my way. It didn't. The story never ran and many of the claims in the book were later discredited.

Washington was that kind of town for me. A year spent close to power but far from its triggers and levers, as well as its repercussions. Acid rain was falling on the lakes of New England but I never actually went to see the destruction for myself. I should have gone to the north-west of the state to see the dead fish and the fouled waterways, just as I should have taken a flight down to Managua and San Salvador to get a first-hand account of Washington's dirty war in Central America.

I was young and out of my depth. One morning Robert McNamara, the architect of the Vietnam War, came striding towards me down Pennsylvania Avenue, his face ruddy from the cold, his jacket collar turned up against the wind, his gimlet eyes fixed on the pavement. For a moment I imagined bailing him up and demanding an explanation for the whole catastrophe that was Vietnam, Cambodia and Laos. I would demand—on behalf of my indignant generation—some answers.

How does it feel to have so much blood on your hands, Mr McNamara? Is it difficult to sleep at night? Do you ever think of yourself as a war criminal?

Nearly twenty years later, documentary filmmaker Errol Morris would illustrate the best way to elicit answers from someone like the former American Secretary of Defense—not by crusading for a cause, using tricks, or behaving like a bloodhound, but rather by waiting and listening, by having the good sense to know that the truth was to be found not by trying to shame a man, but by trying to humanise him.

In *Fog of War* Morris was able to persuade McNamara to expound on the lessons of war in general: that its architects needed to empathise with their enemy, that they needed to be prepared to examine their reasoning for waging war, and that they needed to understand that human nature could not be changed.

I was still a long way from these subtleties and I was a long way from understanding that a deeply complex man such as Robert McNamara might warrant the slightest sympathy. It was much easier to live in a clearly defined world of good and bad, right and wrong, than to have to wrestle with uncomfortable ambiguities.

I didn't like uncertainty, and yet, if truth be told, I was often gripped by it, on big issues as well as small. At night I would sit for hours in my tiny airless basement apartment, wondering what to do with myself. Would I go out for dinner on my own, or cook myself another bowl of ratatouille and rice? Would I watch Ted Koppel interviewing a Washington insider, or read the book that Seymour Hersh had written on the Nixon White House? Would I pour myself a drink or roll a joint, or do both? Would I put a call in to Australia or call the woman I'd met the previous week at the Redskins' game? Would I work the phone in order to try to expand my contact list beyond the perfunctory, or just go to bed?

One evening, at dusk, a family walked past my window and peered down from the laneway onto my little tableau of indecision. I was wondering about the drink or the joint, hoping perhaps the phone would ring, or that my landlord—a leading television producer with CBS—might invite me up for dinner (he never did). I felt the gaze from three pairs of eyes fall on me as I sat on the couch staring at the floor.

Grabbing the newspaper, I began poring over the day's headlines, hoping desperately that they'd seen a young man casually reading the paper after a long day at the office, not some no-hoper staring into space.

That became my strongest memory of my year in Washington, D.C.,—not covering Congress, or visiting the White House, or reporting on dirty wars in Central America, or getting to know one of America's top Middle Eastern experts, or visiting the Smithsonian Institute, or playing my first game of baseball or delighting in the cherry blossoms of spring. Rather, it was getting caught in the act of doing nothing while pretending to be doing something!

When I returned to Australia at the beginning of 1985, after two years in America, one of the things I most longed for was to finally prove myself—and be accepted—as a journalist in my own right.

That might sound like a rerun of the American experience and, of course, in a way it was.

Unfortunately I struck Piers Akerman, then deputy editor of Rupert Murdoch's national newspaper, the *Australian*. I was hired by the paper's editor, Alan Farrelly, to work on news and features but Akerman let it be known from day one that he deplored the decision.

'Why have you got it in for Leser?' the chief of staff, John Lyons (now Middle East correspondent for the newspaper), asked Akerman several months after I'd started. By this time it had become clear to Lyons that Akerman was vetoing most of the stories I was being assigned.

'Because he trades on his father's name,' Akerman replied.

'Who's his father?' Lyons replied.

'Bernard Leser, publisher of *Vogue*.'

'I never knew that,' Lyons said.

Lyons never knew that because I'd never told him. It was the last thing I intended telling him, or any of my other colleagues for that matter, but Akerman had formed the view that I was only on the newspaper by dint of my father.

I suspect this was partly true. Before returning to Australia, I'd asked News Ltd's New York correspondent, Sally Macmillan, if she could pave the way for an introduction to Alan Farrelly. Farrelly and I met in Sydney and he offered me a job. Whether this was because Sally Macmillan had told him I was the son of Bernie Leser, I'll never know. What I do know is that I never mentioned it to him.

What I also know is that from day one Piers Akerman decided to make my life a misery. The tension with him reached its apotheosis in January 1986, when I was sent by the editor-in-chief, Les Hollings, to cover the rise of Islamic fundamentalism in Malaysia, particularly as it was being played out in the eastern state of

Terengganu. I'd been given the assignment on the strength of an interview I'd done two months earlier with former prime minister Tunku Abdul Rahman, who'd been visiting Australia, partly to warn us of the growing threat posed by radical Islam.

My brief was to spend ten days moving among the paddy fields, fishing hamlets, small towns and urban centres of Malaysia to gauge the extent to which the country's Islamic opposition party was winning the hearts and minds of the people. I was to write a 5000-word cover story for the weekend edition of the paper, as well as produce five or six other stories during those ten days, including two pieces on the impending execution of two Australians for drug trafficking.

I was with a staff photographer in the north of the country, heading by taxi to our hotel when, after days of tight deadlines and caustic phone calls from Akerman in Sydney, the tension inside me finally exploded. A curfew was in place because of religious unrest and we only had a short time in which to cross the border from Terengganu to Penang, via Kelantan and Terak. After 10 pm no cars were allowed on the roads. My deadline for the story was the following morning and we were still 100 kilometres from our hotel. It was now 9 pm and the driver was going too slow. I asked him to go faster, but the roads were dark and potholed. The speedometer stayed on sixty. I asked him again to speed up. No response. We then rounded a bend and there, straight in front of us, was a cow lumbering across the road. There was nothing the driver could do. We hit the creature side on and its belly exploded on impact, splattering our windscreen with blood and steaming offal.

'WHAT THE FUCK ARE YOU DOING?' I screamed. 'YOU COULD HAVE KILLED US. YOU FUCKING KILLED A COW. IT'S ALL OVER THE CAR. WE'VE GOT TO GET TO OUR HOTEL BEFORE THEY SHOOT US. JESUS, THERE'S COW ALL OVER THE CAR.'

We got to our hotel at about midnight and for the next eight hours I chain-smoked my way through the pitch hours, tearing out sheets of paper from my Olivetti typewriter and crumpling them up until I finally had a version of the story I liked.

The following morning I spent two hours dictating it to a typist in Sydney and then collapsed in the pool and ordered two cocktails in quick succession. It was the first time I'd relaxed in ten days.

On my return to Sydney, Akerman appeared at my desk one morning, demanding an explanation for the cocktails on my expense account. 'What's the meaning of this?' he said, slapping the Malaysian receipts down.

'What's the problem?' I asked, returning his hateful gaze.

'Since when do you order cocktails on this newspaper's expense?' he snarled.

'Look, Piers, I wrote seven stories for you in ten days. All I had during that time away was you barking at me down the phone. I delivered all that you asked of me and more. Now you want me to justify two cocktails?'

'Yes, I do.'

That was our relationship for two years—mutual hatred—with Akerman unleashing a constant barrage of insults and innuendo, and me occasionally hitting back with whatever feeble firepower I could muster.

Not long after the Malaysian trip I was appointed acting foreign editor of the paper. My task during the 4 pm till midnight shift was to sift through the evening's international stories and then choose the best ones to fill the foreign pages of the next day's second edition.

One evening I decided to remove a photograph from the second edition that had appeared in the paper's first edition. It was of Prince Charles's bald spot. The photo and accompanying caption had been sent from the London bureau and was designed—in my opinion—to gently mock the heir to the British throne because of his vegetarian diet. The more vegetables you ate, so the implication of the photo and caption went, the more hair you lost. That, of course, was the problem with Charlie boy. Too many vegetables.

Even if you thought the photo had some amusing relevance, the main problem with running the photo so prominently in the foreign pages of the national newspaper was that the same photo also appeared towards the back of the paper in a section devoted to gossip and celebrity. Akerman had put the first edition of the paper to bed earlier that evening with the same item on two different pages.

I decided to replace it with a photo of Nicaraguan cripples being wheeled through the streets of the capital, Managua. It was a dramatic shot and, with an accompanying small news item from Central America, more relevant, I thought, to the foreign pages.

'What do you think you were doing last night?' Akerman demanded the following afternoon when I arrived for work.

'What are you talking about?' I replied.

'What were you doing running a story on those Marxist agitators in Nicaragua?'

'It was a good photo,' I said.

'It should never have been run.'

I couldn't contain myself any longer. 'Well, what were you doing publishing a photo of Prince Charles's bald spot TWICE?' I yelled.

'Get in here, you raging little ant,' Akerman bellowed, ordering me to his office and slamming the door. Our shouting went on for several minutes, Akerman accusing me of gross insolence, me responding that he was a bully and a thug. How dare I speak to him like that? Who did I think I was? Didn't I know who I was speaking to? Yes, I surely did. The most loathsome individual I'd ever known, then and now. A man whose bullying management style was the antithesis of everything my father stood for.

And I was far from alone in that estimation. Akerman had targeted many journalists on the *Australian* and, later on, in other newsrooms where he was appointed to edit Murdoch newspapers. To me, however, this was a personal vendetta. Akerman was out to destroy if not my career, then certainly my morale, as if holding down a job on a national newspaper wasn't difficult enough.

I remember one day when Les Hollings walked over to me to ask if I'd read Robert Hughes's *The Fatal Shore*. The book had only just been released. I was finishing off a story on industrial relations, my second story for the day, and no, I had not yet read Hughes's monumental tome.

'Well, you'd better hurry up and read it,' Hollings said crossly, 'because you're interviewing Hughes this afternoon and we're running the story on page one tomorrow.'

It was three o'clock. The interview was in an hour's time, the deadline for the first edition in three hours. The book was 603 pages long.

That was the schizophrenic nature of news reporting. Nothing to do for hours on end, then suddenly an assignment at short notice, a flurry of phone calls, a dash to meet the interviewee, frantic last-minute checking and rechecking of facts, then sitting down to write a crisp, clean, entertaining piece of prose.

The work was thrilling but stressful and the stress was compounded if you happened to be at war with your boss. I'd been experiencing stabbing pains in my chest for weeks. I was thirty years old and already suffering from acute anxiety.

I complained to Les Hollings about Akerman several times, to no avail. The man was a protected species at News Ltd, as Rupert Murdoch would make clear a few years later when he appointed him editor-in-chief of the Herald and Weekly Times Group in

Melbourne, and then vice-president of Fox News in America. Piers Akerman, he said, was one of News Ltd's 'greatest assets'.

Needless to say, during the years of the Howard government, Akerman, along with broadcaster Alan Jones, became the prime minister's pin-up media personality, and it was easy to see why. Akerman's *Daily Telegraph* and *Sunday Telegraph* columns were invariably vicious, partisan attacks on all the predictable Murdoch targets—trade unions, federal and state Labor governments, environmentalists, Republicans, drug reformers, asylum seekers, homosexuals and any commentator vaguely left of centre.

One of Akerman's strengths for Murdoch—apart from his undoubted intelligence and wit—was his willingness to savage those with whom he disagreed politically, and often those with whom he worked. His claim in 1991 to *Sunday Age* journalist Caroline Wilson that if he was 'ever accused of bias' he 'would roll on the floor laughing' was in itself beyond laughable. His bias was—and remains to this day—legendary, and his behaviour even more problematic.

Such was the clamour and indignation surrounding his name during an industrial dispute at the *Herald-Sun* in 1991 that when his face appeared in an office window one afternoon a group of picketing employees below began chanting, 'Jump, jump, jump.'

Akerman refused to do so, but after two years of working with him on the *Australian*, I did just that. I jumped to Jerusalem.

Postscript: A few years later my father bumped into Akerman at Wiltons restaurant in Jermyn Street in London. Akerman apparently saw my father walking past his table and, as my father recounted, was so eager to say hello that when he stood up he knocked a glass of red wine all down his front. 'I thought you'd be pleased to know that,' my father told me the next day.

5

YOU DON'T HAVE TO BE JEWISH

Tell me, now that you are all finished at fourteen being a Jew,
do you know a single thing about the wonderful history and
heritage of the saga of your people?

Jack Portnoy to his son, Alex,
in Philip Roth, *Portnoy's Complaint*

Like Alex Portnoy in Philip Roth's uproarious novel, *Portnoy's Complaint*, when I first arrived in Israel in 1977 I was something of an exile from my Jewish history—not to mention religious traditions and laws.

True, I'd learned all the important Old Testament stories at Sunday school; I'd absorbed a sense of cultural and historical difference through what I'd gleaned from my parents and grandparents; I'd blessed the fruit from the vine and the bread of the earth at my family's Friday night Shabbat dinners, much to the amusement of my non-Jewish friends who were invited to join us. I'd fondled Jewish girls upstairs and downstairs and even learned a few Jewish jokes courtesy of the 1965 comedy album, *You Don't Have To Be Jewish*.

The Astronaut: Isn't it wonderful, Mama, that White and McDivitt went round the world sixty-two times.

Mama (with strong Brooklyn accent): So big deal. If you got money, you can travel.

But to me all this had been largely devoid of spiritual meaning, as had the true human dimensions of the Arab–Israeli conflict that had begun during the late nineteenth century and then spilt over into full-scale war following the upheavals of Israel's creation in 1948.

I'd travelled to Israel that first time in late 1977—after first surviving the opium- and hash-filled dens of South-East Asia, Nepal, India and Sri Lanka—with all the ill-formed ideals of my youth: that here was a young pioneer nation that had reclaimed the swamps and made the deserts bloom; that had turned back the invading Arab hordes not once, but three times, in thirty years; that had restored the Jewish people to their ancient home-land after 2000 years of relentless wandering and persecution; and—here's the important thing—had known how to treat its minorities with compassion and decency.

I'd arrived as a student backpacker on a mission to re-enter the Old Testament. I would visit the ruins of the Second Temple in Jerusalem, climb the desert cliffs of Masada, pay homage in the Cave of the Patriarchs where the tombs of Abraham, Isaac, Jacob, Sarah, Rebecca and Leah were located. I would be welcomed 'home' by my brothers and sisters as a suitor might be invited into the bedchamber of his paramour. That was my self-authored roman à clef—a young Australian Jew exercising his Right of Return, being warmly received in his 'homecoming'.

It didn't turn out like that. I had read Hebrew at Sunday school but I couldn't understand a thing that was being said to me; nor did I know anyone in the country except for my mother's closest friend, Pnina Salzman, Israel's leading classical pianist.

I felt estranged from the moment I stepped into the arrival hall of Tel Aviv's Ben Gurion Airport.

'Where have you come from?' demanded Israeli customs officials. 'Who packed your bags? What is your mother's maiden name? How long are you planning to stay? What are you intending to do here?'

I'd never encountered such brash people in my life, and that was before being pushed out of the way on buses by old people muttering curses, and then having to listen to them quarrel and kvetch with each other for the entire ride. Everywhere an argument—in Hebrew, Russian, German, Polish, Yiddish, Hungarian, Czech: loud, tempestuous, fractious exchanges; shoutings from one side of the street to the other; howls of indignation in restaurants and cafés; finger-pointing and wild, angry gesticulations. And among all this the ubiquitous young soldiers, men and women of the Israel Defense Forces, with their come-hither eyes and their sub-machine guns slung insouciantly over their shoulders.

I didn't like what I was seeing and so a few days later I went to work on a kibbutz near the Lebanese border, where I discovered the joys of getting up at 3 am to haul great clusters of bananas to waiting trailers before the sun rose over the Jordan Valley. That gave me my first taste of the socialist pioneering spirit that had once inspired the founding fathers of the Jewish state.

I grew to like the physical work, but apart from the bomb shelters—where we would often gather to listen to Pink Floyd's *Dark Side of the Moon* on an old stereo at night-time—I had no sense that I was in a war-torn region, hemmed in on all sides by hostile neighbours, or that the country was actually an occupying power disregarding the rights of a subject people—until I heard Egyptian president Anwar Sadat's impassioned plea in November 1977 to the Israeli people and, by extension, to Jews around the world.

The Palestinian problem is the core and essence of the conflict and ... so long as it continues to be unresolved, the conflict will continue to aggravate, reaching new dimensions. In all sincerity, I tell you that there can be no peace without the Palestinians. It is a grave error of unpredictable consequences to overlook or brush aside this cause.

Sadat, arch-enemy-turned-peacemaker, would prompt me to return to Australia two months later and change my arts degree major from psychology to Middle Eastern studies. Having witnessed such a historic event, I was eager to know more about the origins of the Arab–Israeli conflict in general and the Palestinian–Israeli contest in particular; about the ways in which competing nationalisms—and religious absolutism—had entangled two people in a millennial struggle of epic proportions. I wanted to understand better the Arab world's rejection of—and failure to reconcile itself to—the Jewish state. I wanted to understand something that I had simply never considered before: the historical hardships of the Palestinians caused by displacement, rejection and oppression, much of it at the hands of Jews.

And it was Dr Robert Springborg, the American-born Arabist, who was to give me that education on my return to Macquarie University in 1977. Springborg was one of the world's leading experts on the Arab world. He had written books on Egyptian politics, Iraq and the Middle East more broadly. He had been a consultant on Arab governance and politics for American and United Nations organisations, and had worked on democratisation programs throughout the Middle East.

He was hated by the Jewish lobby, and in the late 1970s I fell under his spell. He introduced me to the complexities of the Arab League nations, and gave me a view of Middle Eastern history not filtered through pro-Israeli or Jewish eyes. He was the first person in my life to present the Arab as a human being, rather than as the demonised 'enemy' who would have all Jews thrown into the sea. He laid out for me the extent of Palestinian suffering, how the burden of conquest, expulsion, poverty and humiliation had helped to radicalise a lost and subject people, and how this had happened through one of the greatest collisions in history: a collision between the Jewish and Arab people in the aftermath of the Holocaust and the post-colonial break-up of the Middle East into sovereign nation states.

Some of my Jewish friends were not impressed with this reorienting of my moral compass, among them Martin Indyk, also at that time a lecturer in politics at Macquarie University. Martin was the Australian Jewish son of my parents' friends John and Mary Indyk, and he would eventually go on to become one of the world's most powerful and insightful commentators on Middle Eastern affairs: founder of the Washington Institute for Near East Policy; special assistant and then principal adviser to President Bill Clinton on Arab–Israeli issues, and later, in two separate stints, American ambassador to Israel, these last appointments earning him the distinction of being the first and only Jew—as well as foreign-born diplomat—to ever be appointed US ambassador to Israel.

During those years at Macquarie University—and later during my twelve months in Washington, D.C., in the early 1980s, Martin would attempt to counter what he believed was the egregious pro-Arab bias I had accepted unblinkingly from Robert Springborg. (In 1990–91 Springborg would fall foul of the Hawke government and the Australian Jewish lobby for this perceived bias, particularly following his criticisms on the ABC of the government's support for the American-led invasion of Iraq. This would so incense Bob Hawke that the prime minister would press for Springborg's removal as a Middle Eastern commentator on the ABC.)

My parents were also perplexed by my newfound sympathy for the Arabs. My mother had been a member of Zionist youth groups in Sydney and, from 1941 to 1946, my father had served as founder/president of the Zionist Youth Movement in Auckland. In 1944, he'd actually established the first camp for Jewish boys and girls in New Zealand and, from 1965 to 1971, had been publicity chairman in Sydney for the United Israel Appeal. Their support for Israel was steadfast, but they would always listen to my views with tolerance and patience.

Not so my maternal grandmother, Hansey Simblist, a woman I loved and feared in equal measure, and who believed until the day she died that on the subject of Middle Eastern politics I'd been hoodwinked by the wrong version of history—the Arab version, not the Jewish. Like most Jews of her generation—and indeed later generations—she viewed the creation of Israel through the lens of the Holocaust. She understood the Jewish craving for, and conquest of, Zion as a final deliverance and redemption from a history of vilification and extermination.

In 1940, she and her brother-in-law, Jack Davis, had actually gone to see Arthur Calwell, the then Australian Minister for Immigration, to plead with him for visas for her forty-seven relatives in Latvia. Both of them had believed, as had many people at the time, that the Nazis were preparing to march on Riga and that the country would soon be lost; that their family needed to get out soon or perish. Whatever they'd said to Calwell that day in 1940 must have worked, because by the time the two of them left his office they'd managed to secure the visas. All the aunts, uncles, nephews, nieces and cousins would be allowed to resettle in Australia.

'You won't believe it,' my grandmother told them by telephone soon afterwards. 'We've got them—visas for all of you. You can come to Australia. We'll find you somewhere to live. It will be a simple life at first but you'll see—you'll love it. The beaches, the harbour, the sunshine . . .'

And then the fateful reply: 'But why would we want to come to a godforsaken country like Australia when our homes are here? Everything is fine. The Germans won't come.'

But, of course, the Germans did come and all those relatives—except for one who escaped into the forest—were forced to dig their own graves before being shot in the back of the head.

My grandmother's sense of Jewishness was so entrenched that when her second daughter, my aunty Dinee, asked her for her blessing to marry her non-Jewish college professor, my grandmother stubbornly refused. 'No daughter of mine is going to marry a goy,' she said.

My aunt responded by marrying her professor anyway, in a secret ceremony at a registry office. She eventually left Australia for America, never to grace her mother's doorstep again. My grandmother lived with that regret for the rest of her days, but it never translated into an acceptance of non-Jews into our family.

Her views were primitive, tribal and perfectly understandable, and in the case of Israel, she would brook no dissent. She believed that after centuries of annihilation, it was only right and proper that the Jews finally had a homeland of their own. I didn't disagree with that proposition. What I found decidedly awkward was that any discussion of Palestinian rights was always dismissed with a wave of the hand and a recourse to all the familiar Zionist arguments—that in stark contrast to 1000 years of Arab indolence and backwardness, the Jews had made the desert bloom after a few short years of enterprise; that there was no such thing as a Palestinian nation; that the Jews had wanted them to stay in Israel but that the Arabs had decided to flee; that they'd rejected the 1947 Partition Plan for Palestine; and—here was the big one—there was plenty of land for all the Arabs, except that the Arabs had no interest in helping these so-called Palestinians because they were only hell-bent on waging war against the Jews.

I'd heard these jeremiads time and again, and whenever I offered her a different point of view—yes, one often informed by Springborg's lectures—she'd chide me: 'Then why don't you just go off with your Palestinian friends?'

'Oh, Nan,' I'd plead. 'Don't be like that.'

'Where do you get your views from?' she'd continue. 'We lost everyone in the Holocaust and you should support the Arabs now?'

'But, Nan, it wasn't their fault what Hitler did. They didn't kill the Jews.'

'Well, they're killing them now.'

'That's because the Palestinians were displaced.'

'What Palestinians?'

'The Arabs who lived there prior to the creation of the state of Israel.'

'There aren't any Palestinians. They're all Arabs.'

'Nan, that's their identity. They think of themselves as Palestinians.'

'And you should think of yourself as a Jew.'

In 1982 I visited Israel for the second time, and spent three months there freelancing before taking up the position on the *Times-Picayune*. Depending on one's point of view, my timing was either very good or very bad. The Israelis were about to invade Southern Lebanon in an attempt to destroy the Palestine Liberation Organization (PLO), which had set up a state-within-a-state after its expulsion from Jordan twelve years earlier.

Operation Peace for Galilee began a few weeks after my arrival with a full-scale incursion into Southern Lebanon. It ended with the deadly siege of Beirut and the massacre by Lebanese Christian militia (under the protection of Israeli forces) of more than 800 Palestinians in the Sabra and Shatila refugee camps.

I didn't get to Beirut but I went into Southern Lebanon with Israeli forces, visiting the largely Shiite town of Nabatieh, as well as the ancient Phoenician port city of Sidon, where the PLO had established its bases. As with many 'liberating' armies, the Israelis were greeted at first with flowers and jubilation, until their so-called 'liberation' turned into a disastrous eighteen-year-long occupation.

That was my first limited exposure to war. It was also the year I met the aptly named Talya Press, at that time press liaison officer for the World Zionist Organization.

Talya had arrived in Israel as a sixteen-year-old, hoping to turn a new page in the Promised Land. Something had happened to her back in Philadelphia that had caused such grief and confusion that one day she'd simply decided to pack her bags and come to Israel. What that 'something' was she never told me.

Talya was fluent in four languages and knew Israel intimately. She was passionate, smart and forthright, and had strikingly beautiful lapis lazuli eyes. One evening she invited me to her Jerusalem apartment for dinner following a tour of the Judaean Desert and Dead Sea. After a dinner of couscous and red wine from the slopes of Mount Carmel she asked me to stay the night. I stayed for the next three months.

We became lifelong friends, despite our sometimes conflicting views on the Arab–Israeli conflict. Like my grandmother and parents, and many of the Jews I knew, she believed I'd been hopelessly compromised by my university lecturer and my left-leaning friends in Australia. At night we would smoke Marlboro Lights on her verandah overlooking the rooftops of West Jerusalem, and she would talk about the Jews who had turned the desert into a modern-day Garden of Eden; who had extended the hand of peace to the Arabs many times over; who had, in 1948, when the Jewish state was being created, tried to persuade the fleeing Arabs to stay, in spite of hysterical cries from the Arab capitals that they should run for their lives.

Under a blue-black sky, with the smell of Jerusalem pines all around us, we would dive down into the underworld of the Jewish experience—the early anti-Semitism of Christianity, the blood libels of centuries, the Crusades, the Inquisitions, the expulsions, the ghettos, the pogroms, the death camps, the mass killings . . . and then, after all this, the Great Return to where we now sat, inside this ancient city of holy contest. Still no peace. Still rejected. Still beleaguered. Still misunderstood.

I would listen to Talya and offer my own still forming rebuttals on behalf of the Palestinians, half believing what I was saying, half enjoying being devil's advocate. Our arguments would rage on into the early hours of the morning, when we would fall into bed. I would sleep with my own small army of angels until awakened by Talya's screaming and flailing arms as she did battle with the unnamed ghosts of her past.

When I left the *Australian* to return to Israel in 1987, I was thirty-one years old. After my studies in Middle Eastern politics and my two previous visits to the region I was determined to become a Jerusalem-based correspondent. Piers Akerman, the man who had made the newsroom a living hell during my two years on the paper, made the move easy. Merran Morrison made the move infinitely more difficult.

I'd first met Merran at the age of fourteen, when we'd come together at a garage party on Sydney's Lower North Shore. She'd arrived with a boy called John. I'd fetched up with a girl called

Belinda. We swapped partners halfway through the night, getting high on Black Sabbath's 'Paranoid', dancing and kissing to Van Morrison's 'Moondance'. Then we didn't see each other again for fifteen years.

'Hi, aren't you Merran Morrison?' I said to her in a vegetarian takeaway shop in Paddington one day in 1985.

'And aren't you David Leser?'

I remember the shiver of excitement I felt at seeing her again, even though she was now living in Canada and only in Australia for a short while. She was having a farewell party the following week and asked if I would come. Yes, I would. 'I'll ring you,' she said. And she did, but I never got the message.

Then, eighteen months later, in September 1986, I walked into a party and there she was, in white pants that looked like Jean Miró had gone to work on them, no bra and pert little breasts that brushed up against her purple silk top. Her hair was tied back in a ponytail and her skin was the colour of honey, the curve of her mouth full and sensuous. I knew immediately I wanted to kiss her long and deep and soon.

Later that night we walked hand in hand through Kings Cross, past St Luke's Hospital, and up the stairs of my terrace into my studio apartment where, before undressing, she said to me, 'I'm in love with another man.'

'Who's that?' I answered as casually as I could.

'His name is Pierre and he's Canadian.'

She'd been with him for three months—but did she know that I, too, was born in Montreal and had a Canadian passport? No, she hadn't realised that. Did she not think it better to shop at the local store than the international supermarket? No, not necessarily, she said.

'Well, that's fine,' I replied, 'as long as you don't think of Pierre while we're making love.'

And she didn't, and we did, and that was the night of our first coming together, nearly two decades after we'd danced in that garage as teenagers. Our timing, however, was slightly out. A few days before we'd met again, I'd been in Burma writing a story on the country's forgotten Jews, a community which, during the middle part of the nineteenth century, had reached its zenith with a population of about 3000 and by 1986, the year of my visit, had dwindled to less than thirty. On a train somewhere between the collapsing capital of Rangoon and the old royal seat of Mandalay I had made the decision to return to Israel to do two things: to establish myself as a Middle Eastern correspondent, and to make love to as many Israeli women as humanly possible.

Yes, okay, I wanted to report on the struggle for dominance and truth among the People of the Book and, by doing so, come to better understand my own Jewishness, and my own sense of responsibility towards the Palestinians, but I also wanted to sow a few more wild oats—and, if possible, all the way from the Lebanese border in the north to the Sinai Desert in the south, taking a circuitous route around the Arab villages and Bedouin camps of the Negev, charting a course from the shores of Lake Tiberias over to the Mediterranean, then down to the improbable blue waters of the Red Sea.

I wanted to immerse myself in the Arab–Israeli conflict but I also wanted to drown in Jewish womanliness, in all the delirious combinations made possible by calamity and the consequent in-gathering of Jews from around the world.

I wanted wild congress with blue-eyed Hungarian maidens and dark-eyed Yemenites, many of whose grandmothers had crossed the deserts of Arabia by camel just so I might meet their granddaughters in unholy union. I wanted to drink from the hybrid cup of North African tailors and European merchants and to celebrate all the fine qualities that the Israeli-born Sabra woman boasted—thorny on the outside, soft with the fragrance of a desert fruit inside.

I had been hopelessly tormented by beautiful women ever since my little bullet train had jumped the tracks carrying its night mail into Mrs Robinson's bedroom. And it seemed to me that Israel was the cruellest trick of all to play on a Jewish man from the Diaspora: a nation of sun-kissed, beauteous, athletic females, many of whom were tank, artillery and parachute instructors, non-combat officers from crack commando units, bomb-disposal experts, flight controllers, jet-fighter mechanics and weapons technicians who could speak several languages, kill intruders with their bare hands and make gefilte fish and chicken noodle soup on demand.

Merran had ended her relationship with Pierre soon after our first night together, so this was a difficult thing to admit to the person I'd been with for the previous three months, and with whom I was actually imagining spending years, if not the rest of my life. But the Israel imperative was greater at that time. I had been contemplating going there for years prior to meeting Merran and I needed to get the place out of my system. So instead of continuing to work with Piers Akerman, and instead of continuing my relationship with Merran, I decided in March 1987—amid tears and declarations of love—to relocate to Jerusalem. 'I need to go to Israel and write,' I told her. 'I love you and I'll be back in six months,' although, to be truthful, I didn't quite know whether it would be six months or six years.

A few short weeks after I arrived in Jerusalem, eighty-seven-year-old Father Lazarus made an unexpected entrance into my life. Father Lazarus was a Greek Orthodox monk who had lived as a hermit in a cave on the top of the Mount of Temptation for twenty-seven years. He'd gone there initially because the woman he loved had spurned him. That was in 1952, and two years later he'd found seclusion in a monastery an hour's walk east of Bethlehem, out in the middle of the Judaean Desert. He spent three years there training to be a monk and then, in 1957, ventured further into the wilderness, going to live on the mountain top where Jesus had once waged his almighty struggle with the Devil. Together with a group of Palestinian refugees, he'd fashioned from the rock face a church, three rooms and a kitchen, and this was where he'd done battle with his soul every day for nearly three decades. Had he not fallen one day outside his cave and broken his leg, he might still have been holed up there instead of living in Jerusalem.

He was residing behind the ancient walls of the Old City in St Constantine's monastery, working as an English-speaking guide for the hundreds of tourists visiting the Patriarchate's museum. He still held the keys to his mountain grotto and he agreed to let me take him back there so we might talk about what had prompted him to withdraw so completely from the world.

'I did this for my sins,' he said, as we sat outside his cave sipping coffee and looking down over the scorching desert where, two decades earlier, he'd seen tens of thousands of Palestinians fleeing the conquering Israeli forces during the Six-Day War. 'I was so desperate I came here for my salvation. I felt like the last man on earth.'

Father Lazarus's sin—as he saw it—was to have pledged marriage to a woman he met in Australia in 1925, promising to take her to America. After falling ill, he'd reneged on his pledge because he didn't think he would be able to look after her. 'It was a sin,' he said. 'If she was still alive I would bring her here now. Not for the flesh but for hers and my salvation.'

This young Greek-born man had left Australia for America

after this broken pledge and in Brooklyn a few years later had met another woman, this time a Greek widow with a young son. He'd fallen in love with her and initially she'd accepted his marriage proposal, but after informing her that he wanted a child, she had withdrawn her pledge, just as he had done twenty years earlier with another woman. 'She promised to marry me but when I told her what I wanted she changed her mind. It was then I decided to become a monk.'

For some reason listening to this diminutive white-bearded man talk about sanctity and unrequited love affected me deeply. It made me think about how true love, with all its quarrels and follies, presents itself to us rarely and that to turn away from it would be to risk becoming 'the last man on earth'.

By 1987 my own parents had been married for thirty-five years and somehow they'd managed to create not just a family but also a history spanning decades, from the years immediately after the Holocaust and the creation of the state of Israel, to the Korean War, the sixties counterculture (not that they were ever part of it!) and the Vietnam War, and the transformation of a largely Anglo-Celtic society like Australia into a vibrant multicultural nation.

Father Lazarus had seen the sweep of history from his mountain cave 350 metres above sea level, but for three decades he had been utterly alone. Love had failed him. Love had gone unacknowledged, unanswered, and to me it seemed like I was now being presented with a parable of despair that I could use as a reference point for my own shifting affections.

From the moment I'd arrived in Israel, Merran and I had written each other love letters—sometimes ten, twelve, fourteen pages long, full of missing, hurting, needing, planning and longing. We also spoke on the phone, sometimes for an hour, trying to breathe each other in across the mass of land and water that stretched between us. And through all this missing and hurting and longing I came to realise just how much I loved and admired her, and also how much I relished the contrast between our family backgrounds, and between our differing sensibilities and skills.

Merran was an urban planner and a public-art curator who saw the world in visual, spatial terms. She saw lines and angles and symmetry where I saw nothing, or only vague shapes on the horizon. She could interpret architectural styles, fashions and trends the way a farmer could divine clues in a bank of clouds. She understood the urban environment, how the best cities evolved through a collaboration of artists, architects, planners and designers, and how this collaboration could become a living, breathing work of art.

She was, in fact, a true Renaissance woman. She could design and draw and paint and sew and cook and write love letters as well as academic papers of high distinction, and she could turn her mind to politics, culture, religion, philosophy and art. One night, wearing a body-hugging French creation, she could be the most glamorous woman in the room; the next morning, dressed in gunpowder-stained overalls, she might be brandishing an oxyacetylene welder in the garage.

She was a pyrotechnic as well. She would lay detonators and load mortars on and off barges and choreograph firework shows—exquisite tableaux of light and heat that had audiences sucking in their breath. She was a cultural planner who could map a community's needs from a social, economic and political perspective. She could determine whether a community required a new library or more money for the surf club, or whether the rugby playing fields had become obsolete because the ethnic mix of the community had changed.

She could swim like a dolphin, effortlessly gliding through the water, stroke after beautiful stroke, and she could find her way through a strange city with dolphin-like sonar tracking. She was also a fearless traveller—arriving in Sri Lanka during the civil war, venturing to Central America during the height of the Death Squads, riding a motorbike across Bali.

The fourth of five daughters, she had grown up as one of a pack who had roamed the middle-class idyll of Sydney's Hunters Hill, a suburb where both her parents had been raised, and their parents and grandparents before them—not just in the same suburb, but in the very same street. All the sacred sites of this suburb were firmly in place. The sandstone Presbyterian church, the football fields, tennis courts and bowling club, the jetty down at Woolwich Point where the ferries chugged back and forth each day to Circular Quay.

When she was four, Merran's father had shown her how to build a doll's house, and in this *bambino* Medici nursery he'd actually helped her install a miniature flushing toilet. My father would not have known what a toolshed looked like, let alone been able to guide me towards hammers and screwdrivers. Merran had gone on to study architecture at university before shifting to a planning degree, receiving high distinctions for most of her subjects.

By the time I was in Israel she was a highly paid public-art consultant for Darling Harbour, commissioning artworks for the redevelopment of what was still a largely derelict Sydney precinct.

Three months after I left for Israel she came for a two-week holiday. We had a glorious time together, wandering the souks of the Old City, visiting the Wailing Wall and the Dome of the Rock, driving through the still-to-erupt West Bank; floating on the Dead Sea and lunching on the shores of the Galilee.

And then, a few weeks after she'd returned to Sydney, everything suddenly changed.

'Hi, darling,' she said when I picked up the phone one night. 'You wouldn't believe what's happened—there's no job for me.'

'What do you mean there's no job?'

'He sacked me.'

'He can't sack you.'

'Well, he did. It's over. Can I come back to Israel?'

'That's terrible. Shit. I can't believe he's sacked you.'

'Yes . . . Can I come back?'

'Look, I don't know, give me a minute—yes, I think so—I'm not sure. Oh, that's terrible. Let me call you back . . .'

The problem was I'd met Rosie the week before in a bar in West Jerusalem. She'd slept in my bed that first night but we'd stopped just short of going too far. Still, I liked her, and I wanted more.

Now Merran was asking, 'What do you mean you don't know?'

'Well, you've only just left and psychologically I'm just getting over the fact you're not here—plus I've got all this work to do, and . . . Can I think about it for a day or two?'

It was the wrong thing to say. Merran was distressed by my hesitancy, and understandably so.

My father happened to be in Jerusalem that day. In March 1987, at the same time I was arriving in Israel, he had been appointed the first non-American president of Condé Nast USA. He'd flown to Israel to spend a long weekend with me at the King David Hotel, that marvellous pile of pink limestone overlooking the Old City that Menachem Begin and his cohorts from the Irgun had blown up in 1946.

'What do you think, Dad? Should I tell her to come?' I asked him later that evening, pacing up and down his suite.

For a long time he didn't answer. Then he said, 'Well, it seems to me you've never loved anyone as much as you love Merran, and you've probably never been as loved by anyone as much as Merran loves you.

'That's one point. The second point is she's deeply upset. This would be a huge blow to her, losing her job, and she's asking to come and see you. I don't see how you can say no. If you do, you risk throwing everything away.'

He was right. Merran was the love of my life. We'd known each other since we were fourteen and even though there'd been sixteen years between meetings, it was like we'd lived inside each other's skin forever. We shared the same love of books, films, music, people, politics and food. We were both Australian. We both spoke English. We both came from middle-class homes in Sydney. We had a lot going for us.

On the other hand there was Rosie—free and desirous of me in her little sandstone apartment on Mount Scopus. 'Come over on Tuesday night,' she'd said in her thick Hebrew-accented English.

Life is a series of choices and these choices determine everything that follows. Here was my choice: one road leading into the heart of Israeli society, via Rosie's bed; the other pointing towards home, back to Australia.

To say no to Merran would have meant the end of the most important relationship I'd known. It would have meant, in all likelihood, starting a relationship with Rosie, and if things had worked out, probably coming to know her family and friends, learning Hebrew, becoming more entrenched in Israeli society, possibly staying for years.

I was partly receptive to this, and already imagining the possibilities of an Israeli wife, Jewish children and a roving brief as a Middle Eastern correspondent. That was the right fork, leading through wounded, haunting landscapes, past ancient cities and armistice lines, along valley rifts and on to coastal plains soaked in the blood of the ages.

The left fork pointed towards the bays and beaches of Sydney, towards family and friends and all that was comfortable and familiar. 'I could never live in Australia,' the spokesman for the

Israeli foreign ministry had told me one day. 'Too boring. Nothing happens there.'

By Israeli standards nothing did happen there. A people at peace in a big brown land on the edge of the world.

I chose the left fork. 'Darling, of course you can come back,' I said the following night when I called. 'I'm sorry I hesitated. When can you get here?'

And then afterwards to Rosie: 'Look, about Tuesday night—I'd love to, I really would, but my girlfriend is coming back from Australia. I'm not sure where we can take this.'

'Oh, that's too bad,' she replied. 'Perhaps we won't see each other again, no?'

'I'm not sure.'

'So have a good life, yes?'

'Yes. You too.'

6

WELCOME TO GAZA

Shortly after arriving in Jerusalem in March 1987, I wrote my first article for the English-language Hong Kong newspaper, the *South China Morning Post*. It was on the looming international peace conference being sponsored by the Americans, one that was causing bitter divisions within Israel's 'national unity' government over whether to exchange land for peace.

I wrote the story on a Toshiba laptop, printed it out on a machine that weighed nearly more than my packed suitcase, presented it to the military censors and then sent it by express post to Hong Kong for the princely sum of thirty-four shekels, which was nearly a hundred Australian dollars at the time.

Two weeks later I received a copy of the story in the mail and, to my utter joy and amazement, there it was—spread out as the lead feature in the foreign section of the Saturday paper. ISRAEL AT THE CROSSROADS . . . David Leser, in a special article for the *South China Morning Post*, reports from Jerusalem.

What did I do when I saw the results of my labour? I'll tell you what I did. I jumped on my bed and started doing a jig. If you'd happened to be looking in the window from outside you would have seen a short man with thinning hair, his eyes closed and hands raised aloft, crying, 'I've done it! I've done it!'

And had you knocked politely on his door and asked him what he was doing and who he thought he was at that moment, he would have told you the unvarnished truth—that, at this moment, he was nothing less than the reawakened King David, son of Jesse, slayer of Goliath, conqueror of Jerusalem, harpist, poet, adulterer and uniter of warring tribes. It was *he* dancing on a bed in West Jerusalem in 1987 disguised as an Australian Jewish journalist; *he* who had returned to write modern-day psalms in the form of feature articles for an English-language newspaper in Hong Kong—because these articles were finally going to bring peace to the Middle East.

Okay, the man had a dose of 'Jerusalem syndrome'. It was a well-known psychological condition often afflicting tourists, particularly men, who got too close to the holy places. In this case, however, there would be no lasting psychopathology. He would not claim to be the Messiah. He would not deliver a sermon at the Wailing Wall, nor wear a toga down the Via Dolorosa. He would simply get off his bed after about five minutes and make a cup of tea.

And then he would travel throughout Israel and the Occupied Territories writing other features for his new masters in Hong Kong—as well as papers in Australia and America—on the turmoil in the West Bank, on the ructions within the national unity government, on the battle over sacred sites in the Old City, on the rescue of Jews from Ethiopia, on the merits of the Baha'i faith, on the dispossession of the Bedouin, on the ancient techniques of desert agriculture, on the growing power of religious Jews and on the allegations of torture and perjury within the country's internal intelligence organisation, Shin Bet.

And then, together with the woman he loved, he would venture into one of the most heavily populated and miserable places on earth, in order to write the story he'd been threatening to write ever since arriving in Israel six months earlier.

∽

Now an angel of the Lord said to Philip—Go south to the road—the *desert road*—that goes down from Jerusalem to Gaza!

Acts 8:26

The Gaza Strip is not a pretty place, and back in 1987 the signs of its infirmity were everywhere. Wedged between Egypt and Israel, on Israel's south-western flank, it was a teeming corral of 500,000 disaffected and angry souls, almost half of whom were living in eight squalid refugee camps scattered throughout the territory.

In October, a few weeks after Merran's return, we decided to go there on assignment, with Merran taking the photographs and me doing the interviews and writing the story. We would drive the 100 kilometres south-west from Jerusalem to Gaza in my new Swiss Lancia, passing through the Erez Crossing separating the Strip from Israel. In Gaza I would talk to Palestinian activisits, lawyers, members of the Red Crescent Society and refugees inside Jabalaya, the largest of the eight refugee camps.

There was only one problem. I forgot to listen to the military radio before leaving. Had I done so, I would have known that tensions were still boiling over the death of three Palestinians at a roadblock two weeks earlier. I would also have known that a large protest designed to shut down the Gaza Strip was scheduled for that very day.

We didn't know trouble was coming until it actually arrived, and that was just minutes after we'd seen the sign that said WELCOME TO GAZA, and we'd turned into Omar al-Mukhtar Street, the main thoroughfare running from Palestine Square to Port Gaza on the Mediterranean. We were looking for the office of the Palestinian lawyer whom I was scheduled to interview.

Within seconds I realised my mistake. All the shops were shut and the eyes of the street were upon us. Hundreds of people were now staring at my very shiny new Swiss car with Israeli number-plates and two people inside who looked very much like Israelis.

'Oh fuck,' I said, as much to myself as to Merran.

'What do you mean?' she replied. 'The cultural difference?' She thought I was responding with alarm to the way the Arabs looked, compared to the Jews of West Jerusalem.

'No,' I said, terror suddenly taking hold. 'No one is doing anything and everyone is looking at us.'

And that was when the first brick came flying through the front windscreen, missing my head by centimetres. The second brick broke the driver's window, landing at my feet, showering glass on my hands and legs. The third shattered the pane on Merran's side, missing her head by a whisker. Then came a volley of rocks and stones and suddenly we were without windows, surrounded on all sides.

The car began to idle in second gear. We were just about to stall when I jammed it into first and tore out of there, tyres screeching, nearly knocking down two demonstrators in the process. It was over in seconds.

'Are you alright?' I cried, as we headed towards the sea.

'Yes,' Merran replied. 'I'm fine.'

Fine? We were nearly bloody killed. What on earth was I thinking coming here without a Palestinian guide?

We went to the Israeli military headquarters at the western end of Omar al-Mukhtar Street and reported what had just happened (we did this for insurance purposes, not to bring retribution on the population). Then I called the Palestinian lawyer whom I was supposed to have met half an hour earlier and he came to collect us, apologising profusely on behalf of his people as he drove us back to his office.

'Did you have a sign on your car saying you are a journalist?' he asked.

'No,' I replied, ashamed of my own stupidity.

'This is necessary, my friend,' he said. 'Especially today. Today you drive into demonstration because of killings.'

'What killings?'

'You did not hear? The Israelis shot four Palestinians yesterday. This is a demonstration for the killing.'

We then went from the Palestinian lawyer's office to the office of the Gaza Red Crescent Society, and on to the Jabalaya refugee camp. To me, a child of Zionists, raised on the comforting images of suntanned Jewish pioneers reclaiming their ancient birthright, treating their Arab cousins with a democratising benevolence, this was as confronting a sight as I had ever seen—as many as 100,000 Palestinians living under the most appalling conditions in an area of no more than 1.5 square kilometres. This was Israel's Soweto, and definitely not what my Jewish upbringing had taught me.

We spent the rest of the afternoon in Jabalaya and at dusk returned in our windowless car to Jerusalem, where I went straight to my desk to write what I believe was the first story of the uprising to come.

On 6 December, an Israeli businessman was stabbed to death while shopping in Gaza, and two days after this four Palestinians— three from Jabalaya—were killed in a 'traffic accident' when an Israeli army tank transporter crashed into a row of cars.

So incensed were Palestinians at what they saw as a deliberate act of revenge for the stabbing that on 9 December Jabalaya erupted, triggering a chain reaction of violent protests throughout the West Bank and Arab East Jerusalem. An entire nation was now rising up in a spontaneous act of revolt. The first uprising, or intifada, was to last for six years.

Two months before these events my story was published in the *South China Morning Post* with the headline: FLAMES OF ANGER ROAR IN GAZA. It made me look like the right man for the right story at the right moment. I knew better. I knew it had been pure fluke on my part, in concert with breathtaking naivety.

I was deeply troubled by having gone with Merran into Gaza without having first observed the proper precautions. In my defence, I could claim that the demonstration was the first of its kind against Israeli occupation; until that point in the history of the Palestinian–Israeli conflict, no Israeli cars had been attacked in the Occupied Territories.

This was no defence at all. I'd set out for Gaza because it seemed from various reports—although not the ones I failed to listen to on the day of the attack—that the place was about to explode. Here was a desperate people living in squalor and without hope, denied access to basic health and education, detained without trial, family members deported, homes demolished and no rights to union membership or fair wages. There was obviously going to be a tipping point, and this had been it.

After finishing my 3000-word article I took a long bath, and as I sank into the warm water I began shaking uncontrollably. For at least an hour I lay there shivering and obsessing over what might have happened, imagining Merran injured, or worse, if one of those bricks had hit her in the head and/or the car had stalled. I believed the crowd would have pulled us from our car and beaten us to death—just like they were to do in the ensuing months and years when other cars strayed into the wrong area at the wrong time.

Merran thought I was being overly dramatic. She thought that to say we could have been killed was to say we could have been flattened by the truck that roared past us seconds after we'd stepped onto a kerb. Or that, had we still been leaning against the tree when lightning struck, we'd have been toast. We'd been in trouble, yes. The crowd had been angry, yes. It was a close shave with those bricks and rocks and stones, yes. But it was over in seconds. We'd got away. End of story.

For years afterwards nothing I said would ever convince her that my reading of what happened that day was right—that as probably the first Israeli car to drive into the Gaza Strip on the eve of the first Palestinian uprising, we were in mortal danger—not just because of who we were (or who we were presumed to be), but because of where we were and when we happened to be there. It was about timing, and our timing had been disastrous.

Two weeks after Gaza I asked Merran to marry me. I had taken to heart the story of Father Lazarus's twenty-seven years in the desert because of love's misfortune. I had absorbed the tragedy of Merran's sister Jill, whose partner John had dropped dead a few years earlier in London from a cerebral haemorrhage. Jill had never been truly honoured as his widow because they'd never formalised their union with a wedding.

Our near escape had me thinking about my love for this doctor's daughter from Hunters Hill, and how, if one of us had been killed that day, I would have wanted to have been her husband, not her boyfriend, and for her to have been my wife. That sounds like the reasonings of a Jewish catastrophist, but in those weeks with Merran in Israel, which had turned into months, something new had claimed us both; something beyond the love and the longing, which had to do with the writing of a shared mythology, a shared history, here in the Holy Land. I wanted to walk through this world with her.

Shortly after our Gaza incident we drove in my newly repaired car to Taba, the resort town at the northern tip of the Gulf of Aqaba, where the desert meets Egypt's Red Sea Riviera. Today Taba is a border crossing between Israel and Egypt, but in 1987 it was the cause of a major international dispute—a 600-metre sliver of shingle and sand coveted by both countries but controlled by Israel.

Israel had built a US$20 million hotel on the shores of the Red Sea and, together with the nearby Bedouin camp and the End of the World nightclub, it was one of the most popular tourist destinations in the region for both Israelis and Europeans.

Such were the delightful distractions of Taba that you could sit on the verandah at the Sonesta hotel, the translucent waters of the Red Sea and the mountains of Jordan and Saudi Arabia shimmering beyond, and completely ignore the fact that this was a no-man's-land of bitter contention between two frontline states. (Two years after our visit, Taba was returned to Egypt and seventeen years after this the Sonesta hotel was blown up in a car-bomb attack by an al-Qaeda affiliate. Thirty-one people died and another 159 were injured as ten floors of the hotel collapsed.)

'Would you marry me?' I asked Merran one evening as she sat on my lap.

'Of course I would,' she replied, as if the question were absurd.

'Really?'

'Really.'

'Did you think I would ask you?'

'I hoped you would.'

When she'd said yes a third time we went back into the room to seal our pact and activate our oxytocin receptors in the time-honoured way of lovers, and then called our families to tell them the news, despite Merran's suggestion that we wait till morning.

'Why would we do that?' I asked.

'To be sure. To sleep on it. You might change your mind,' she said.

'No way . . . let's call them. It'll be fine in the morning.'

So we did—just to eliminate any backsliding. If I was going to take this giant leap of faith into wedlock, it would have to be seized without hesitation down here in the Sinai Desert.

'Hello, Mum . . . it's us. We're here overlooking the Jordan River. I just thought you'd like to know we're getting married. Yes. We just decided. We wanted you to know. Thank you, yes. I know, it's great, isn't it? Are you surprised? Really? Happy? Oh, that's great. Is Dad there? Hi, Dad, I just wanted you to know we're getting married. Yes, we decided a little while ago. I don't know. Possibly March next year when I'm back. Yes, we are too . . . over the moon.'

Merran's father Jim had died when Merran was twenty-three. We called her mother, Jeanne. 'Hi, Jeanne, it's David here in Israel. I just wanted you to know that Merran and I have decided to get married.'

There was a long pause.

'Aren't you going to ask my permission?' she replied, only half joking.

'Yes, of course. Sorry, Jeanne. Would you mind if I married your daughter?'

'Not at all,' she said. 'I would be delighted.'

And with that I took the left fork home instead of the road less travelled.

7

CARD GAME

On 31 March 1988, Merran and I were married in the grounds of a sandstone manor in Sydney in front of one hundred and seventy people. Merran was a picture of loveliness in raw-silk damask pants and a body-hugging taffeta dress split to the waist. She looked like an Indian princess as she glided towards me to the sound of Sting's 'Fragile', a song that captured for both of us the perishable nature of life and love.

I wore a white suit and purple tie and looked like the proverbial cat that had swallowed the cream. I still had hair.

It was an evening—as Paul Simon might have said—of miracle and wonder. Kathryn Selby, the Australian classical pianist, played Debussy's 'L'isle Joyeuse'; a swing band had us dancing to Duke Ellington and Tommy Dorsey numbers till 1 am; and in the garden Merran's 'Torch Brothers' created a beautifully choreographed fireworks display that rained happiness on our heads.

The period leading up to our wedding had been difficult. In January, I'd gone to see my grandmother, Hansey Simblist, to inform her that Merran would not be converting to Judaism as we'd originally planned.

Merran had grown up in a Presbyterian family, but for most of her adult life her sympathies had lain with Buddhism, although her curiosities extended beyond Buddhism to other faiths, like Judaism and Baha'ism. It was this curiosity about other faiths, coupled with her love for me and my Jewishness, that had made it possible for her to contemplate something I'm not sure I could ever have done—convert to the faith of my spouse. She was doing this for no other reason than to make me happy.

We'd begun Jewish conversion classes at the liberal-minded Temple Emanuel synagogue, but after three excruciatingly diffi-cult forays into Jewish studies and the Hebrew language it had become clear to me that if we were to continue this together, we would both end up being far more Jewish than I'd imagined. I didn't even know how much I really wanted Merran to be Jewish, or why. According to Jewish law, it would mean that our children would be Jewish and this would make my parents and grand-mother happy. But to arrive at that place required so much study on Merran's part that I was not prepared to make her go through it, so I pulled the plug on our classes and announced this to my parents before going to confront my grandmother on the subject. This was never going to be an easy conversation because—unbe-known to Merran—my grandmother's affection for her had largely been predicated on her becoming Jewish. Obviously, she had still not learnt from the tragic consequences of her opposition to her second daughter's marriage.

It was the eve of Rosh Hashana, the Jewish new year, and as my grandmother and I sipped tea served to us by her Scottish housekeeper, she reached into her purse to present me with a twenty-dollar note for the new year.

'Nan,' I said to her, 'I just need to tell you . . . I hope you'll understand . . . that Merran is not going to convert after all. It was my decision, not hers, but I felt after the three classes we did that she'd end up being more Jewish than I've ever been, and it didn't feel right.'

My grandmother stuffed the twenty dollars back into her purse, snapped it shut, then looked at me with sad, reproachful eyes and said, 'I see, dear. Very well then.'

That scene had been wrenching but not catastrophic. Catastrophic was two months before our wedding day, when Merran's house in Rozelle, in Sydney's inner west, burnt to the ground. I'd been living there since my return from Israel in January. One night we went out for dinner with my parents and returned later that evening to find the street cordoned off and firefighters dousing the last of the flames that had devoured her weatherboard cottage. Apparently, we'd left the halogen lamp on too close to the back of the couch and, given that the couch was made of a highly flammable polyurethane foam, the whole thing had gradually overheated before igniting into a fireball.

Our friend and flatmate Susan Biggs, soon to be one of Merran's three bridesmaids, was on the phone when she heard crackling in the living room. She knew we weren't home but she ran upstairs to our empty bedroom screaming for us to get out of bed, disoriented—she realised later—by all the retardant chemicals. Susan only narrowly escaped herself before the flames licked the living room ceiling and stairwell, causing the phone to melt into the table. Everything Merran owned—furniture, clothes, books and photos—was reduced to cinders.

That was the beginning of our life together after Israel— a house of ashes and a white wedding that brought together an upper middle-class Jewish family of European roots and a fifth-generation Presbyterian family from Hunters Hill in Sydney.

At the beginning of 1988 I returned to the *Australian* as a feature writer for the soon-to-be-launched weekend magazine. Merran had taken a job with the Crafts Council of New South

Wales and, with the insurance money from her house and some much needed help from my father, we were able to buy a terrace in Darlinghurst, across the road from where junked-out hookers and transsexuals plied their unhappy trade.

In January the following year we discovered Merran was pregnant. She was late in her cycle and had just handed me the home pregnancy test from the bathroom when I asked her, 'What colour does the stick go if you're pregnant?'

'Pink,' she said.

'It's so pink it's purple,' I replied.

Merran came rushing from the bathroom and burst into tears. I grabbed the banister to steady myself. Only four weeks earlier she'd said to me, 'Let's try to have a child in about a year.'

A year? You can't be serious, I'd thought. *We only got married last March. I'm still getting used to being a husband. That will take at least another three years. And surely we'll want time to enjoy ourselves. Alone. How would we travel? How would we go out on Saturday nights? What would happen to Sunday mornings in bed? And, for that matter, Mondays, Tuesdays . . .*

These, of course, were peripheral questions. The real question was: how could I, who at times considered myself too free-spirited even to be married, become a parent? I was too selfish. The idea seemed preposterous, the risks for the child too high.

Naturally I needed to consider Merran's biological clock. According to the one-year-from-now plan she would be thirty-four by the time our first child arrived, about thirty-six for our second. The timekeeper was saying, 'Do it soon!' but the pit of my stomach was saying, 'No, wait.' I needed an accident—and that's what we got.

Somehow, life conspired at this time to give us a sabbatical in paradise. Twelve months after starting with the *Australian Magazine* I resigned to pursue freelance writing, while Merran completed her contract as an arts consultant. The timing was perfect for a working holiday. I had commissions for two months in the United States and, after that, the offer of a friend's cottage in Greece for as long as we wanted. 'Come, make babies,' the friend had said warmly.

∾

The island of Cephalonia is not a bad place for procreation, even if you've already accomplished that. The Ionian Sea wraps around the setting of *Captain Corelli's Mandolin* like a turquoise quilt and the fir tree-covered mountains loom from behind every white-washed wall.

Our cottage sat in a garden of daffodils and poppies on the side of a hill, and each day we would wake to the tinkling of goat bells as the local shepherd, a dashing Greek god-like figure, guided his flock up and down the rocky incline. For six weeks we heard from virtually no one else.

One brisk early morning we hired a car in order to see the island. We took the mountain road and on that treacherous strip of tar, with its sheer vertical drop into the limestone sea and no safety fence, I had a very long look at mortality.

I had feared death two years earlier in the Gaza Strip, but this was the first time I had been scared of dying because of someone else.

On the one hand, there I was in an open jeep with the woman I loved—part of a blissed-out family-in-the-making. On the other hand there was this yawning drop into the sea, barely two metres away.

There is no way you can look into an abyss and not thank the gods you're alive and that your brakes are working. There is no way you can ignore the fact that there are three people in a car on a mountain road, not two. You just don't know the third person yet.

This was the moment that the swell of Merran's stomach became the object of my unconditional love. This was where the notion of fatherhood really began to take hold and a selfish life began to make way for a wonderfully old-fashioned—and much better—idea: that somebody else might matter more than myself. And this was where, not long after this mountain drive, I began writing a letter to my unborn child:

I wanted to photograph your mother's face this afternoon, there in the field surrounded by yellow and purple flowers, or else in the front of the house where pink oleanders matched the colour of her shirt.

I am only now beginning to see how perfectly suited I am to a life with her. She is the only woman I have ever really imagined being my wife, and your mother. She is the only woman I have ever known who is as strong as she is gentle, who laughs as hard as she cries, who bestows on others a rich but subtle nourishment and wisdom.

I have felt this since we met, but in the first year after our wedding it was sometimes dimmed by my own forebodings. She, too, wrestled with the constraints of marriage. Believe me, there were times when she wept and wept and there was nothing I or anybody could do. She was weeping for a life passing and for a new one that imposed on her demands which anyone who cherished their own freedom would find daunting. It had nothing to do with love. It was just that thing called marriage.

You must understand that, certainly in the age in which we lived, in the age we now live, it was not, nor was it ever going to be, a simple matter for two people like your mother and I to marry. Marriage was the great compromise; children the ultimate shackle. At least, that's what we thought until we found one another and decided, independently, that we were each worth the risk.

I know I love you already without having seen you, and yet I shudder at my own incompetence, at the failings I hope never to pass on to you but which you will inevitably be touched by.

I have no answers, only questions.

I sit here at my desk and ask myself: how can I father a child in an age such as this? What kind of world will I bequeath to you? What will your judgement be? And when you've judged the world, how will you then judge the people who brought you into it? Will we be friends, like my father and I? Will we understand one another, or will you turn around in ten years' time and say, 'Dad, you're fucked.' And will my father—your grandfather—stand behind me and laugh, and urge you on, because in life's great cycle it's now my turn to get from you what I gave to him?

You see, I have no answers. Only questions.

I think our daughter was fifteen when she read this letter for the first time. 'That's nice, Dad,' she said.

We returned to Sydney and went almost straight from the airport to our birth class. This was not just any birth class; this was the New Age variety, replete with beanbags, ambient music, chamomile tea and two beaming instructors whom I shall call Brad and Janet.

Within minutes of our arrival Brad was instructing us in communication through massage. With a gentle voice and a clear set of of instructions he showed us how to relate to one another through touch—how to 'feel at one' with our partner and, for us men, how to imagine there was a real person inside the woman next to us. That's right: 'a baybeee'.

For me, it was time to leave, but Merran insisted we give the class longer than fifteen minutes. I agreed, reluctantly.

141

Brad wasn't finished, though. He next went down on all fours, holding a plastic doll called Matilda to his crutch. He started pelvic rocking with Matilda firmly in hand. Matilda's head then started crowning and, *bingo*, within seconds the doll was born, straight from Brad's jeans.

Brad was then standing up. Squatting. Bending forward over the cushions. Brad was doing impossible things and Matilda was presenting as posterior, anterior, breech. You name it, Brad was doing it. This was truly an act of God—but it was the first and last New Age birth class we went to.

As it turned out our child was breech and no amount of exercise or cajoling seemed to budge it from its preferred buttocks-first-into-the-world direction. We sang. We talked. We rubbed. Nothing.

Someone had told us an old wives' tale about why infants went into a breech position. It was because the parents expected the baby to be one sex over another. In protest, the baby presented its genitals first instead of its head.

It wasn't that we preferred a boy to a girl. It was just that all those people who claimed to have special intuition about these things said categorically: 'It's a boy.' And when friends, family and Greek peasant women tell you with such certitude that you are going to have a son you start believing them.

So we waited for this son of ours to come. We had been told that 4 September was the due date. At 11 am on 19 September, after inspecting the CTG results, the obstetrician told us to 'go home, have some lunch and then come back and have a baby'.

And that's what we did. We went home, had lunch and then returned to the hospital for the birth of our first child.

Even now, as I write this, I can hear the screams. They are bloodcurdling—as though we are on a battlefield and Merran's leg is being amputated. She is having an episiotomy and I am helpless in the face of this. This is my first experience of the everyday miracle of birth.

It's 11.30 pm. A minute ago it was two o'clock. Give her the gas. She wants the gas. Where's the doctor? She wants to push. Why won't you let her push? Okay, not fully dilated yet. Come on, we're nearly there. Here's the doctor. Why does he look so calm? Look at the pain she is in! Please don't scream. Okay, scream. Scream as hard as you want. Yes, he says you can push. The bottom's showing. Goddamn it, that's my child's bottom. Push. That's right, the bottom is coming. Please don't scream. Darling, he's telling you to feel the bottom. You don't want to? Okay. You do want to? Okay. The doctor wants to cut. Jesus, he's cutting. That's right, push, push, PUSH. Here it comes. The trunk is coming. My God, it's blue. No it's not, it's white. The head's still inside. The head's coming. It's out. It's bloody. It's a baby. Look at this! My God, here it is. We've done it! You've done it! We've got a baby! What is it? I forgot to ask.

It was a girl, not a boy. A girl. Jordan, our first daughter. The name was bound to cause a stir, especially on my side of the family.

'Are you really going to call her Jordan?' my grandmother asked me straight after the birth.

'Yes, Nan.'

'Well, let's hope she brings peace to the Middle East.'

In the year of Jordan's birth I wrote two of my first stories for *Good Weekend*, stories that would change my thinking, and my journalistic compass, forever. When I'd returned from Jerusalem at the beginning of 1988, I'd become despondent at the thought of ever finding a subject as gripping as the Middle East conflict.

For me, the Middle East still had everything. The desert and the souk, the Hindu Kush, Fertile Crescent and the Garden of Eden. It was the stories of the Bible and the traumatised aftermath of the

Holocaust. It was where the forces of colonialism, Pan-Arabism, Zionism and Islamic fundamentalism converged. It was where some of the worst features of the Cold War had been fought out between superpower patrons and their client states. It was where Jew confronted Muslim, Arab confronted Israeli, Persian confronted Arab, Afghani confronted Persian, Kurd confronted Turk, Shia confronted Sunni, Lebanese Christian confronted Lebanese Muslim, Sephardic Jew confronted Ashkenazi Jew, and where thousands of other tribes and clans confronted one another: Uzbeki, Hazara, Turkmen, Pashtun, Baluchi.

It was where the Bedouin roamed, and from where refugees still fled, across borders and oceans to countries like ours. It was the birthplace of some of the great advances in mathematics, architecture, literature and science, and it was also the birthplace of the assassin, the Fedayeen and the suicide bomber. It was the place that had appalled, intoxicated and confounded people for centuries and, for many years, me too.

And here I was returning to Australia to write about what? The re-enactment of the First Fleet voyage? The World Expo in Brisbane? A newly deregulated economy?

Towards the end of Australia's bicentennial year I answered my own question after being commissioned to write two profiles on two people I thought worthy of feature-length articles. The first was A.D. Hope, the grand patriarch of Australian poetry; the second, Petrea King, a woman who had counselled thousands of Australians with life-threatening illnesses.

It was ten years since I'd read the confessional poems and sonnets of the American poet Robert Lowell at university, and over the years I'd also penned a few passable poems and lyrics myself. I was a stranger to the more subterranean conversations that took place in the poetic imagination, but I can see now how just reading poetry was an act of deep contemplation. It was a questing after different truths, an attempt at a conversation with some part of yourself that didn't take place in everyday life.

I met Professor Alec Hope at his Canberra home in December 1988. He was eighty-one years old and had just finished his first comic play, while also translating three other poets into English. Hope read eleven languages, including Old Icelandic, and had been awarded an OBE, a Companion of the Order of Australia, as well as numerous other prizes for his contribution to Australian literature.

He had started early. At the age of eight he'd written a fifty-two-stanza poem for his mother on the virtues of Christianity, and by the time he was nine was so well acquainted with the works of Wordsworth, Tennyson, Keats and Shelley that he likened them to 'familiar friends'. At ten he'd devoured Milton and confronted Byron and, by the age of twelve, had written a novel. At fourteen, his first poems were published, but it was not until he was forty-eight that his work was first published in book form.

The poet's torch had been passed to him more than twenty years earlier, around 1932, by another great Australian of the European tradition, Christopher Brennan. Their encounter one day in the toilet of the Mansions Hotel in Kings Cross was as fantastically bizarre as it was brief.

Hope was standing in a cubicle one afternoon when Brennan appeared beside him. Hope tried to engage the ageing drunkard in dialogue, but when this proved futile, he pulled out a felt pen and began writing on the toilet wall. It was an inscription from the fortifications of ancient Pompeii: FUTUITUR CUNNUS PILOSSUS (the hairy cunt) . . .

Brennan took the pen out of Hope's hand and finished the quotation: MULTO MELIUS QUAM GLABER (fucks much better than the plucked one).

'He didn't talk about the contents at all,' Hope told me. 'He gave a fascinating short talk about the metre. He said, "You know, it's a septenary, of course." His talk only lasted five or six minutes. And he slumped away again and I had my pee and came back to find him . . . collapsed. That was the only time I met him.'

I was nervous about meeting Alec Hope because of his reputation for verbal savagery. After reviewing Max Harris's first novel, *The Vegetative Eye*, Hope had written that Harris was 'morally sick', and couldn't write. (Harris told me later that Hope had gone in for the kill—almost like 'shooting baby rabbits in their burrows'.)

He'd given Patrick White a mugging too, for which White was never to forgive him. Hope wrote that arguably Australia's greatest author had three disastrous faults as a novelist. 'He knows too much, he tells too much and he talks too much.' White's novel *The Tree of Man*, Hope wrote, was 'pretentious and illiterate verbal sludge'.

David Martin's selected poems had also copped a hiding, with Hope describing them as 'crude and debased art', while Mary Gilmore's verse was likened to 'a daily batch of scones'.

When I arrived at Alec Hope's house the front door was open and the old man was shuffling down the hallway to greet me with a notebook of unpublished poems in his hand. We would end up talking at the dining table for hours over a half-flagon of red wine, with the late-afternoon shadows dancing in the window and his 120-year-old cat, Abyssinia, brushing past our legs. We talked about other poets and about poetry and about the role of dreams in poetry until, finally, I asked him whether he was scared of dying.

He responded with a story about Jonathan Swift who, in his old age, pointed to a tree that was beginning to go brown at the top. 'I shall be like that tree,' Swift said. 'I shall begin to die at the top.'

'And so he did,' Hope told me. 'He went mad and he knew he was going mad and that is something that one has a horror of. I am pleased that my legs give way and the top end seems to be all right so far.'

And then, in a moment akin to Bob Dylan pulling out his Martin guitar and singing 'Not Dark Yet' for you, Professor Hope opened his notebook, cleared his throat, and with a slightly slurred but resonant voice, read me one of the last poems he would ever write.

It was called 'Card Game'.

Club, diamond, heart and spade,
Under these the game is played.
Warfare, wealth, love and death
Dominate our every breath.

Players are not free to choose
Suit assigned nor hand refuse
Dealt them careless of their skill
Shuffled blindly, well or ill.

Wealth I had no talent for;
Lacked all aptitude for war;
Death at most might set me free;
Hearts were always trumps to me.

Looking back on that meeting with Alec Hope twenty-five years ago, I can see now I was trying to open my eyes and ears to new lines of inquiry, hoping that journalism could help me answer some of those questions.

Many of us embark on unconscious pilgrimages to places without really understanding why. We gravitate to wells, churches and battlefields, to caves and ceremonial sites, because they speak to parts of ourselves that are longing to connect to something bigger, to fables, myths or songlines, to mystical traditions of which we might have only the barest understanding, but are drawn to nonetheless. Our brains are firing us to *know*, but our souls are demanding that we *feel* something.

A.D. Hope's line 'Hearts were always trumps to me' spoke to my own predisposition. As a teenager I had looked for ways to voice these things, but my own poetry and feckless love songs were no substitute for the masters themselves—Lennon and McCartney, Dylan, Paul Simon, Leonard Cohen and Bruce Springsteen, men who were able to write about their hungry hearts without wincing.

In 1977 I'd actually gone looking for Leonard Cohen on the Greek island of Hydra. Cohen had owned a house there since 1960 and written songs like 'Bird on a Wire' in his cottage overlooking the Aegean. He also met Marianne there, the woman who was to inspire one of his most unforgettable paens to the allure of women, 'So Long Marianne'.

I arrived in Hydra with my backpack and acoustic guitar and set off in search of my hero, believing—for some reason that still eludes me—that Cohen would be pleased to meet me.

'*Yassou, kalimera,*' I called out to the farmers and goatherds I passed on the winding coastal road leading out of town. 'Do you speak English? Do you know where Leonard Cohen lives?' No, they didn't speak English and if they understood my request, they weren't about to reveal the whereabouts of the Canadian poet and songwriter. After walking about ten kilometres without sighting my man, I did what any self-respecting Cohen acolyte would have done. I sat on a rock with a view of the cliffs of Hydra, took out my guitar and sang 'Suzanne', hoping that Cohen might appear. He didn't.

❧

Petrea King was the second person to help guide me into these long-cordoned-off places of the heart. I profiled her for *Good Weekend* shortly after interviewing A.D. Hope, but her influence would prove far greater than that of the genius poet.

Six years before our meeting, Petrea had been diagnosed with acute myeloid leukaemia and told by her doctors that she 'wouldn't see Christmas'. She was offered chemotherapy that would neither cure her nor give her a remission, but might extend her life by a few weeks. That was September 1983 and she was thirty-three years old.

Petrea had been studying yoga and meditation in America when she was diagnosed, and once she was back home with her young children she made plans to die. 'I wept buckets,' she told me at our first meeting. 'I knew that if I had died my father would have gone on at length about my accomplishments, but inside I still wouldn't have known who I was. I didn't have any peace. I still didn't have any kind of resolution about the events of my life, and I think that was the hard part.'

Petrea had worked as a roustabout in New Zealand and a boundary rider in western Queensland, then with Winston Churchill's family in Sussex as a nanny, during which time she catalogued his library and letters. But she had also known great suffering.

At the age of twelve she'd spent nearly three years in hospital because her knees rotated inward so severely that they kept dislocating. Her first sexual experience had been at seventeen when she was raped by a friend at a church fellowship meeting while she was in a back brace. In her early twenties she'd become so crippled by arthritis she could only walk with crutches. In 1982 one of her beloved brothers took his life and then, eighteen months later, she was given her own death sentence.

Petrea felt she hadn't lived yet, and this was what she applied herself to when she was diagnosed.

'It wasn't so much doing anything to stop myself from dying,' she told me. 'It was just trying to find some peace before I did. I fully expected to die. I packed my internal bags. My children were only four and seven and they went to live with their father.

'I moved in with my parents and they looked after me, and then I went to Italy. I literally had all my life packed up in this little suitcase.'

Petrea made her way to a place she had always dreamt of visiting: Assisi, in the hills of Umbria. She was taken in by a monastery a few kilometres outside the city where St Francis had isolated himself in prayer and contemplation. There, in a cave built into the rock face on the slopes of Mount Subasio, Petrea followed St Francis's example, meditating and praying for up to eighteen hours a day.

And she found peace. When she returned to Australia she was told she was in remission but that it was unlikely to last. She had no conscious plan to work with people with life-threatening illnesses, but having trained as a naturopath and with some nursing in her background, there seemed to be an inevitability about this new calling: to work with the sick and dying.

Within weeks of beginning her new practice, people with cancer and AIDS began seeking her out. She came alive in their presence. She understood many of the issues they faced. They needed to talk and cry and rail and scream. They needed, after the doctor's diagnosis, to be treated as human beings with their own unique stories, personal histories and futures. They needed advice on exercise and diet and meditation and various other ways of addressing the discord in their lives. Many people, having been told they were going to die, discovered how to live properly for the first time. And to love. 'I have arranged my public schedule so that I can kill myself in November,' a leading Australian conductor told Petrea several years before his death in 1991 from an AIDS-related illness.

'But I'll be damned if I will die before I've learnt how to love.'

This man was a gifted artist, comfortable on the world's stages, a man at his best when expressing himself through his music. It was the only way he was able to truly give voice to his emotions because he didn't feel safe speaking of what was truly in his heart. Before he died, Petrea helped him find the profound peace he'd been aching for. She was to end up doing this with more than 100,000 Australians over the succeeding years—not just people diagnosed with life-threatening illnesses, but also people who had suffered a crisis of hope or purpose; who, in some cases, had been crucified publicly in the media, or had feared some dark secret being made public. Some were prepared to take their own lives rather than see this happen. Petrea counselled them all.

Her reputation spread. At one point she was seeing an average of 200 people a week in her lounge room in Crows Nest—young, old, nearly dead, the not-yet-ready-to-die. When I first met her, a woman had just telephoned to ask for an appointment. Petrea told the woman she couldn't see her for three weeks.

'But the doctors have only given me four,' the woman said.

'Alright,' Petrea replied. 'I'll see you on Saturday morning.'

Her first teacher in this magnificent vocation had been a nine-year-old boy called Charlie who had died three years earlier from cancer. Petrea had been invited into Charlie's home to see if there was something, *anything*, she could do for his family, as they were falling apart.

'I think this was a major turning point in my life,' she told me. 'I witnessed that while Charlie had his hand held and his brow stroked, he was never actually cuddled anymore because of the tubes and the pain. So we sat him forward in bed and I straddled the bed behind him, and from then until the day he died a couple of weeks later, twenty-four hours a day, he lay in the arms of people who loved him.

'I used to sit in bed with him at night so his family could sleep and he had a nurse as well, and then the family used to take turns during the day. So instead of his mother disappearing to draw up the morphine and his father disappearing because he couldn't stand feeling so helpless in the presence of his beloved son in so much pain, the brother and sister not knowing what to do and disappearing, and Charlie going down with his pain, we found tools and skills so we could work through that hellish situation together.

'I used to hold both his hands and look into his eyes and we would breathe through the pain. It didn't change it. It didn't make it go away, but we were able to participate in it and that was very, very valuable.

'His father had been very resistant to being in bed with his son because it was so hard to be so close to so much pain without escape. Yet, finally, he got in the bed. Just to see him hold and stroke his sleeping son, weeping, it was very painful, but it got to the very essence of what being human was about, a willingness to simply be present to the whole agony and richness of life.'

Petrea King's approach to life was a form of investigative vulnerability—a way of probing the essence of what it meant to be human. This was one of the reasons I joined her Quest For Life Foundation soon after writing my article. I had grown to love her, and I wanted her as my friend.

In her presence it was enough to be who we were, not who we were pretending to be. In fact, it was of urgent, life-affirming importance that we do so. And, conversely, it was important that we all stopped being who we were not in order that we might live more meaningful, authentic, integrated lives—*before* a medical diagnosis forced us to take stock and look at all our misdirected priorities or unresolved issues.

'Ask yourself,' Petrea once said to me, 'not whether you're good at your job, but whether your job is good for you.'

8

THE JOURNALIST AND THE MURDERER

In 1989, after a year of freelancing, I joined the staff of a new bimonthly magazine, *HQ*, and for the first time in my working life—notwithstanding the Southern embrace of New Orleans—I began to feel as though I was surrounded by true allies.

With the exception of art director Bruce Daley, my new colleagues were all women. Shona Martyn, the red-headed dynamo from New Zealand with the warm bustling person-ality and the razor-sharp intelligence, was the founding editor, fresh from a five-year stint at the helm of *Good Weekend*. Fenella Souter, her deputy, was the as yet undiscovered Dorothy Parker of Australian journalism—a woman of penetrating brainpower, the stillness of a Zen monk and a withering, uproarious turn of phrase. She would later become editor of both *HQ* and *Good Weekend* and, eventually, executive editor of *Marie Claire*, while also proving herself one of the best feature writers in the country, not to mention one of my dearest friends.

At *HQ* Roz Gatwood was the chief subeditor and resident guardian of the Queen's English. She knew nothing about popular culture post-1970, but everything about the classics and how a sentence could be consistent, clear and rhythmic. If there was a spelling mistake, grammatical error or structural incongruity within a story, Roz's scrupulous eye would detect it. She was a one-woman editorial surveillance system.

Together these three women, along with the irrepressible Susan Skelly and, later, Jane Wheatley and Amruta Slee, comprised, at the time, arguably the best editorial magazine team ever assembled in Australia. No subject was taboo. No lines of inquiry were ever left unexplored. No 'facts' were ever left unchecked. No story was ever good enough, until it was.

There was no publication like it, no forum more contemporary, intelligent, irreverent, provocative and committed to in-depth journalism than *HQ*. It was Australia's answer to *Vanity Fair* (minus the bumper advertisements) and for nearly five years I had the privilege of being its feature writer, although one day the owner of the magazine, Kerry Packer, made me doubt this privilege.

'Hello, Kerry,' my father said to the Big Man when we bumped into him one morning at the southern end of Palm Beach. Standing on the shoreline in his swimming togs, Packer was a formidable sight.

'Hello, Bernie, how are you?'

'I'm fine, Kerry, thanks. Have you met my son David? I'm not sure if you know, but he happens to be working for you.'

'Is that right?' Packer said. 'And where would that be?'

'*HQ* magazine,' I replied.

Packer looked at me as though I'd just told him I liked to cross-dress after dark. 'Well, I don't think much of it,' he said, turning back to my father. They were the only words we ever exchanged.

It took me a few months to adjust to the *HQ* experiment. I was not used to the meticulous scrutiny, the hands-on editing, the intense collaboration. And so, in the early stages, I agitated.

'What's wrong with the way that sentence reads?' I demanded angrily of Roz Gatwood one day.

'It doesn't make sense,' she replied, too evenly for my liking.

'How doesn't it make sense?' I blustered.

'You can't use a verb like that because it's a transitive verb and it has to take an object. And by the way, the phrase "inverse proportion" can't be used like that either because the situation you're describing is directly proportional, not of inverse proportion.'

'Oh bullshit, Roz.'

Roz had an instinct for language that I'd never encountered before. In another place and time she might have been James Joyce's literary editor. Sometimes, however, she went too far. On one memorable occasion she had the temerity to delete the opening line of my story. She thought it was overwritten, too flowery. She said she'd been planning to break the news to me at a later, more opportune moment, but I'd pre-empted her by stumbling across the laid-out pages in the art department MINUS THE LEAD I'D LABOURED OVER FOR HOURS.

'What the hell are you doing, Roz?' I demanded, storming over to her desk.

'David, I think the lead is better like that,' she replied, again with infuriating equanimity.

'You can't just change the lead of my story,' I insisted.

'I'm making your story better, David. It's my job.'

'*Better*? You've got to be kidding . . .'

The argument raged for another ten minutes before the entire *HQ* staff headed out to the end-of-year Christmas lunch in Darlinghurst. Roz and I entered the bus through different doors and sat at opposite ends of the lunch table.

We eventually made our peace over a couple of bottles of wine and, in retrospect, I came to see that she was right and that the four women with whom I was now working were actually trying to help me.

'You know, David, we're all on your side,' Susan Skelly said to me not long after this incident, with the reassuring tones of a palliative nurse.

On my side? She couldn't mean that. All of them. On the same side as me. I had grown so accustomed to working for (mostly male) News Ltd editors in general, and Piers Akerman in particular, that I'd become convinced that the biggest enemies came from within one's own ranks. Death by 'friendly fire'. But not at *HQ*. This was journalism at its best and the reason why I began to flex my still underdeveloped writerly muscles.

By this stage, my father was two years into his job as president of Condé Nast Publications Inc, the US parent company of the international *Vogue* empire. During his years running British Condé Nast, he'd grown the business from three publications— *Vogue, House and Garden* and *Brides*—to six, with the addition of *Business, World of Interiors* and *Tatler,* the 270-year-old British society journal that had been losing money until Condé Nast bought it in 1982 with twenty-five-year-old Tina Brown as editor. It had been the beginning of an enduring friendship between my father and Brown, as well as her husband Harry Evans, the legendary editor of Britain's *Sunday Times,* whom my father would later appoint the founding editor of *Condé Nast Traveler,* the magazine whose guiding principle would be 'truth in travel'.

In London, between 1976 and 1987, my father had also formed Britain's largest independent magazine-distribution company, in partnership with a Hearst Corporation subsidiary, as well as launched German *Vogue.*

Such was his success that one of his main competitors,

Terry Mansfield, managing director of the Hearst Corporation's nine-magazine British subsidiary, remarked on his departure to the United States: 'When Bernard Leser came from Australia, he slowed down our growth dramatically at *Harpers & Queen*. I'm delighted he's going to America. I'll be one of the first people to stand on the jetty and wave goodbye.'

My father's contact book was the envy of any journalist and his networking skills that of an artist. 'He's the only fellow I know who goes to three or four parties a night,' Brian Walsh, managing director of Harrods, London's upscale department store, observed. 'Bernie went to the royal wedding [of Prince Andrew and Sarah Ferguson] in July [1986]. He escorted the American actress Claudette Colbert, and they sat at Nancy Reagan's table. On the way he stopped at the hospital to visit a sick Australian friend.'

But it was more than just consummate networking skills that made my father who he was. It was his consideration for those who worked for him that distinguished him from most other media titans, and yes, I know that must read like the blinkered view of a fawning son, but it is not just my opinion.

'He was so warm,' Sandy Boler, the woman my father appointed editor of *Brides* magazine, told me one day. 'He believed in people, where others didn't. I remember one woman who worked for *Brides* fell down the back stairs and broke her collarbone and, twice, he called to see how she was. When I had my ulcer operation, he rang the surgeon to ask what the risks were to me. He rang my mother and grandmother to tell them how I was, how my husband [Adrian Hamilton] was and how the children were. That's not something you learn out of a book of good manners.

'And he had a deep respect for editors. If you went to him with an issue, he would say, "That's a real problem. Give me time to think about it." I call that seriously grown up. He made British

Condé Nast such a happy place to work. He let the light come in, the warmth come in, the air come in. He opened up the house.'

By the time he and my mother left for New York in 1987, he was known in the Australian media as the 'King of the Glossies', the '*Vogue* man' who was going to take 'an elegant bite at the Big Apple'.

'Think of the male models in *Vogue* magazine: tall, lean, lightly tanned, languidly elegant. The epitome of drop-dead chic,' wrote Jane Cadzow, a friend and former colleague of mine at the *Australian*—as well as a future colleague at *Good Weekend*. 'Now think of Bernard Leser: mild-mannered, middle-aged, myopic. An awfully nice fellow but hardly the Greek god type. Which just goes to show that looks aren't everything.'

By this stage, he was on a first-name basis with most of the world's great fashion designers and photographers, with the editors-in-chief and proprietors of pre-eminent American, British, Canadian, Irish and Australian newspapers—men like Rupert Murdoch, Kerry Packer, Sir Warwick Fairfax, Kerry Stokes, Conrad Black, Robert Maxwell and Tony O'Reilly. He dined regularly with figures like David Frost, Harold Evans and Tina Brown, and spent more than one memorable evening with Margaret Thatcher at a London reception, as well as Queen Elizabeth and the Duke of Edinburgh at Buckingham Palace.

On arrival in New York he was given reserved tables in restaurants like the Four Seasons, the Royalton and Le Cirque, tickets to the Metropolitan Opera and entree into the living rooms of people like Barbara Taylor Bradford and Dominick Dunne. He spent weekends in the Hamptons with the *New York Times*' managing editor A.B. Rosenthal and his wife, Shirley Lord. He was on friendly terms with *Cosmopolitan* editor-in-chief Helen Gurley Brown and her film producer husband David Brown, and Evelyn and Leonard Lauder of the Estée Lauder family.

He flew by Concorde from Paris to Marrakech for a Christian Dior event where he was transported in a flower-decorated, horse-drawn carriage to his hotel before a reception at the Royal Palace hosted by Morocco's King Hassan II; there were vacations in St Moritz and the villa in Cap Ferrat where Somerset Maugham had once lived. He was put up in hotel suites overlooking Key Biscayne, the Virgin Islands, Lake George, the outcrops of Montana, travelling first class wherever he went. He was given the world, and then some.

Often I used to feel that my father was so dazzled by all this that manners, bearing and beauty meant more to him than the uncomfortable, messy reality of things. You didn't get to the Christian Dior party at the Royal Palace in Marrakech by wanting to publish a story on the political dissidents who'd been arrested, executed or 'disappeared' during your host's rule. You got there because it was the last thing on your mind.

And yet throughout this time his ability to behave decently never seemed to desert him. One day, in 1993, his goddaughter, Kate Ayrton, asked him to host a luncheon for her in New York to mark her graduation from university. Neither her father nor her stepfather were able to attend. There was one slight problem. My father had been invited that same day to a small luncheon hosted by Bill and Hillary Clinton at the White House. Faced with the exquisite dilemma of his goddaughter or the leader of the free world, he chose the former.

While we both worked in magazines, we came at our jobs from different angles. My father's was a quest for excellence in publishing; mine was a quest for the 'truth', whatever that was supposed to mean. Certainly, at *HQ* magazine in the early 1990s, it was about trying to probe people and issues that we thought deserved relentless scrutiny.

And one of the people to fall into this category was Lady (Mary) Fairfax, the perceived villain at that time in the ruin of

John Fairfax Ltd, the oldest family-run media company in the world, publishers of the *Sydney Morning Herald,* Melbourne *Age* and *Australian Financial Review.*

I'd first met Lady Fairfax in 1990 when she'd invited Merran and myself to accompany my parents to dinner at Fairwater, her sprawling mansion overlooking Seven Shillings Beach in Double Bay. My parents had known Lady Fairfax since the late 1940s, ever since her marriage to—and subsequent spectacular divorce from—Sydney lawyer Cedric Symonds. Mary Fairfax had then gone on to marry Warwick Fairfax, the chairman of John Fairfax Ltd. Over the years, she had transformed Fairwater into one of Sydney's premier salons, particularly after Sir Warwick Fairfax's death in 1987.

I'd spent twelve months trying to persuade Lady Fairfax to agree to an interview, given what was happening to the once-proud company that she and her son Warwick Fairfax had controlled. Warwick Fairfax's takeover of John Fairfax Ltd in 1987 had stunned the financial community, not only because of the amount he'd borrowed to do it—$2.5 billion—but also because he'd pursued this mad venture even after the stockmarket crash of 19 October 1987.

By the time Lady Fairfax and I sat down to a lunch of braised chicken and apricot soufflé at Fairwater, her and Warwick's company was being placed in receivership with debts totalling $1.7 billion. It was not an altogether pleasant meeting. Lady Fairfax wanted to see my questions in advance. (Four were rejected before I arrived, including one about her religion.) She also wanted to read the story before it was published, a request which was not granted.

The story I wrote was not a flattering one, as it explored details of her scandalous love affair, her harrowing divorce trial, her celebrated remarriage to Warwick Fairfax and her role in the decimation of the Fairfax empire. In the process, I also, against her express wishes, delved into her conversion from Judaism to Christianity and the fragility of her relationship with her first-born son.

'Is she one of the most monstrously misunderstood women in Australia,' I wrote, 'or is she as deceptive as she is clever? Is she a manipulative, scheming woman, hungry for power, wealth and status? Or a tireless worker for the arts and charity, as well as a generous, fun-loving hostess and friend? Is she a family maker or an empire breaker? A proud matriarch who frequently owns up to only three children or a tormented mother of four? Is she a Jewess or a Christian? Does she sit atop staggering wealth or horrendous losses? Is she a figure of romance or of vengeance? And is it Mary or Marie?'

Needless to say, my parents were deeply embarrassed and Lady Fairfax never forgave me; she turned her back on me the next time we saw each other. (At least she kept sending my parents an annual Christmas card.) But I did this with a certain relish. I did exactly what Janet Malcolm had accused journalists of doing in her book, *The Journalist and the Murderer*. I played 'the confidence man, preying on people's vanity, ignorance or loneliness, gaining their trust and betraying them without remorse'. That is a harsh version of my own motives but there's more than a kernel of truth to it. What I didn't do, of course, was expose (some of) my own motives for writing that story. I couldn't see then that in tearing down Mary Fairfax I was subconsciously fulfilling an even more compelling brief—tearing down the walls of my parents' impossibly rarified social life, particularly my father's.

As I gained experience I would end up writing my first book—a devastating critique—about Bronywn Bishop's rise to prominence in the Liberal Party, at a time when it looked possible—surreally so—that she might become Australia's first female prime minister.

(Who would have thought that twenty years after this book was published in 1994 she would still be in politics, now as Speaker of the House under a Tony Abbott-led government?)

My mother had shared a love of classical music with Bishop ever since their days together at musicologist James Murdoch's Australian Music Centre. What better sounding of the bugle could there have been than for me to spend six months writing a book that would unmask Australia's Boadicea as the political pretender and shallow ideologue she was?

I did this for years—to people like Mary Fairfax and Bronwyn Bishop—and, later, to John Howard, Alan Jones, Ron Walker and Gina Rinehart—as part of a journalist's prerogative to challenge those with real or putative power, wealth and status. But I also did it to make myself feel better about having come from the same side of the tracks as many of them. By challenging them I could defy my father, and by defying my father I could define myself in opposition to him. It was all rather sad and predictable really.

This smouldering rebellion didn't temper my love for my father, but it certainly informed it. I didn't like the way he carried his authority, the way he divided the world into those who'd succeeded and those who hadn't. I didn't like the skin-shallow world of fashion and its elitist presumptions, and I certainly didn't like the fact that *Vogue*, in particular, was the gold standard for how one looked and behaved. If I rummaged deeper into myself, I didn't like the fact that my father was seldom at home when I was growing up and that I could barely remember playing with him as a child, let alone having dinner with him during the week. (My parents were out almost every night.) I didn't like his Teutonic silences; in fact I recoiled in the face of them, and I didn't like the fact that my mother was always under such huge pressure to accompany him to events rather than stay at home with me.

I also didn't like the fact that he'd never flown economy, not once in his life, or caught public transport, or built a toolshed where we might have communed silently over a lathe or electric saw. I didn't like how this fostered an impracticality in me that continues to this very day. I also didn't like the fact that when he went to England in 1976 and joined his Tory circles and private clubs like the Garrick ('a club where actors and men of refinement might meet on equal terms'), he sent my nine-year-old brother to a boarding school in the English countryside, far away from his home, his brother and sister, his school, his friends, his dog, far away from everything he ever loved—and very much against his will.

I had no idea how much my parents had agonised about this decision; how much advice they'd sought from various educators in the United Kingdom. All I could see, from my vantage point, was that my brother Daniel—whose entry into the world nearly twelve years after me had aroused the first fatherly instincts I'd ever known—was not where he wanted to be: with his family. This brother of mine who, as a little boy, would scream for our parents not to go out to another dinner party, and then come crawling into my bed when they did; this same brother who would write me desperate letters from boarding school and who, later in life, would become my friend and confidant and help me through my own turbulent times.

I forgave our father all this because what was there not to forgive? *Tout comprendre, c'est tout pardonner.* But it fuelled in me a desire to do battle. Battle with my father's values. Battle with the 'truth', as I saw it. Battle with falsity and pretence. Battle even with my heroes.

While still at *HQ* I went to Florence to duel—and that's exactly what it turned out to be—for ten heart-stopping hours with Oriana Fallaci, until that day one of the world's most famous journalists and certainly one of my idols. She'd been a giant in her profession, had covered wars, insurrections and famines, and interviewed everyone from Bobby Kennedy and Henry Kissinger to Indira Gandhi and the Ayatollah Khomeini. She'd always done what we, as reporters, had been taught not to do: she'd led with her heart in a completely partisan, hot-headed, indeed *Italian* manner. She'd torn her chador off in an interview with the Ayatollah Khomeini, describing it as a 'medieval rag'. She'd told a Catholic priest to 'go and shit on your mother'. She'd once said to Alfred Hitchcock: 'With all your cordial humour, your nice round face, your nice innocent paunch, you are the most wicked, cruel man I have ever met.'

Now Fallaci had cancer and didn't want to do the interview, but if she did, she only wanted to talk about her latest book, *Inshallah*. She didn't want to talk about journalism because, for her, journalism was finished and she felt nothing but contempt for most of its practitioners. She didn't want to talk about her private life either, and in the twenty faxes we exchanged before I went to Florence, she reinforced that over and over again.

But after welcoming me into her book-lined apartment just beyond the Ponte Vecchio, the famous old bridge that crosses the Arno River, she then decided to talk about everything. She talked—and wailed at the same time—about the death of her father, mother and sister, all from cancer. She talked about her own cancer and how she believed she'd become sick when covering the first Gulf War in 1990; how she'd accompanied the marines into the desert and been forced to sit under a black cloud of toxic fumes as the oil fields burnt out of control.

She talked about how books were her children, how few women she'd befriended, and how she refused to see men as the antagonists of some feminist mythology.

At one point I asked her why she thought she was able to disarm so many people during the course of her journalistic career. Was it because she had offered something of herself? Her terrifying response made me see how ambiguous my question had been; she'd construed a sexual meaning that was never intended (although I later discovered she'd once likened a good interview to coitus).

'What should I have offered, for Christ's sake?' she exploded, pointing her finger at me. 'What should I have offered these people?'

Well, I'm suggesting . . .

'No, no, no!' she said, standing up, her voice filling the room. 'What could I offer to the people I interviewed? In your opinion?'

Are you asking a rhetorical question or do you want . . .?

'Yeah, you said, "Is there something you offered them?" What do you expect me to offer?'

I'm asking what it is that you think makes . . .

'No! No! No! *I want you to clear this incredible question.* You said, "Is it something that you offered them?" To what were you referring? Offer what?'

Offer something . . .

'What?'

Of yourself, some experience, something that makes them feel as though they are dealing with a human, someone they can relate to . . .

At last she understood what I meant. She sat down, put her daggers away, and then said: 'Everybody knew who was Oriana Fallaci. Those who wanted to give [the interview] to me were very respectful. They were a little surprised when they saw me arrive in flesh and bones because they expected me to be a big woman. I entered and, eight times out of ten, they would say, "Is it you?" . . . because I am so small. They expected to see a Viking.'

At dusk, Fallaci took me into the hills above Florence and we walked arm in arm through the same wooded country where she'd spent evenings with Alexandros Panagoulis, the Greek poet and resistance fighter who'd died in mysterious circumstances. Panagoulis had been her one true love and the subject of arguably her finest book, *A Man*.

Later that evening, in a restaurant in those same hills, she'd talked about her relationship with Deng Xiaoping, China's former leader, and how it had been 'a love story at first sight' between them. I then asked her whether she had any interest in interviewing Bill Clinton or Boris Yeltsin. Once again, she erupted, heedless of the fact we were in a packed restaurant.

'Do you think I would waste a second of my short life to do interviews? I HAVE CANCER, AND YOU WANT ME TO SPEND TIME WITH CLINTON AND YELTSIN?!'

After Oriana Fallaci, I stepped knowingly into the serpent's pit of the Australian rock industry to attempt to get the measure of the godfather himself, Michael Gudinski. I tried pulling teeth from my songwriting hero, Paul Kelly, and I parodied myself unashamedly when writing a story on Peter Garrett, which began thus: 'I once applied to be the lead singer of Midnight Oil. I'm five foot six with nearly a full head of hair, and I can carry a tune. Instead, they chose a guy who's six foot six, completely bald and sings like Dylan on a bad day. They made the right choice.'

It was all true. On leaving high school I'd auditioned as lead singer of the band that would become Midnight Oil. Rob Hirst, my friend from Sydney Grammar, was the drummer and he'd invited me to come and give a rendition of Jethro Tull's 'Locomotive Breath'. Peter Garrett did his version too. The better man got the job.

Writing for *HQ* during the late 1980s and early '90s was the ultimate training in learning how to pen long feature articles without boring the pants off your reader. Sometimes, though, it was the pants of the writer that needed to come off, as it did when

I went on assignment one weekend to a nudist colony south of Sydney.

This was a significant moment. I came to see that if I could take my clothes off with complete strangers, there might be other baggage I could dispense with, although this realisation only came later. At the time, there was just the sheer dread of the assignment. It was late autumn and I was going to a nudist camp near Mittagong to write about why it was some people preferred to live without their clothes on. What seemed perfectly clear from the outset was that at some stage during the weekend I was going to have to take my clothes off as well.

'I'd rather resign than do something like that,' Roz Gatwood offered by way of reassurance before I left the *HQ* office. And then: 'Don't forget to wear an apron when you're cooking.'

'And be careful. There's frost on the ridges at this time of year,' Fenella Souter chimed in. My colleagues had fallen about, weak with laughter, and I carried their collective hilarity all the way down into the Southern Highlands of New South Wales.

What to pack, though? If Fenella was right and there was frost on the ridges, did that mean beanies and socks? Would I need underpants or a jacket? What about hankies?

Prior to my arrival I hadn't grasped the fact that the naturalist movement was effectively divided into three wings: the Stalinist wing, where you were required to shed your clothes at the gate; the anarchist wing—represented by the nudist beach movement—where you would find little, if any, policing; and finally the progressive wing, where parents could come to a resort and take their clothes off while their teenage children kept theirs on.

That was the resort we entered, a progressive one, although I didn't know that until it was too late. For half an hour I stood in my caravan paralysed with fear. Then, finally, tentatively, I undressed and walked naked towards my first interview, with photographer Tim Bauer walking jauntily by my side. We were heading poolside to meet the daughter of the resort's manager, and her partner, and we were to talk to them about the joys and perils of, well, being a nudist.

The only problem, and it was a significant one, was that when we got to the interview I saw to my horror that our interviewees—who were in their early twenties—were the children of nudists, not nudists themselves. They were fully clothed. We were completely naked.

'Hi there. David Leser from *HQ* magazine. How are you doing today?'

'Fine,' the young woman said. 'How are you?'

'Great,' I replied. 'Great to be here. Fantastic place. Tell me, how long have your parents been nudists?'

'Quite a while.'

'And have you ever been nudists yourselves?'

'No, it's not really our thing.'

I looked at Bauer, one of Australia's finest photographers. He was butt naked except for a camera around his neck. I was sitting shirtless, pantless, underpantless, with my legs crossed and a notebook balanced on my knee. There was a pen perched behind my ear. I was a study of mortification.

'Do you think nudism is a way of demystifying sex?' I asked.

'Not sure, mate,' came the reply.

Silence.

'Right, well do you think the body is the great leveller? Is this a way of removing tired old measurements of status and wealth?'

I approached the subject as if I were an anthropologist touring the backblocks of Burkina Faso. It was the most excruciating interview of my life. I stayed for half an hour, then slunk back to my caravan to put my pants back on. It was a cold day beside the Wollondilly River, just as my colleagues had predicted.

Hundreds of people were arriving. They were setting up barbecues, picnic tables, playing table tennis and mixing drinks at the bar. No one had their clothes on. What to do? Would I interview people with my clothes on or off? Would I turn up to dinner in just my underpants? What about the guy in the spa with no neck I'd seen when I arrived? Would I have to get into the tub with him?

For hours I stood in my caravan—fully clothed and stricken. Then I summoned the necessary courage. I'd done one interview naked. It couldn't get worse. I took my pants off, picked up my notebook and pen, and went striding out into the bush, my manhood shrinking with each footfall.

'Hi, how ya going?' I called to my neighbours as they approached me from under the blue gums, all loins and grins. 'Great day.'

Keep walking, David. Check out the river. Look at nature's bounty. Here's another couple walking towards you with nothing on. They're grinning too. Act like everything is fine. Keep walking.

'Hi, how ya going? Great day.'

In retrospect, it's not surprising that what eventually brought me undone was the one-hundred-year-old Arab–Israeli conflict.

Even though I was no Middle Eastern expert in the way of reporters like Robert Fisk, Thomas Friedman, the late Marie Colvin or our own Paul McGeogh, I had been wrestling with the subject for years. And notwithstanding my newfound fascination for writing psychological profiles—along with naked self-parodies—to me there was still nothing quite like the shuddering events on the streets of Cairo, Damascus, Baghdad and Jerusalem.

This seemed especially true in 1993, after Israel and the PLO signed their historic peace accord on the White House lawn, opening up yet another extraordinary chapter in the history of this blood-soaked region.

One evening I sat in the comfort of my living room on the northern beaches of Sydney and watched—like millions of others around the world—the extraordinary moment when Israeli prime minister Yitzhak Rabin hesitated, then shook hands with his arch-enemy, PLO chairman Yasser Arafat. I burst into tears, much to the horror of my then four-year-old daughter, Jordan.

'Why is Daddy crying, Mummy?' she said.

'Because they're making peace in Israel,' her mother replied.

I remember thinking, *This could be it. This could be the miraculous moment.*

A few weeks later, Ali Kazak, the Australian representative in Canberra for the Palestine Liberation Organization, called me at home to inform me that if I could get to the West Bank by Monday morning, Dr Hanan Ashrawi, the Palestinian team's chief negotiator at the Madrid peace talks, would see me. Any later than Monday morning and she would be returning to PLO headquarters in Tunis. There was no time to lose. It was Thursday afternoon.

Within a few hours I was booked on a flight departing Australia on Saturday morning, arriving in London at 5.45 am the next day. I then had an eighteen-hour wait in London before my connecting flight to Israel at midnight. I would land in Tel Aviv at 5 am on Monday, take an Israeli taxi to Jerusalem, change to a Palestinian taxi in East Jerusalem, and hopefully get to Dr Ashrawi's home in Ramallah by 9 am.

Ashrawi was a formidable interviewee. She'd been dubbed 'the diva of the West Bank' because of her haughtiness and the fact she was regarded as the individual most responsible for igniting former US Secretary of State James Baker's sense of moral outrage over the treatment of Palestinians.

She held a Master's degree in Renaissance English literature and a doctorate in medieval English literature, and in her radical student days had been appointed Lebanese-based spokesperson for the General Union of Palestinian Students. It was in that capacity she'd first met the then rising star of the Palestinian resistance, Yasser Arafat.

In 2003 Dr Ashrawi would be the cause of near-apoplexy among members of Australia's Jewish community when she was awarded the Sydney Peace Prize. Accusing her of having failed to condemn Palestinian terrorism, the Zionist movement and its supporters boycotted her lecture and sought to prevent her from speaking in Sydney University's Great Hall.

I was on edge before I boarded the plane in Sydney. I had Dr Ashrawi's considerable résumé demanding my attention. I had United Nations resolutions and previous failed peace conferences rattling around in my head. I had my own experiences of the Lebanon War and first intifada to reflect on. I had my time as a correspondent there six years earlier, when I'd left Merran in Sydney to pursue a wild dream. I had the joy of the first story I'd written for the *South China Morning Post* on the Arab–Israeli conflict, in which I'd attempted to explain the competing claims of two people vying for the same piece of land.

In my economy-class seat en route to London I was thinking about this and the origins of colonialism, Zionism, Pan-Arabism and terrorism. I had my old lecturer in Middle Eastern politics, Dr Robert Springborg, weighing in on patron–client relationships in the region, the use of proxy wars and the role of the military in Arab society. I had Father Lazarus up there on the Mount of Temptation. And I had the entire history of the Jewish people pressing its considerable claims on me: my father and his family departing Germany in 1939 with barely months to spare before the gates of hell slammed shut; and then, two years later, on my mother's side, in that Baltic land of pine forests and fast-flowing rivers, the extermination of her family.

Also in the frame was the honour that had been bestowed on my father a few months earlier by the American Jewish Committee, an organisation dedicated to safeguarding the welfare and security of Israel and Jews worldwide. On 2 June 1993, before 650 guests at the New York Hilton, the committee had presented my father with the Human Relations Award in recognition of his (implicit) lifelong commitment to Zionism, and his (explicit) achievements in the publishing industry, in international political and business circles, and in the world of philanthropy.

Many of the city's movers and shakers were there to pay tribute, among them Abe Rosenthal, columnist and former executive editor of the *New York Times*, who gave the keynote address; James Wolfensohn, soon to become the president of the World Bank, who had presented my father with his award while declaring him to be 'a man of unique character, loyalty, warmth, integrity and independence'; and Leonard Lauder, president and CEO of Estée Lauder, who had offered the toast and raised my father's hand aloft, describing 'the joys and pleasures of watching Bernie do great things [during our] long and dear relationship of more than thirty years'.

Four days later, my father had written to Alfred Moses, the president of the American Jewish Committee, thanking him for what had been a spectacular—and deeply moving—night.

'But now we move on,' he wrote, '[because] nothing stands still. In this life and in this world, we have to prove ourselves over and over again, each day, each hour, and demonstrate that we have the qualities of character and professionalism expected of us.'

So this trip of mine to Jerusalem three months later felt like no ordinary assignment. It felt like some kind of sacred mission. 'This is the story you have to write,' I kept telling myself, 'because this is your role as a journalist, this is your privileged position as a chronicler and as a Jew, and as the son of Bernard and Barbara

Leser—to help explain this conflict to Australians and, yes, just like your grandmother told you on the birth of Jordan, to help bring peace to the Middle East.' *You have to keep proving yourself over and over again, each day, each hour . . .*

And only now can I look back and say of this deranged person who happened to be me, 'You poor, sick and sorry fuck.'

I didn't sleep a wink on that twenty-four-hour flight from Sydney. Nor in the eighteen hours between landing at Heathrow and taking the midnight flight to Tel Aviv. Nor, again, in the five hours that followed, en route from London to Tel Aviv's Ben Gurion Airport, where I was meeting my brother Daniel, who would photograph this assignment.

By the time we arrived at Dr Hanan Ashrawi's house on that October morning at 9 am I had gone nearly fifty hours without sleep. This was just the beginning.

After the interview I returned to my room at the American Colony Hotel to try to rest. It was late morning and, after the adrenalin rush of talking to Dr Ashrawi, impossible to switch off. I decided to eat something, lie by the pool, visit the Old City, bide my time until I could head to bed for an early night.

At around 8 pm I took a sleeping tablet and lay there waiting for sleep to rescue me, but I kept returning to the interview and to the story I was beginning to craft in my head.

Dr Hanan Ashrawi was born in Ramallah and educated at the American University of Western Beirut . . . No, too prosaic a beginning. What about: Dr Hanan Ashrawi is a Palestinian woman and Christian . . . No . . . The Middle East peace process hangs in the balance and its final outcome may well depend on a Palestinian Christian woman educated in Beirut . . . No, it's too . . . Look, come back to this in the morning—it's time to sleep and the story's not due for another week and the interview is in the can. But don't forget this is truly historic. There might be peace for the first time between Arabs and Jews. Remember when you were . . . yes, the rocks and stones of Gaza, my God we were nearly killed . . . I shouldn't have gone there without checking the military radio first. How could I have been so stupid? I can still see that man with the brick in his hand . . . and Merran thinks I'm being melodramatic about it! And to be Jewish and a journalist here, now—who would have thought? Those Palestinian flags flying in the streets today, those photos of Arafat. Unbelievable . . . here in East Jerusalem. Stop. Breathe. Count sheep. Make that goats; this is the Middle East. My God, the Middle East. The Middle East stands at the crossroads. No, way too clichéd. Dr Hanan Ashrawi leans back in her chair, takes a deep drag on her Marlboro Red and says: 'The Israelis are prisoners of their own pathology.' Yes, that's it . . . Have a look at it in the morning. Well why not write it down now you're awake? Yes, but you need sleep. What time is it? It must be morning in Sydney. Merran will be getting Jordan ready for school. I hope she's alright—she seemed so terse on the phone the other day . . . How on earth am I going to get to sleep? A jerk-off, that'll help . . . Yes, a good long stroke, that's it . . . Oh what about that raven-haired beauty in the shop this afternoon? And the way she looked at me. That half-smile, that tilted head, those dusky legs under that tease of a skirt. Oh yes, those thighs . . . yes, yes, yes, this will get me to sleep . . . Fuck the Middle East and fuck everything in it . . . Fuck the Arabs and the Druze and the Maronites and the Moabites and Hittites and Shiites and Yemenites. Fuck them all and fuck that woman in the shop. Fuck her fuck her fuck her fuck her fuck her . . .

A Jerusalem dawn can be a divine experience—a blazing orange ball rising up over the Mount of Olives, bathing the dolomite of the city and the desert beyond in burnished gold. Then the call from the minaret—an insistent, cleansing, confessional cry from the back of the soft palate . . . *la illah illa Allah . . .la illah illa Allah . . .* reverberating across dust and cobblestones, calling the faithful to prayer.

I'd been awake all night when dawn's lament broke that second morning. *Next year in Jerusalem.* Ever since I was a little boy I'd heard these words spoken with reverence and hope, the wistful pleas of my grandmother and mother and aunts and uncles at the end of every Passover and Yom Kippur. After all the years of sorrow, *next year in Jerusalem,* we would meet in this place of sacrifice, pilgrimage and false prophecy, in this contested, fractious, beautiful, holy land.

For the previous six years, during the intifada, the streets of Jerusalem's Arab quarter had been unnaturally quiet, the people seething with resentment, their main weapon of protest a commercial strike or hanging washing from clotheslines in accordance with the colours of the outlawed national flag.

On this day the Old City was a festival of Palestinian flags, the colours of the Arab revolt fluttering from thousands of rooftops. PLO signs were daubed over the walls of the city and T-shirts emblazoned with Yasser Arafat's grinning face were being sold openly.

Years of secret talks, many of them in secluded homes in Norway, had forged links between these former enemies. Jews and Palestinians had begun talking to each other in ways never seen before, and for all the deep flaws, for all the perceived pro-Israeli biases of the peace process, it seemed to be yielding unimagined results: an end to a conflict that had convulsed a region and traumatised the world for nearly half a century.

For the next six nights I stayed awake: worrying about the story, worrying about not sleeping, worrying about Merran juggling work and children, worrying about whether I was going mad, which I was. No amount of alcohol, sleeping tablets or self-worship seemed to work. I dragged myself around East Jerusalem and the West Bank interviewing other Palestinian women with a rising sense of panic. And this only made the fear of bed more acute.

By the time I flew out of Israel with my brother Danny, a week after my arrival, I hadn't slept in 194 hours. Any sleep I'd managed could only have been calculated in microseconds. Even on the plane back to London I couldn't switch off. I'd seen the Israeli opposition leader (now prime minister) Benjamin Netanyahu three rows in front of me and had spent two hours devising ways of approaching him for an interview. (In the end I just walked up to him, introduced myself, and asked him if we could talk. He said no.)

When I got to my parents' apartment in St John's Wood I collapsed on their huge double bed, drew the curtains and listened to the faint ticking of the living-room clock. 'Just sleep and we'll see you in a couple of hours,' my sister Deborah said.

I stretched out on the bed and lay there for an hour beseeching sleep to come. I began talking to myself as though I were an infant. *There, there, little one, it's okay. Just relax and lay your head down to sleep. Everything is alright. Go to sleep, little baby, don't you cry.*

But baby did cry because it was at this point that the horrifying thought occurred that I might never sleep again, that I would have to be hospitalised in order to have sleep induced, that I would need to be narcotised out of commission or I would surely die of sleeplessness.

And it was then that loud, racking sobs began rising out of the depths of me, from somewhere I'd never known existed. Wave after wave of anguished tears turning into moans.

My brother and sister found me there two hours later, curled in a foetal position and whimpering into my pillow. My sister seemed bewildered by my state, and all the more so when I declined her suggestion of going out for dinner that night to a Russian restaurant. My brother, who had watched my slow descent all week, could see I was in no state to go out, borscht or no borscht.

Finally my cousin Annette arrived at our apartment with Indian takeaway, a large joint, two strong sleeping tablets and the sweet benediction of a neck massage. She broke the insomniac circuit and I passed out for six blessed hours. I was never quite the same again.

9

TO BEGIN TO NOT KNOW

There are many ways a man may fall through the floor of his own life. He might suffer a serious accident. His wife might leave him. His boss might sack him. His friends might betray him. His son or daughter might reject him or, far worse, fall ill or die. He may experience one or more of these calamities and know he no longer has control over his existence the way he once did, or thought he did. He hears a click in his head, he feels a grinding deep in his bones, a change in the frequency of his biorhythms, and he knows he is no longer the man he was.

The crack in my road opened up during the Middle East peace process of 1993; after that I became more like a crazed beast in my bed than a man in repose, sleeping sometimes only two hours a night, if at all. Until this moment I'd never questioned sleep. I'd never thought of it as something I could or could not do. I was tired. I went to bed. I read a few pages of my book. I fell asleep. I didn't think about it. I didn't will it. It just happened.

After Jerusalem I was plunged into my own Divine Comedy: *Nel mezzo del cammin di nostra vita mi ritrovai per una selva oscura ché la diritta via era smarrita.* 'In the middle of the road of my life,' wrote Dante, 'I awoke in a dark wood where the true way was wholly lost.'

Dante was thirty-five when he found himself in his dark wood, assailed by leopards and she-wolves. I was thirty-eight. Something in me had snapped. Some level of confidence or competence in my own recuperative abilities had been lost to me. I began dreading the night. I began thinking about sleep the way some people view a difficult assignment. Could I solve the riddle of the sleep logorithm? What would happen if I didn't? What was the best and quickest formula for success? I had enough sense to know that the very act of posing these questions was a guarantee of failure, but I had no way of arresting my fall into Dante's *basso loco*, his low place.

I stopped sleeping in the same bed as my wife. I moved into the cottage adjoining the house. I began wearing a sleep mask and stuffing plugs into my ears. I created a tomb for myself, making sure the doors were closed tightly and the curtains drawn. I stopped drinking coffee. I started taking valerian tablets—and sleeping tablets when the valerian didn't work, which it never did. I took to playing relaxation tapes for an hour before lights-out— ambient lullabies that dulled my senses with their appalling massage-room monotonies. I started doing yoga. I began seeing a sleep psychologist, then another after the first one was killed stepping off a kerb in Manhattan and looking the wrong way. I saw a doctor, an osteopath, a kinesiologist, a Chinese herbalist, an acupuncturist and a homeopath, who asked me if I ever got angry with myself.

'Sure,' I said. 'Doesn't everyone?'

'Maybe,' he replied. 'But I'm interested in *your* anger. How do you get angry with yourself and when?'

'When I am trying to write the lead of a story and can't find my way in,' I told him.

'What do you do when that happens?' he asked.

'What do I do?'

'Yes, what do you do?'

'I scream at myself.'

'How?'

'What do you mean how? Do you want me to show you?'

'Yes.'

'Well, I say, "You fucking arsehole, David."'

'How do you say that?'

'I scream it.'

'Do it.'

'Now?'

'Yes—do it.'

'Well, I say: "YOU FUCKING ARSEHOLE, DAVID, YOU FUCKING FUCK. YOU'RE THE BIGGEST FUCKING LOSING FUCKFACE ON THE FUCKING PLANET. YOU FUCKING FUCK."'

Long silence.

'Would you speak like that to a child?'

'Absolutely not,' I replied. 'Never. No way.'

'Do you have a photograph of yourself as a little boy?'

'Yes, I do.'

'Put that photo next to your computer, and the next time you're tempted to speak to yourself like that have a look at that little boy.'

It was good advice. It didn't cure my insomnia but it got me looking at aspects of myself that I'd been ignoring for a long time. It also stopped me screaming. Mostly.

I needed to stop thinking about sleep. I needed to take more rest breaks from my computer. I needed to stretch. I needed to redress my chi—I was way too overheated. I had to change my diet. No chilli. No tomatoes. No capsicum. No alcohol before bed. I took to buying dope again and to rolling medicinal spliffs after dinner. I reverted to childhood cups of Horlicks with hot milk, sometimes adding—against advice—tumblers of cognac or whisky. I began running on the beach in the morning, up and down, north and south, for forty-five minutes, then swimming laps of the ocean pool, up and down, east and west, hoping the physical efforts of the day would pay dividends by nightfall.

I would sleep three or four hours, then wake and not be able to go back to sleep. Sometimes I would scream out in frustration.

Then I would read, but lose concentration, being too tired to follow the narrative. I would count sheep, goats, dogs and cats. I would turn on the television with the sound down, following shapes and imagined dialogue for hours on end. I would creep into the house to make myself a cup of tea, stand by the bedroom doors of my wife and daughter, listening to their gentle, enviable stirrings. I would return to the gloom of my bed and start counting all over again, until the first cracks of light began filtering into my room and I would crawl out of my boneyard, head down to the beach and then return to my family for breakfast.

And all this had begun happening as the warrior queen of the Liberal Party, Bronwyn Bishop, was entering my life, and the birth of our second daughter, Hannah, was drawing close.

At the end of 1993, Michael Heyward, head of Text Publishing, commissioned me to write a book on Bishop, believing—as I did at the time—that the Australian Liberal Party, after a decade in opposition, might just be stupid and desperate enough to put its faith in a soprano-singing disciple of Ayn Rand.

As it transpired, of course, they were not, but they might have been had not larrikin writer and filmmaker Bob Ellis stood against her as an independent for the safe Liberal seat of

Mackellar. With a dramatic swing against the Liberals in the March 1994 by-election, Ellis ensured not only the death of Bishop's grandiose ambitions, but also the commercial death of my book as well.

The country had been saved from a political absurdity but, for me, six months of furious research and writing would end in publishing oblivion. Apart from a cover story in *Good Weekend* and the odd positive review, the book sank without a trace.

And then came the birth of our second daughter, Hannah, at the Sydney Adventist Hospital in Wahroonga, an effortless birth by comparison with her sister's buttocks-first entry into the world nearly five years earlier.

'Jordan, your sister is about to come,' I ran out to the waiting room to tell her as her mother pushed down into the second stage of labour.

'Hang on, Daddy, I've just got to finish my noodles,' she said.

'Forget about the noodles,' I replied. 'Don't you want to see your sister arrive?'

'Okay, I'm coming,' she said, stuffing another big spoonful into her mouth as I lifted her out of her seat to witness the miraculous arrival of her little sister, Hannah Lilly Morrison Leser, in the early hours of 29 July 1994.

We were living in a restored farmhouse in Mona Vale on Sydney's northern beaches where, a year earlier, Merran had been appointed the cultural planner for Warringah Shire Council, responsible for helping devise policies and strategies for the cultural life of nearly 150,000 people living in one of the most sought-after areas of Sydney.

Anne Summers had just offered me the job of staff feature writer for *Good Weekend*. There, for the next five years, I would come to enjoy more professional success than I'd ever known, writing cover stories on social and political issues for the most widely read weekend magazine in the country, while at the same time heading personally in a diametrically opposite direction.

While juggling working from home with two young children, I would take on the now-late Richard Carleton from *60 Minutes* to see whether he could absorb scrutiny the same way he gave it. *Tick tick tick*. I would break bread with Pauline Hanson at her home just after her incendiary maiden speech to the House of Representatives, drink Bundy and Coke with her in her kitchen and then rifle through her CD collection when she wasn't looking. (I found a Gene Pitney CD with the song 'Town Without Pity' on it. Perfect.) I would spend five hours with Alan Jones in his Newtown warehouse—while his black manservant served us tea and scones—and then another nine years dealing with the lawsuit that followed. I would enter the locked ward of Rose Porteous and Gina Rinehart's bizarre and poisonous feud in Perth. I would fly with John Howard aboard the prime minister's plane and talk to him about his faux love for Bob Dylan.

'Who's your favourite musician, Mr Howard?'

'Oh, Bob Dylan.'

'What's your favourite Dylan album?'

'I reckon *Blowing in the Wind* would have to be.'

'And do you like Dylan more for his lyrics or his music?'

'Oh, the music for sure.'

I would joust with Michael Kroger, the ultimate networker in Australian Liberal Party politics, and spend an excruciating time with the then Liberal Party treasurer Ron Walker at Florentino's restaurant in Melbourne, where I sneezed all the way through lunch. He would sit there like a man pinned to the wall, my questions making him angry, and most probably sick, in equal measure.

I would love the job, all those extraordinary characters, the tremendous exposure, the fuel-injected adrenalin each morning. I would even have a book of some of these profiles published called *The Whites of Their Eyes*, just in case anyone had any doubts that the writer had got well and truly behind enemy lines.

But by 1999 my boat had capsized. Wind squalls first, then dark nights of rolling thunder. Apart from losing the ability to sleep, my arms had started to pack it in too. No sooner would I sit down at the computer to write than tingling sensations would shoot through my hands up to my neck. Given that I couldn't sleep and now couldn't type, it felt like my career and life were dangling in front of me.

During this period—and perhaps not by accident—I went to Melbourne to interview Peter O'Connor, the Jungian therapist who'd had a bestseller in the 1980s with his book *Understanding the Male Mid-Life*. As a family therapist, psychotherapist and dream analyst, he'd seen a lot of men undergoing mid-life crises. Many of them were aged between thirty-five and forty-five, and their stories often overlapped or resonated with each other.

Their relationships had broken down but they had no idea why. Their careers had stopped providing fulfilment, or had come to a screeching halt. They were happily married but felt their lives were effectively over. They were constantly having affairs but remained dissatisfied. They'd begun feeling jealous of their children—their successes, their youth. They'd begun contemplating death.

'If there was a general pattern,' O'Connor told me, 'it was the loss of meaning. They realised that what were once goals could no longer sustain them. Many of the men found themselves withdrawing from family and friends or, alternatively, engaging in manic activity—anything to avoid looking at their inner lives. Their social conditioning had led them always to equate action with strength. Now they didn't know what to do.'

To Peter O'Connor this uncertainty was the key. 'The whole

art of that second half of life is to begin to not know,' he said. 'I think our culture mistakenly thinks that knowledge and wisdom are the same thing, so it's very hard for men to say, "I don't know." In the workplace it's banned.

'Real growth comes in the feeling life, in the inner life, by being able to tolerate uncertainty and ambiguity long enough to find out what it is that you need to know. It's what Keats once called "negative capability"—the ability to sustain oneself in doubt and uncertainty without an irritable reaching for reason.'

In 1994, my father also began to fall through his own exalted floor at Condé Nast. He was sixty-nine years old and for nearly half a century all he'd known was the upward trajectory of a remarkable career.

Since moving to New York in 1987, he'd not only presided over established magazines like *Vogue, Glamour, Mademoiselle, Self, GQ, Gourmet, Vanity Fair* and the *New Yorker,* he'd also launched *Condé Nast Traveler, Details, Allure, Architectural Digest* and *Bon Appetit,* as well as spearheaded in 1993 the launch of *GQ* Japan, in association with Chuokoron-sha, Japan's leading publishing company.

I'd witnessed him in action during these Japanese negotiations after he invited me to join him in Tokyo for a week of boardroom meetings and dinners: during the day, the two of us sitting opposite six to eight Japanese executives with an interpreter translating each side's position, then at night sitting on cushions in the finest restaurants eating delicacies from the sea washed down with endless bottles of warm sake. I was amazed by my father's grasp of the issues, the precision of his words, the formality and courtesy with which he dealt with our Japanese hosts.

S.I. Newhouse was also impressed by my father. Over the years he'd written him notes, often at Christmas time, expressing his delight with their working relationship, words which, for a man almost congenitally incapable of small talk, had given my father great comfort and pride.

Five years into his New York posting, at the end of 1992, Newhouse had written to all Condé Nast's editors-in-chief, publishers and corporate executives, seeking to quash rumours of my father's imminent departure, announcing instead that my father would be continuing as president of the company until the end of 1995.

'I want to mention my own great pleasure with Bernie's decision,' Newhouse wrote. 'His fine judgement and his network of close friends, within and outside Condé Nast, are unparalleled. Therefore, I expect that Bernie's presence will help to maintain the stability and maturity in our business affairs that have been invaluable to Condé Nast in the past and will now continue for many years.'

Imagine my father's shock when, in January 1994, on his way back to New York from a family holiday in Sydney, he received a late-night phone call from Newhouse at the Okura Hotel in Tokyo.

'There'll be an announcement in tomorrow's *Ad Age* [*Advertising Age*] saying that you're stepping down as president and that Steve Florio is taking over,' he told my father.

'We've heard these rumours before,' my father replied. 'Just deny them like you always do.'

'I'm afraid this time it's true,' Newhouse countered.

There was an awful silence before my father said, 'You shit,' and slammed the phone down on the man he'd served faithfully for thirty-five years. He'd told Newhouse on a number of occasions that he would be prepared to step aside—with due and fair notice—whenever the time came to hand the reins over to a new generation.

Newhouse probably doubted this, and with good reason. As Carol Felsenthal pointed out in *Citizen Newhouse*, published in 1998, 'Newhouse knew that Leser, a tremendously gregarious man, loved the people, the pace, the business, too much to retire voluntarily any time soon.' Besides which, S.I. Newhouse Jr was never very good at the niceties of a dismissal.

In 1987, shortly before my father's appointment as president of Condé Nast, Newhouse had sacked William Shawn, the legendary editor of the newly acquired *New Yorker* magazine, after initially telling Shawn he could stay in the job as long as he wanted. In 1988 he'd sacked Grace Mirabella, editor-in-chief of American *Vogue* for the previous seventeen years. Mirabella only learnt about her dismissal when her surgeon husband, William Cahan, called her to say that her removal was at that very moment being aired by Liz Smith on the evening news. My father was not party to the decision; in fact, he learned about it from his doctor, the same Bill Cahan.

'I was appalled by the way that was handled,' he told me, 'and I told Si that at the time. He said to me, "Well, that's my way. We had to get rid of her quickly."'

Never in my father's wildest dreams did he imagine he would suffer the same treatment. Years later he would reflect on this and be deeply grateful for Si Newhouse's generosity towards him, particularly after his retirement, but at that time he was more shaken and dismayed than I'd ever seen him.

What he didn't know was that his successor, Steve Florio, president of the *New Yorker*, was impatient for his job and was finding it increasingly difficult to work with Tina Brown, then editor of the magazine. Tina Brown couldn't stand the brash and boisterous Florio, and Newhouse was worried he might end up losing both of them.

On 13 January 1994, Newhouse announced 'with great

pleasure' that my father had been appointed chairman of Pacific operations for Condé Nast and would be returning to Sydney to take up the position in June. He later gave a warm and generous speech in my father's honour at a farewell dinner at the 21 Club, lauding my father's achievements.

He failed to mention, however, that at the age of nearly seventy, my father was now being asked to report to S.I. Newhouse's first cousin, Jonathan Newhouse, a man my father liked immensely but who was thirty years his junior and someone who had always reported to *him*.

Twelve months later, my father resigned from the day-to-day Australian operations and handed over the managing director-ship to Didier Guérin, a Frenchman with a penchant for pink bow ties and personalised numberplates; his two cars were 'Voila' and 'Voila 2'.

My father remained chairman until 1997 before resigning his position, thereby entering a post-Condé Nast universe where the planets not only shone less brightly but actually seemed out of alignment. For the next few years he served as senior adviser and then non-executive chairman to Eric Beecher and his Text Media Group in Melbourne, while also serving on the Australian National Gallery council under both Lionel Bowen and Kerry Stokes. He was then appointed chairman of the National Gallery of Australia Foundation and, from 1996 to 2003, chairman of the council for St Vincent's Centre for Immunology.

My father welcomed these opportunities to give something back to Australia after so many years away, but the truth was this period never quite matched the dazzling lights that had illumi-nated his world for the better part of four decades.

What made matters worse was that by the time he departed from Condé Nast in 1997, Australian *Vogue*, the magazine he'd founded thirty-eight years earlier, was in a state of crisis, with plunging circulation, a revolving door of editors and poisonous internal politics. It was a subject my friend Jane Cadzow described for *Good Weekend* because God knew it was not a story I was going to touch.

'*Vogue* sales are falling sharply,' she wrote. 'In five years, the one-time style bible appears to have lost close to a third of its readers. Most of its staff too. At Sydney head office, where the fashion department recently flounced out en masse, no one knows who's going next.'

Cadzow had sought an interview with Didier Guérin, by this time chairman of the Australian company, but her request was denied. So too was her request for an interview with Guérin's managing director, Peter Gaunt, who referred to Cadzow in a phone call to my father's office as 'the girl from *Good Weekend*'.

My father chose to speak to Cadzow, but it was a decision that did not go down well with his successor.

'I am most disappointed to hear that you decided to communicate with the reporter [from *Good Weekend*],' Guérin wrote in a letter to my father on 30 November 1998. 'We have good reasons not to cooperate with this reporter, and I wish you would have discussed those reasons with us before deciding to ignore our request.'

My father was clearly unimpressed. 'I think the tone and substance of your first two paragraphs are totally out of order and unacceptable,' he wrote to Guérin four days later.

Peter [Gaunt] did not request that I should not speak to 'the girl'. Whilst he did explain that you had chosen not to speak to her, he added that I would obviously act as I saw fit, or words to that effect.

Peter's verbal reference to 'the girl' conveys ignorance of the fact that Jane Cadzow is a highly respected senior writer for *Good Weekend*. She interviewed me several years ago on behalf of the

Australian and treated both *Vogue* Australia and me in a generous and fair manner.

You are out of order in stating that I decided to 'ignore your request'. There was no request. But had such a request been made I would have had no hesitation in explaining to you courteously and openly that I would cooperate. I did make it clear to Jane, however, that I would not comment about current or recent matters but confine myself to reflections about the history and philosophy of *Vogue*.

My main point is, has always been, and will always be that Condé Nast and *Vogue* are the best and that my belief and loyalty to Condé Nast Publications and to the Newhouse family are permanent!

There it was again. My father's deep respect for the craft and calling of journalists. There was more, too, but it was the two last paragraphs that ended up capturing best for me the kind of man he was, and the kind of values that he'd always fought for, and that I had fought so mightily against for a good part of my life.

'Perhaps matters of courtesy and custom have changed and I am old-fashioned,' he told Guérin.

However, communication of the kind you have sent me should have been in the form of a letter with a proper salutation and a proper conclusion.

May I suggest that when, in future, you have concerns, or there are matters in which you seek my support or cooperation, you call me and discuss your thoughts with me directly, in the manner in which we seem to have been able to communicate in the past. The kind of discourteous memo you have sent me produces exactly the opposite to what is in Condé Nast's best interests.

My father might as well have been quoting from *Debrett's Guide to Etiquette and Modern Manners*, the so-called 'contemporary guide to civilised living' that passed out of fashion with the top hat and monocle.

10

FIELDS OF GOLD

Paul Gauguin discovered in his mid-thirties that he no longer wanted to work in a bank; he wanted to paint. He moved to Tahiti. Albert Schweitzer realised at thirty-eight that he couldn't continue his career in music. He wanted to be a missionary doctor in Africa.

In my case, I wanted to live in Byron Bay. By the end of 1999, I had been with *Good Weekend* for five years. During the previous eighteen months I had worked myself to a standstill profiling, among others, Neil Finn, Roger Woodward, Michael Kroger, Ron Walker, Kim Beazley, John Howard, Rose Porteous, Gina Rinehart and Alan Jones, not to mention a clutch of stories on issues like drug law reform, the environmental destruction of Bali and Rupert Murdoch's takeover of the National Rugby League competition.

I was forty-three years of age and I still couldn't sleep. My elder daughter, Jordan, was ten years old and her sister Hannah five. They loved their home and their Steiner school deep in the bush of Frenchs Forest, where they had nap time and felted their own slippers and used pencils rather than pens and sang songs about the seasons and the magical world of elves and fairies. Merran loved her work too and our lives in Mona Vale. She'd recently coordinated new public artworks for Campbell Parade in Bondi and worked as a public-art consultant for the Sydney Organising Committee of the Olympic Games. All that passion and expertise in integrating art and culture into the urban environment was finding expression.

And yet I was aching for something else. I was filled with the kind of fantasies a man experiencing a mid-life crisis might be expected to be having and that Peter O'Connor and I had talked about years earlier.

I was thinking about becoming a farmer and waking before dawn to milk the cows or sit by a stream with a knife and whittle a stick—even though I didn't know any farmers who actually had time to whittle sticks. I was pondering the simple joys of planting vegetables and growing shrubs and fruit trees, and making jams from all the cumquats, apricots and sour cherries that were inevitably going to fall into my well-irrigated earth.

I was contemplating going to Rwanda, Bosnia or Cambodia, helping out in the refugee camps, learning how to build bridges and dams and mudbrick homes—something, anything, to assist a people in crisis.

I was conjuring up the great Australian novel, or at least the great New South Welsh novel, so I could sit in daily commune with my creative, intuitive side rather than the rational, logical side of my brain. I was imagining dropping out completely, just leaving the whole capitalist enterprise behind and playing my guitar in a café like I'd done when I was eighteen and still had hair.

And so, with twelve months' leave of absence from *Good Weekend* in mind, I said, 'Let's go to Byron Bay for a year.' I'd been moonstruck by the place since first visiting in 1972 as a seventeen-year-old. It was there I'd felt the first stirrings of connection to land and sea. I'd never before seen a coastline and hinterland so staggeringly beautiful—emerald-green country spilling onto pearl-white sands and a turquoise bay and, yes, I admit, those gold-top mushrooms from the local cow paddock definitely enhanced the picture.

For the next few years, Byron Bay would become a kind of soul home. It was rain-soft and green and full of music. People didn't come to Byron Bay to further their careers. They came to surf on perfectly formed waves, and to get stoned, and to play music and to save the rainforests, to grow their own food, perform their own home births, set up farmers' markets, wildlife corridors and worm farms, and to build homes from recycled timber in hamlets and towns all the way from the Bay to the fringes of the Nightcap National Park.

Much of this had been made possible by an injection of funds from the Whitlam government into the Australian Union of Students in 1973 to host what became not just the Aquarius Festival—the biggest alternative musical event the country had ever seen—but also the birth of the hippie movement in Australia.

For the son of the founder of *Vogue* magazine, this was a great parting of the waters, at once a deliverance from the plague of bon voyage cocktail parties and after-theatre suppers, and a rolling back of the tide of conservatism and elitism that I had come to associate so closely with my father's world.

But what a faux hippie I had been. In 1975 I spent a week with friends at Wategos Beach ruminating on life, smoking enormous 'Mullumbimby madness' joints, eating three-course meals, consuming numerous bottles of wine, all within a stagger of one of the most exquisite beaches in the world. None of us at that time had jobs, or ever looked like getting one. We were privileged, middle-class Australians experimenting with sex, drugs and ill-formed ideas, and even though we thought we had a firm grip on the world, in truth we had absolutely no idea whatsoever. Richard Nixon had just resigned in disgrace because of the Watergate scandal; Cambodia was entering a new time zone called Year Zero, which we were to later learn was a Khmer Rouge euphemism for genocide; in neighbouring Vietnam, Saigon was falling to the North Vietnamese; and across the Timor Sea Indonesia was on the verge of invading East Timor. Meanwhile, the Whitlam government's three years of quixotic reform were heading towards an abrupt and spectacular end and my friends and my only contribution to this epoch-defining moment was to send a telegram to Whitlam saying: WHAT'S GOING ON?

But Byron Bay had changed radically in the ensuing twenty-five years. It was still a place for hippies, but it was much more than that. It was an Aboriginal meeting place, a women's place, a healing place, a place where the counterculture rubbed up against the city. It was a place where Australia first greeted the sun, and where the streets were named after poets and the plumber took his shoes off at the door.

It was also, of course, an easy place to parody, especially when self-parody was within plain view. Within those first few weeks of arriving in 1999, I grew a goatee, put a stud in my left ear, joined a yoga class, purchased a bag of dope from Nimbin and took up surfing at the Pass. I also had a tea-tree and peppermint concoction rubbed into my scalp by a nubile blonde called Ambrosia with rings in her nose.

I weighed up doing rebirthing with Daniella, dolphin energy healing with Ansula, and a tantric sex workshop with Oceana and Icarus (all in the name of investigative journalism). I baulked at crystal bowl therapy, numerology and singing lessons with Prakash, mainly because my plate was already alarmingly full and I didn't like the sound of crystal bowl therapy. Nor did I think I'd remember the name Prakash, even though I now know it is the Hindi word for 'luminous'. My enthusiasm reached fever pitch in those early weeks and months, so much so that old friends in Sydney thought I'd begun sounding more like a Christian revivalist or hippie snake-oil merchant than the discerning journalist I'd once been.

I think it was about three weeks into our stay when I spied a woman across the road, semi-naked in the reflected light of a crescent moon, swaying in her bedroom window.

I was on the verandah playing my guitar and, from where I sat, it appeared she was moving gently to my music, absorbing the melodies, shivering and floating towards me. It was only when I stopped playing and she continued to quiver and bend in the moonlight that I realised she was actually listening to the stereo in her bedroom. But such was the splendour of the moment— the warm frangipani breeze, the blanket of stars twinkling in the firmament, the sweet intoxication of the joint—that I was fully prepared to believe it was me and my guitar that had caused her to partially disrobe and drift into my field of vision.

'Darling, I think we should live here,' I said to Merran as she stepped out to join me in the inky night.

'We've only been here three weeks and you already want to move,' she replied, a little too crossly for what I thought was such a spell-binding moment. 'What about our lives in Sydney?'

'I know, I know,' I replied. 'It seems a hasty decision. But it could be the right one.'

I wanted to elaborate but I could hardly tell her the main reason for this abrupt change of plans was the willowy form across the road.

Plus I'd given an undertaking to return to my magazine job; our daughters, Jordan and Hannah, were counting on resuming their lives at their old school, with family and friends around them; and their mother, my wife, was eager to pursue her passions in the city and complete her Master's degree in urban design. She had no interest in rural design.

'I don't want to talk about it now,' she said. 'We've just got here. Let's discuss the matter in six months' time. If you still feel like this we can talk about it then.'

'Fine,' I said, peering over the balcony. I had numerous questions demanding immediate answers. If this woman was dancing in this window across the road from me, then what about all the other windows in the Shire? Might there not be moondances taking place everywhere, on beaches and hillside properties, in old community halls?

Was it not possible we were meant to be here, at this time in history, as the great shift in evolutionary consciousness was apparently occurring, as Mars was lining up with Jupiter for the most extraordinary celestial event of the millennium? (That's what the guy in calico pants with the big fat joint in his mouth had told me at the Mullumbimby markets the previous week!)

Was it not possible, therefore, that we needed to change postal addresses, to move in permanently across the road from Aphrodite and her girdle of finely wrought gold in order to live differently?

My yearning for something different had nothing to do with the external, reflected glory of career success, or scaling the lofty heights of logic and reason, but everything to do with accessing the parts of myself that I felt might have been lost to me.

I could detect this in others far more easily than I could detect it in myself; men like Alan Jones, whose life I had pored over for six weeks and who, by his own admission, scorned introspection. Time was too short, he told me, to spend on self-analysis. 'I know what I'm about,' he said. 'I haven't got time to be saying, "Who am I?"'

For me that was the most interesting question of all. Who

was I—or who would I be—if all else were stripped away? Who was I, for instance, when I was not working, achieving, striving, succeeding, performing the tasks—and playing the role of—father, husband, son, brother? Who was I if my primitive will or my limited intellect failed me? Who was I when I was trying to sit still in a room? *A restless lunatic, that's who.* Who was I if my health failed me or I lost my children, wife, home, job, bank account, mental acuity—all the things that propped up my sense of personhood? Who was I if I no longer had the community's respect, or if I no longer had my job, or my right arm? Who was I in the afternoon of my life—to quote Carl Jung—if the 'program of life's morning' had passed?

These were probably the kind of self-indulgent questions only a new arrival to the shores of Byron Bay might have the time and inclination to ask, but they were also age-old questions that mystics, theologians, philosophers, psychologists and scientists had been asking since the dawn of time. *Who are we?*

> We are unknown to ourselves . . . and with good reason. We have never sought ourselves—how could it ever happen that we should find ourselves?
>
> Friedrich Nietzche

Sometimes, in my deeper reflections, I realised I was not just one person, I was many. I was Tommy, the Irish rogue, full of poetry and shite; and Jean-Claude, the adventurous libertine; and Heinrich, the German Jewish intellectual; and Hyme, the neurotic Jew; and Clint, the handyman (very rarely in evidence I might add); and Herbert (my middle name), the responsible family man. I was the driven careerist, the people-pleaser, the seducer, the frightened little boy, the aggressive interrogator, the lazy sod—all of these characters sitting at my own table, housed in the politburo of my own personality, vying for space and recognition, devising strategies for coping in a chaotic world.

Was I all of these people or none of them, and if I was none of them, then who the hell was I? The sum of my life experience, my brain functions, my thoughts, my DNA, my diet, my culture, my personality, my relationship to others? Or was I connected to some deeper non-physical reality that was apprehendable, knowable?

At university I'd loved this kind of stuff, rejecting all economics-related subjects in favour of psychology, philosophy, comparative religion, and Middle Eastern history and politics. In philosophy I'd studied Descartes, Rousseau and the existentialists and I'd found most of it bloodless, except for the weeks of furrowed-brow contemplation where I'd been forced to consider questions like: 'Is Life a Dream, Yes or No? Discuss in 5000 words.'

'No, it's not,' I wrote, but how the hell would I have known, given where I was in my own life at that age? Today I look back at my childhood friends, at the places I used to play as a small boy, the family holidays we went on, my parents, once so young and vigorous. I look at the girlfriends I once had—what were their names again? I look at the opinions I once held, so resolute and firm; the books I was so absorbed in, yet can't remember a line of today; the stumbles and bruises, the little triumphs . . . and all this now just a faint echo in the canyon of my life, as though it might even have been someone else's life, just as Shakespeare described with this immortal line in *The Tempest*: 'We are such stuff as dreams are made of.'

At university, I'd studied comparative religion, dipping into the spiritual traditions of all the major religions—Buddhism, Hinduism, Judaism, Christianity and Islam—and on my first major overseas trip through Asia, the Middle East and Europe, I'd found myself drawn to the well-known and out-of-the-way temples, shrines, synagogues, churches and mosques. I loved the pageantry and colour of the Balinese Hindus; the sense of light and space of the mosque; the hushed reverence of the Buddhist temple; the familiar austerity of the synagogue; the splendour and iconography of Europe's churches. I loved listening to the various calls to prayer—the bells, the trumpets, the hand drums, the exhortations and invocations. And then watching the act of prayer itself: the believers coming through their various doors, east and west, in search of communion with something higher and deeper, something beyond themselves but connected to some kind of collective consciousness or intelligence.

Maybe they were all just fucked-up, lonely souls clutching at the idea of a deity so as to feel less desperate about their lives, or maybe there was something bigger, something truly mysterious, going on. Who the hell knew? But I was fascinated by these questions and the older I got the more important they seemed to become.

In 1992 I'd managed to secure an interview for the *Bulletin* with the Dalai Lama, Tibet's spiritual and political leader-in-exile. He'd arrived in Australia for what was to be only his second visit to the country and was offering just one interview to the print media.

I flew to Perth with Merran with the kind of childlike excitement I might have reserved for an audience with the Beatles. I was not just meeting a world leader, a great political and spiritual figure; to my mind I was also entering a fable—one that spoke of a legendary country known as Shambhala, where the forces of religion and atheism had eventually collided.

During our interview the Dalai Lama talked about the gratitude he felt towards his 'enemy', the Chinese, who had, since their invasion of Tibet in 1959, obliterated villages, burnt men and women alive, forced children to shoot their own parents, compelled monks to publicly copulate with nuns, mutilated the land, desecrated a culture . . . and here he was feeling gratitude?

'I'm trying to promote the value of compassion,' he said, 'and not just based on attachment to those who are close to you, but rather for all beings, irrespective of what that person does to you, or whether they are your enemy or not. Compassion and tolerance are not a sign of weakness but a sign of strength.'

The Dalai Lama offered up many other pearls of ancient wisdom that May morning in 1992, but it was not these pearls I remember most clearly. What I remember most is the Dalai Lama holding my hand and Merran's after the interview.

'Can we have a photograph with you?' I'd asked him as we were preparing to leave.

'Why not?' he replied, giggling. 'With my glasses on or off?'

'What about both?' I said. And with that the Tibetan leader took both our hands in his, turned to the camera, and posed like a movie star, with his sunglasses on and then off.

An hour later I was on a Perth sidewalk with a vast media contingent waiting for the Tibetan leader to arrive for his first and only press conference in the country. One of the journalists, a former colleague of mine from the *Sydney Morning Herald*, was waiting with me after having been called away from covering WA Inc, the Royal Commission into corrupt state government-business dealings.

He wasn't happy about having to turn his gaze East.

'Fucking Dal-aye fucking Lama,' he said.

'What do you mean?' I asked.

'Well, what a load of shit this is, don't you reckon?'

'No, not really,' I replied. 'But you're obviously underwhelmed.'

'Are you kidding? Who gives a shit about the Dal-aye Lama anyway?'

'I don't know. You might be surprised.'

'Not bloody likely, mate. They've got to be fucking kidding.'

Twenty minutes later the room was full—newspaper, radio and

television reporters up front, camera crews towards the back—when the world's most famous monk entered unannounced. Smiling and bowing, his hands cupped in the traditional Buddhist greeting, he walked along the front row, taking in the faces of the Fourth Estate. Suddenly he stopped in front of my former *Herald* colleague and for at least ten seconds looked into this journalist's eyes with a beaming smile, while the journalist, big, burly and fresh from his Royal Commission, blushed like a little boy.

During my years of tortured sleeplessness I'd begun to study Buddhist texts in an attempt to learn to meditate. I wanted to still my mind, but every time I focused my attention on my breath my mind began to boil and hiss. One compulsive, out-of-control thought followed another, speeding towards me from a million directions. I couldn't sit still for more than five minutes. My body ached. My nose itched. I'd count my in-breath, then my out-breath, and before I knew it there'd be another saturation bombing of thoughts, fantasies, projections, recollections and anticipations. This was the uproar no one else could hear when I decided, a year before we left for Byron Bay, to go on a week-long meditation retreat with Sogyal Rinpoche, the author of the spiritual classic, *The Tibetan Book of Living and Dying*.

The retreat was held on the shores of Myall Lakes, about 200 kilometres north of Sydney, and every day we spent endless hours in a large white marquee festooned with flowers, prayer flags and paintings of reincarnated Tibetan spiritual masters.

We were there to learn about the 'nature of mind', karma, rebirth, compassion and impermanence, but most of all we were there—or at least *I was there*—to learn how to stop being ambushed by incessant thoughts.

There were three ways, apparently, to do so. The first was to use an object of beauty or inspiration—a flower, a crystal, an image of Buddha or Christ—and then rest the mind lightly on that object. A second technique was to recite a mantra so that the truth of the words could vibrate through the body, thus purifying both mind and body. The third technique was to watch the breath, focusing lightly on the awareness of the out-breath and, at the same time, letting go of all the grasping and desire. That's the one I chose to follow and this is how the outer stillness sounded from the inside:

Breathing in, breathing out, breathing in, breathing . . . you see? You can meditate, David, it's not that hard, you just have to follow the breath and know that everything is fine and God why doesn't that guy shut up and stop asking questions every time we have a break? Shit . . . breathing in, breathing out, and surely it's time for dinner soon because I'm absolutely starving . . . oh bugger: the breath. Bloody hell, David, you can't even follow your breath for a minute, what kind of brain-dead idiot are you? . . . Breathing in breathing out breathing in breathing out—there you go, that's easy. I wish Merran was here too, this is fantastic, so good for you, I can feel things shifting, but I wish I'd finished that story before I left because that middle section just isn't working and oh for fuck's sake breathing in breathing out but that last story wasn't one of my best so I have to make this next one a killer because I can't afford to get forgotten and shit if only I'd won two more Walkleys when I was nominated that would have been incredible instead of Liz Jackson winning 500 of them—I mean she's good, she's really good, but oh right, okay, breathing in breathing out—this is crazy I need to call Dad and see how he is 'cause he has no idea what this meditation business is all about and bloody hell breathing in breathing out . . .

❧

Victor Hugo once said there was nothing more powerful than an idea whose time had come, and by the turn of the century we were renting a house on the edge of Arakwal Country, home to the traditional custodians of the Byron Bay district for the past 22,000 years.

Our house, owned by Rob Hirst and his wife Lesley, was a beautifully renovated little fibro shack in a garden of newly planted grevilleas with sweeping north-east views to Cape Byron and the wetlands behind Tallow Beach. The house had been bought from the royalties Rob had earned co-writing Midnight Oil classics like 'Beds Are Burning', 'Power and the Passion' and 'Dead Heart', and it was now ours for a 'mate's rate' for the next twelve months—although these twelve months would turn into five years. My old drummer friend from Sydney Grammar School had granted us our own little patch of glory on the rim of the Australian continent.

From day one, Merran and I began walking to the Cape each morning, then swimming in the copper-blue shallows of the Pass before breakfast. I began noticing things I'd never noticed before and, yes, for an urban Jew boy nature was a revelation. We would follow the path of bush turkeys collecting leaf litter for their nests and stand fascinated for minutes at a time as the lace goannas tried to steal eggs from those nests, scuttling away like naughty children. We'd watch ospreys and white-breasted kites soaring above the bald rocky cliff face and dolphins leisurely patrolling the bay.

On a good day—and there were many staggeringly good days—we would watch boardriders, kayakers and bodysurfers vying for the perfectly formed point break, and we would watch flocks of seagulls dive-bombing schools of pilchards swarming nearby, mackerel circling the pilchards, and then, on one occasion, a pod of twenty or more dolphins herding them closer to shore.

'That's the most incredible thing I've ever seen,' Jordan shrieked with delight that particular morning, before dreaming that night of a dolphin kissing her on the end of her nose.

On one of those morning walks to the Cape I met a woman standing under the lighthouse, looking slightly befuddled, as if she'd lost her compass. Her long hair was silvery and wild, and under her wide-brimmed hat you could see a wind-blown face and a pair of piercing blue eyes.

'Do you know what time it is?' she asked me.

'Ten o'clock,' I replied.

That was the extent of our conversation. The following morning, at the very same spot, she repeated the question.

'Same time as yesterday,' I replied, grinning, but she had no idea what I was talking about.

On the third morning, before she could even utter the words, I told her she was half an hour early; it was 9.30. She gave me a baffled look and trudged on up to the lighthouse, looking like a figure from a Scandinavian folktale.

Only later that week, at a dinner given in Byron Bay for Canadian environmentalist David Suzuki, did I find out that my lighthouse acquaintance was Helena Norberg-Hodge, a friend of Suzuki, the Dalai Lama and Prince Charles, and that she'd been taught by the American linguist Noam Chomsky. She was a linguist herself and the only Westerner in the world who could speak the language of Ladakh, the mainly Tibetan Buddhist enclave in north-west India.

Far from being the befuddled fairy woman of my imaginings, Norberg-Hodge was a highly intelligent and committed anti-globalisation campaigner, determined to build awareness of how deliberate government and business-led economic policies were separating people further and further away from their food sources.

She'd moved to Byron Bay not just for its natural beauty but also because she could see this was home to one of the largest concentrations anywhere in the Western world of people trying to live outside the paradigm. She wanted to be part of the great experiment, and she wanted to crusade from here.

I suppose after about six months that's what we decided too. We wanted to stay. We wanted to be part of our own experiment in living outside the city, although it's true that, given the transportable nature of my work, this was a far easier transition for me to make than for Merran. But she'd agreed eventually—and willingly—because she felt the pull of Byron and, more than that, the pull of community in ways I'd never even contemplated.

In the ensuing years she would draft a cultural plan for Byron Shire, curate and project manage sculptural shows, deliver a range of art and cultural ventures for public and private organisations up and down the coast, help steer tree-planting and park reclamation programs, join 750 other women on a hillside to protest—naked—the looming war in Iraq, join a women's group and generally get involved in dozens of community-based strategies. So committed was she to her sense of civic responsibility that in the early years a small group of her female friends even formed a pseudo committee to stop her joining committees.

Until our arrival in Byron I'd never really thought much about what a community was, let alone imagined I could be part of one. It's true that as a journalist I'd always felt part of the noble collective enterprise that was good investigative reporting; and as a Jew, despite my deep disquiet about Israel's treatment of the Palestinians, I felt—culturally at least—part of a tribe that I could call my own.

But that was not the same thing as being part of an alternative rural community where people felt bound to each other through their children's schools, their community halls, their farmers' markets, their pub nights, their bush dances and, more grandly, their collective sense that here was a place worth preserving and celebrating; a place worth tying themselves to trees for, lying in front of tractors for, demonstrating, picketing and agitating for, playing backroom politics for, railing, agitating and never resting for.

Merran had always understood this and, more particularly, the role that local government had always played in knitting people's lives together, but to me this had always been far less interesting than whatever was going on in the capitals of the world—Washington, London, Jerusalem, Cairo or even Canberra.

In our first few years on the North Coast I came to see community as a party in the forest under an equinox moon. It was about building a village in the sand with my daughters. It was the beach at high noon, among the surfies and hippies and mohawks and joggers and bare breasts. It was Aquarius balls just for Aquarians. It was women with five children to five different men. It was a flotation tank opposite Woolies.

It was about a sense of place, spirit of place, *genius loci*, and the living, breathing record of Aboriginal elders who could tell us what it was like before DDT and 245T and CFC and KFC and GMO. It was about a once-proud old abattoir town of blood and guts that had turned itself into the non-conformist capital of Australia, where people like George the Snake Man drove around in his van full of caged carpet and brown snakes (he was the one you called in the middle of the night when something long, dark and sinuous had slithered across your floor); where Zenith Virago, the Buddhist celebrant, helped people embrace death and dying in more conscious ways; where former US surfing champion Rusty Miller taught people something of the philosophy and joys of the sea; where Colin Heaney transplanted—and I'm guessing here—his acid experiences of the 1960s into kaleidoscopic glass; where Mandy Nolan, often pregnant but always uproarious, entertained people as the town's resident comedian; where Di Morrissey, the highest-selling female author in the country, wrote her novels;

where Ian Cohen, the man who'd single-handedly tried to stop an American nuclear-powered warship from entering Sydney Harbour, had his home; and where political writer Mungo McCallum was always cooking up trouble for our political masters, not to mention a few local government figures. 'You're despicable,' he told councillor Ross Tucker one day. 'Well, you're despicable too,' Tucker retorted.

I was still on a year's leave of absence from *Good Weekend* when Deborah Thomas, editor-in-chief of the *Australian Women's Weekly*, called me in late 2000 with an intriguing offer. 'Come over to the *Weekly* and write profiles for us,' she said. I thought she must be joking or, perhaps, have mistaken me for someone else. I'd never read a copy of the *Weekly* before, let alone contemplated writing for it.

'I'm still an employee of *Good Weekend*,' I replied. 'And we're living in Byron Bay.'

'I don't care where you live,' she said. 'Just come over to the *Weekly* and do for us what you've been doing for *Good Weekend*.

I told Deborah I'd think about it and a week later bought a copy of the magazine at Sydney Airport. I hid it under the *Economist* as I strapped myself in for the flight home. ('How are you ever going to write for the magazine if you can't be seen reading it in public?' Merran chided me later.)

I returned to Sydney a few days later to meet Deborah for what turned out to be a delightful lunch, one in which she promised me the world if I would join her team.

Deborah was true to her word. She delivered if not the world, then a world exclusive with my first major story for the magazine: an interview with Anna Murdoch, former wife of Rupert Murdoch.

'[Rupert] behaved badly,' she told me on a golden northern

summer's afternoon on New York's Long Island, 'and I've waited all this time for him to make it right again, but he never took the opportunity.'

Anna Murdoch was talking, of course, about the break-up of her nearly thirty-one-year marriage to the world's most powerful media magnate, and his relationship with Wendy Deng, the Chinese-born former intern at Murdoch's Star TV in Hong Kong.

She told me she had tried to save the marriage but that her former husband had no interest in salvaging it. 'He was extremely hard, ruthless and determined that he was going to go through with this no matter what I wanted, or what I was trying to do to save the marriage. He had no interest in that whatsoever.'

I might have now been living in Byron Bay doing salutes to the sun under the she-oaks, but I still knew a good story when it dropped in my lap, and this one was a scoop of the first order being delivered with deadly aim by a woman finally deciding to break her silence and set the record straight.

Two months later Deborah had me flying over the Pyrenees and the snow-capped Atlas Mountains into Marrakech to interview Malika Oufkir, the adopted daughter of King Hassan II who, along with her mother and five brothers and sisters, had been jailed by the Moroccan king for fifteen years before managing to escape with two of her siblings. (They'd spent three months excavating a shaft and tunnel using a spoon, an iron bar from one of their beds and the lid of a sardine can.)

Malika and I had met in Los Angeles on my way back to Australia from interviewing Anna Murdoch. She was having lunch at the Beverly Hills Hotel with Tina Brown, and my father and I were there for one night, flying in opposite directions—him to New York, me back to Byron Bay.

Tina Brown was by this stage the editor of *Talk*, a monthly glossy that had been launched two years earlier on Liberty Island with 800 guests, including Demi Moore, Salman Rushdie and Madonna. *Talk* was owned by Harvey and Bob Weinstein of Miramax films and Brown was in Los Angeles to talk to Malika about a movie based on her life.

Malika and I met and spoke for no more than thirty seconds. Two months later, after first clearing it with Deborah Thomas, I called Malika in Paris, to see whether she would agree to an interview. She did, and from the moment we met again—first in Paris, then flying together to Marrakech to attend her friend's wedding—I knew we had formed one of those unshakeable bonds that occasionally occurs between journalist and subject. Once again, I owed this meeting to my father.

For eight rarified years, Deborah Thomas flew me around the world to interview some of the most remarkable women I've ever met. Susan Sarandon in New York, Anjelica Huston in Los Angeles, Helen Clark in Wellington, the McCartney sisters in Belfast, and even Dame Edna Everage in Denver, Colorado, where she (he) managed to bring the house down three nights in a row with her time-honoured ability to turn suburban banalities into theatrical uproar.

In Australia, the *Weekly* gave me access to other extraordinary women too—people like the blind writer, poet and former salon-keeper Barbara Blackman; Rupert Murdoch's mother, Dame Elisabeth; the two Fionas—Fiona Stanley and Fiona Wood, both Australians of the Year; Janet Holmes à Court; and painter Judy Cassab.

All through these years I was reminded time and time again of how much pleasure I had always derived from my relationships with women—wife, daughters, mother, friends, colleagues, interview subjects—and how this driving impulse which I had always witnessed in my father was now finding full expression in his son as a profile writer of women for Australia's leading women's magazine.

Perhaps the woman I came to love and admire most during that time was Irina Baronova, the former Russian dancer who, at the time, was eighty-six years old, nearly blind and living on a glorious ridge in the hills above Byron. She'd greeted me at the door with her feet turned out like Charlie Chaplin's and a kiss on either cheek.

At first glance she appeared as fragile as porcelain, but when she spoke her voice was gutsy and her manner full of the kind of dramatic flourishes you'd expect from a former White Russian prima ballerina.

We sat opposite each other and I commented immediately on the beauty and blueness of her eyes. 'I don't know what my eyes look like,' she replied, in her still-thick Russian-Romanian accent, 'because I can't see myself in the mirror. That's why I don't put makeup on, because I can't see where the skin finishes and the lips start . . . where are the eyelashes, if there are any left. Maybe it's good. I can't see any wrinkles, hooray.'

She laughed, then fixed me with her beguiling but near-blind gaze and said, 'I see you have something light on top, but you have no head, no face [laughing some more], so if I want to see what you look like, I have to come nose to nose really to inspect your face.'

'Would you like to do that?' I asked.

'Yes, please.' And with that she pulled my face towards her, grabbed both cheeks and gave them a squeeze. 'Yes, nice,' she cooed. 'Good, now I can see you.'

That was the beginning of our little love affair. We talked for hours throughout the afternoon and into the evening about the joys and sorrows of her remarkable life. At one point she spread that life out for me in photo form on the table between us.

'That's me in *Swan Lake*,' she said. 'I played Odile . . . And that's me in *Bluebeard*. I was the last of the six wives—the one who got the better of the husband. And that's Aurora's Wedding, part of *Sleeping Beauty*, and I was Princess Aurora . . . and here I am as the Queen of Shemakhan.'

In another era—seventy years earlier—Irina Baronova had been one of the three so-called Baby Ballerinas with the legendary Ballet Russe de Monte Carlo, performing on the most illustrious stages of the world. She'd danced in London for King George V and Queen Mary (and their successors King George VI and Queen Elizabeth); as well as Adolf Hitler and Joseph Goebbels. The Nazi Minister for Propaganda, bearing flowers, had visited her backstage in Berlin in 1936.

She'd collaborated with the greatest choreographers of the twentieth century—Leonide Massine, George Balanchine, Bronislava Nijinska and Michel Fokine—and artists such as Pablo Picasso, Henri Matisse, Joan Miró, Marc Chagall and Salvador Dali, who designed her costumes and stage sets.

She'd known everyone: Charlie Chaplin, Marlene Dietrich, Shirley Temple, Clark Gable, Grace Kelly, Cary Grant, Noël Coward and Marilyn Monroe—and, of course, the pre-eminent dancers of their time, Rudolf Nureyev, Margot Fonteyn and Mikhail Baryshnikov. Vivien Leigh and Sir Laurence Olivier had been godparents to her two daughters. She'd had a wild affair with a young Yul Brynner and an eighteen-year marriage to the great love of her life, Cecil Tennant, London's leading theatrical agent of the 1950s and '60s.

And here we now found ourselves, in another century, in another country, taking in the gathering dusk, drinking straight bourbons, smoking Alpines and talking of life, death, love and music. I couldn't get enough of her—nor could my mother who, on meeting her, felt as if she'd found a true companion in the world of music, culture and European refinement.

When I later interviewed Irina at the Byron Bay Writers

Festival I saw 300 people fall in love with her as I had. For an hour one could have heard a pin drop as we picked our way through her life—her escape from Russia as a child during the Bolshevik Revolution, her subsequent life of destitution in Romania, her arrival in Paris as a nine-year-old to study ballet, her meteoric rise to international stardom, her marriage to Cecil Tennant and then his sudden, tragic death. All of this had the audience captivated.

'Do you ever miss the roar of the crowd?' I asked her as we came to the end of our interview.

'Oh no,' she said, 'it's too late for that. That was a long time ago.'

'Would you like to hear it one more time?' I then said . . . and before she'd even had the chance to say yes or no, the crowd had risen to its feet, clapping and roaring. As I stood there, arm in arm with Irina, there was not a dry eye in the house. Certainly not mine, and certainly not hers.

These were the stories I now dreamt of as a journalist. Stories that connected. Stories of the heart. For years I'd gone looking for dirt, so much so that Ian 'Molly' Meldrum had once said to me during the course of my profiling his then business partner Michael Gudinski: 'I've heard about you. You come across as a nice guy, then you turn into a cunt.' Admittedly Molly was drunk at the time, but maybe he'd had a point. Stuart Littlemore QC said much the same thing a couple of years later when I called him about his friend Richard Carleton for a *Good Weekend* profile. He told me he deplored the kind of profiles I did, and then accused me of being a 'prick', sneaking around in the dark looking for dirt to dump on people.

Perhaps that was true. Perhaps that was the only way I felt I could get under the guard of tougher pricks and cunts than myself. Be a prick and a cunt too. I'd liked to think I was a fair prick and a balanced cunt, but that might have been wishful thinking on my part.

Some journalists are addicted to war. Some can't leave their nation's capitals for the thrill of political combat. Some want to write about food or music or architecture. A new way of baking chicken with guavas perhaps; a break-through album from a rising star; a new post-modernist structure that redefines a city.

In Byron Bay—and with the *Australian Women's Weekly*—I wanted to write about people whose lives added something to the collective human endeavour. I can see how earnest that looks on the page, but it was the truth. I wanted connection, and the *Australian Women's Weekly* made that possible.

With few significant exceptions I'd never really profiled people of true goodness before. I'd mostly written about rogues and rascals, people with giant egos and massive flaws and often a good many things to answer for. It was impossible to spend five weeks in the sinkhole of a Gina Rinehart and Rose Porteous feud and not feel sullied yourself. Or to spend great chunks of your life trying to size up Pauline Hanson, Bronwyn Bishop or Alan Jones and not think the world was full of monumental hubris and self-delusion. In doing that one could easily forget that the world was potentially as good a place as it was bad; that for all the people betraying the public trust, committing the indefensible, wreaking havoc and misery in their own and other people's lives, that there were also those producing works of art, writing poetry, making music, tending the sick, reaching out, giving up time and money for something far bigger than themselves. It was easy for journalists to forget this, or at least it was easy for me. It was easy to think the only stories that really mattered were the ones where someone was getting killed or maimed or stitched up or doublecrossed or dispossessed; that lying, cheating and dissembling were the norm.

Even during the course of covering the Bali bombings for the *Weekly* in 2002, even in the face of all that murderous, unspeakable horror, what struck me most were the acts of heroism and the outpouring of love that followed.

Actually, that's not right. What struck me first was the chilling arbitrariness of life and death. You hated the song that was playing in the Sari Club that night so you left the dance floor and died.

The song just happened to be Sophie Ellis-Bextor's 'Murder on the Dancefloor'.

Or you dropped your wallet at the bar of the Sari Club, bent down to retrieve it, and you lived while the guy next to you lost his head. Or you decided on an extra-long shower before stepping out into the night and you woke to a new dawn. Or your taxi dropped you off outside the nightclub and you walked straight into the arms of death.

How easily the tears flowed during those days. The night before my flight to Bali I'd had a farewell drink with one of my closest friends, Jennifer Byrne, who throughout the previous thirty years had reported on just about every human catastrophe one could think of—genocide, war, famine, insurrection, terrorism, natural disaster—and she'd managed to cover them all with distinction and, it should be said, a fair dose of necessary detachment as well.

Not now. Not during this period. Now she couldn't stop the tears. Now she felt she was crying for every human horror she'd ever witnessed, for every child she'd seen lose a parent, for every parent who'd seen a child go before them.

My father and I had been thinking much the same thing on that day before my flight to Denpasar, as we'd sat in a car listening to 'Fields of Gold', recorded by the late Eva Cassidy. My father had just come out of hospital following a hip operation and I wanted to drive him home before leaving for Indonesia. We'd sat there moist-eyed as the melody wrapped us in its afternoon glory.

It's twelve years now since that dreadful week in Bali. It took days for the horror of what happened to sink in, although there's a strong chance that it never will. Families destroyed in an instant. Parents and children annihilated, maimed or permanently traumatised. Classmates, best friends and lovers torn from one another. That group of children who lost their mothers. That man who lost both his wife and daughter. The man who lost his two brothers. The family whose two sons and daughter-in-law were ripped from them. The football club that lost seven of its finest. On and on the roll call of dead and missing. Bridal parties cut down, birthday parties mercilessly cut short or never held. Beds never slept in. Last declarations never made.

During the days I spent on the island after the bombing I came to the conclusion that it was perhaps only in grief, or in the face of death, that we find ourselves drawn to the devotional. Perhaps these are the times, rather than when we feel vaguely happy, that we share our common humanity most strongly. We have less to hide, less to defend, and so we allow ourselves the possibility of being more open to the pain of others, to the pain of the world.

On my second day in Bali I'd joined a large public ceremony as it made its way along Jalan Legian, the once humming life-line of Kuta and Legian, towards the burnt out shells of the Sari Club and Paddy's pub. All around me were floral wreaths and messages of condolence, and hundreds of Balinese people in sombre procession—men carrying flowers and wearing T-shirts saying 'Together For Life'; women holding hands or carrying their infants; older children in their slipstream, so quiet and so beautiful it was enough to bathe your eyes clean.

Suddenly the silence was broken by an anguished scream. It was a Balinese man wailing himself into a trance for his lost wife. All you could do was stand and listen and bow your head.

Next to me, a Balinese woman stared blankly into the ruins.

She was in the Sari Club too that night, but somehow escaped with just burns to her arm.

Eventually we found ourselves at Ground Zero, and as police and security looked on, we sat down in front of the twisted wreckage to pray or meditate or simply pay homage to the lost and broken-hearted. It felt, as Allan Rogers from Portland, Victoria, said to me later that evening, 'like everybody had just become one'.

'As much as it has taken a tragedy for this to happen,' he said, 'everyone has come together. It doesn't matter whether you are Americans, Australians or Balinese . . .'

I'd felt this when I met two Australians of Turkish Cypriot extraction, Mustafa Sumer and his cousin Kursat, in the after-math of the bombing. Three of Mustafa's brothers had been in the Sari Club that night, two of them managing to escape with shocking burns, gaping shrapnel wounds and permanently shat-tered eardrums. The third brother, Behic, was not found, and even though Mustafa, his eldest brother, was clinging to the faint hope he was alive—he might have lost his mind and wandered off into the paddy fields—in his heart of hearts he knew Behic was gone.

'We loved each other so much,' Mustafa told me, his eyes brimming with tears. 'Everyone said they'd never seen a family so tight . . . He was green-eyed and always smiling . . . he had a fourteen-year-old son . . . he loved life . . .'

These men had been strangers to me and photographer Marc Gerritsen half an hour earlier, but suddenly the four of us were crying together and hugging one another as though we'd always been part of each other's lives. Our hearts had suddenly cracked open and in that raw, tender, unforgettable moment their suffering had become ours.

So many acts of heroism, small and large. One man was walking towards the Sari Club when he was knocked to the ground by the force of the blast. When he looked up there was someone in front of him on fire. He rolled around in the mud to get wet, donned a motorcycle helmet, and walked towards the flames to pull the man out. How many people risked their lives in such a manner?

And then, later, there were the volunteers, like Sydney schoolboy Shane Ullman, who took time out from his family holiday to help in the morgue; or Australian trainee doctors Vijith Vijayasekaran and his wife Priya, who abandoned their holiday to save dozens of blast victims, help set up a network of other volunteers and give crash courses on administering fluids to burn victims.

Hundreds of others did what they could, in some cases actually helping to amputate limbs or peel off burnt skin, in other cases compiling lists of the dead and injured, opening their homes to the families of victims, donating blood, using their language skills to translate, sitting vigil all night with the wounded and traumatised, or telephoning distraught family members back home.

'Your little boy is on his way,' Jill O'Connor from Downtown Apartments told the mother of one young man after he was airlifted out on a Hercules.

'How does he look?' the mother pleaded. 'You have to tell me how he looks.'

'I've only just met him,' Jill replied, 'but apart from a scratch above his eyebrow, he looks exactly as he looked the last time you saw him.'

The mother had burst into tears.

Up in the foothills of central Bali, Janet de Neefe, the Australian owner of the Casa Luna guesthouse and bakery, set up a hotline and an Ubud Relief Disaster Fund. Within hours, money started pouring in from all around the world, from people who had been to Bali years earlier but had never forgotten the warmth and generosity of the Balinese. Hotels and restaurants began sending food, ice, disinfectant, clean sheets, towels, anything they could lay their hands on for the overflowing and overwhelmed hospitals of Denpasar.

Many of the people coordinating the transport came from the Balinese scooter club who, with their motorbikes and mobile phones, suddenly transformed into modern-day knights in shining armour.

There were outpourings of sympathy and compassion on a grand and, at times, unexpected scale. One journalist I spoke to said he would never forget seeing an Indonesian military intelligence officer crying his eyes out and apologising to his Australian counterparts for what had happened. Many of his colleagues were equally distressed.

'You really saw the potential for humanity at this time,' Judy Chapman, an Australian woman helping out in the hospital crisis centre, told me. 'It made me fall in love with humans again.'

Just before I left Bali I went into the central highlands to speak to the most revered Hindu priest on the island. I wanted to know how the Bali bombings might be understood in spiritual terms.

The eighty-two-year-old man received me in the grounds of what was once the royal temple of the Tabanan dynasty, built 900 years earlier.

'Why do you think this has happened to Bali?' I asked him.

'Kali Yuga,' he answered simply.

I shook my head. 'What is Kali Yuga?'

He explained through an interpreter that, according to Hindu scriptures, Kali Yuga was the fourth and last stage in the cycle of the world, a time of apocalypse associated with the demon Kali.

'Everything can happen in Kali Yuga,' he said. 'People can blow up nightclubs. Parents can defile their children. Children can kill their parents.'

'When will it end?' I queried him.

'When the world has washed itself clean.'

11

'SO YOU THINK YOU CAN DANCE?!'

I am standing in front of twenty people, most of them strangers, in a large dance pavilion set in the rice paddies of central Bali. I am wearing my underpants, and I am about to perform as the great Russian dancer, Mikhail Nikolaevich Baryshnikov, the explanation for which will become clear shortly.

It is five years since the first Bali bombing, two years since the second wave of terrorist attacks in 2005, and I am on a break from the *Women's Weekly* to attend a week-long writing/yoga retreat that begins each morning at dawn with the roosters badgering us from our beds, then an hour of salutes to the sun followed by a breakfast of tropical fruits and banana pancakes.

After breakfast, with our bodies limbered, our writing coaches, Sarah Armstrong and Alan Close, take us through a series of exercises called 'freewriting' which, as I am soon to discover, means learning to write without stopping; learning to lose control; learning to allow the first thoughts to be the ones you commit to the page; learning not to know where you are going—either in life or on the page.

I'd always stopped and started, backspaced and edited, ruminated endlessly on what was worth saying and what wasn't. Screamed at myself when I couldn't craft a sentence; stewed endlessly over a line or paragraph that felt populated by clichés and old tricks. And here I was being told not just to let it go, but to begin with the following sentence: 'The story I really want to write is . . .' And then with no time to hesitate or self-edit, to begin writing:

> The story I really want to write is the story of a lucky man born to unlucky parents in the luckiest of times. My father lost his mother when he was three years old. 'I have to go now darling,' she had said to him, and that was his first memory—his mother packing her bags and leaving . . .

And then I was told to stop and to begin with the negative version of the same sentence:

> The story I really don't want to write . . . is the story of my pain and vulnerability and fear and lust and anger and jealousy; the story of my shadow which creeps out of sullen, half-buried corners . . . the story of all the things I don't like about myself, and let's think . . . where to start? Perhaps as a small boy, with being short, although that's not even coming close to it, is it? But yes, seriously, it's a good place to start—with being the shortest in the class, although there was one year where I was the second shortest, but no matter because being the second shortest didn't make me feel man enough or boy enough and how unoriginal does this sound, you might say, but let me continue because this is a free write, right? And so I think I became in all likelihood more competitive in sport than I would have been had I not been 167. 64 centimetres (okay, 166.37 centimetres, short) . . . and what about that match where I pulled off all

those try-saving tackles and then cut through the opposing back-line to sprint sixty metres for the try-line but was pulled down centimetres short, just on full-time, because the opposing full-back managed to clip my heels in a diving tackle just as I was about to WIN THE GAME, and how I relished my father coming to watch me play, although he wasn't there that day, or most days actually, because then I would try and win the game single-handedly with little kicks over the opposition's heads; picking the ball up on the rebound; getting the opposition running in the wrong way with those deft little flick passes and then, in defence, launching myself at a rampaging opponent by taking his feet from under him. So, yes, competing in sport but also competing to be the most defiant, the most insolent ('Leser, get out of this class now and go and tell the headmaster I want you given three of the best,' and that was three straps on the bottom with a bamboo cane) and competing to get my father's attention, but how could I ever compete with the important demands of *Vogue* magazine and the Lady Potters and Lady Fairfaxes and Lord Kenilworths of this world, and competing to get the girl because if you were the second shortest in the class and you could get the girl, then that would make you feel like you were ten feet tall in the saddle and then, later in life, wanting to be the best at everything. The best writer. The best lover. The best father. The best husband, the best provider, best son, best brother, best friend. And all this pressure of being the best when of course you know you are anything but the best and yet your father lives by this credo so how can you let him down: 'In this life and in this world, we have to prove ourselves over and over again, each day, each hour . . .'

I wrote a lot more that needed editing that day in Bali about the story I didn't want to write, and it was full of things that were hard to put down on the page then, but even more so now—all the characteristics I disliked in myself that I might have adopted from my father but were truly mine in spades too: all the egotistical, puffed-up, overly ambitious, pontificating, defensive, highly critical, workaholic, judgemental, self-referencing, self-righteous, censorious, dismissive, insecure, selfish bits . . . And that was just for starters, because once you disappeared down that kind of foxhole it was difficult to find your way back, even when you were reminding yourself that all the negative traits had their equal and opposite positive ones too.

But along with this lacerating self-critique was the companion thought that I actually liked myself quite a lot too, and so if I was having these thoughts then what about every other poor fucker—and let's face it, that's a good portion of humanity—who never grew up with privilege and opportunity; who never had a sense of belonging; who never knew they were loved; who were never told—repeatedly, endlessly—that they were capable of anything; who were never exposed to a world of books and music and interesting people; who were never made to feel anything other than inadequate, abandoned or ashamed?

That was the other thought. If I, the privileged firstborn son of a magazine publisher growing up in the luckiest of homes in the luckiest of countries in the luckiest of times in human history—*Lucky Leser*, one of my friends had even dubbed me—if I had these feelings of inadequacy, then what about everyone else?

Psychology 101, you say? Yes, but then wasn't that the whole point of being alive? Of being conscious? To ask the right questions, not just as a journalist but as a human being? To examine not just other people's dark, cold, self-hating, contradictory, disconnected places, but to examine one's own, given that this was possibly the most uncomfortable inquiry one could ever undertake? To begin to tolerate uncertainty and ambiguity. To begin to hold opposite sides at the same time, not to rush to one position or another, but to allow disparate ideas to coexist, within ourselves and within others. To begin to know oneself, and to begin to know that we don't know.

Other people's flaws, hell, they were easy to recognise, easy to turn into a blood sport at any social gathering, but what about drilling down into the depths and truth of one's own pain? What about taking the journalist's impulse for burglary and rifling through the drawers of one's own conspicuous shortcomings and strategies, then uttering the unutterable, printing the unprintable *about oneself*? What kind of darkness resided in that inner country and how on earth could we ever sit with someone else's pain if we couldn't begin to touch our own?

Courage comes from the Latin word for heart, *cor*, from the old French word *corage*, meaning 'heart, innermost feelings'. To speak one's mind by telling one's heart.

During my interview with Oriana Fallaci in 1993 she'd said to me: 'Courage and fear are associated.' Mind you, she was referring to the time she was covering the Israeli invasion of Southern Lebanon and had refused to sit inside the Israeli tank as it was edging towards battle with the Syrians. Instead, she'd perched on the edge of the hatch.

'I know how you die in a tank,' she told me. 'It's the most horrid death. It takes four or five minutes to die and you cook like an omelette . . . so I stayed outside, because if I was caught inside I would have cooked slowly. I gained the admiration of everybody for what was an act of fear.'

Now, fourteen years later, I am thinking of Fallaci and courage and bearing witness to other people's hearts, as well as my own, on this, the end of my yoga retreat where I have come to the rather dubious decision to try to impersonate the great Soviet-born dancer and choreographer Mikhail Baryshnikov.

I have chosen Baryshnikov—as opposed to, say, Quasimodo—because during the yoga retreat I had suddenly remembered that I'd once studied ballet as a five-year-old and that this had been the earliest remembered moment of my childhood humiliation.

For reasons I am now deeply regretting—reasons of candour, self-confession, 'personal growth'—I'd revealed to the group how it was I came to do ballet and how one morning in 1961 this fact was discovered as I was sitting in my first school assembly at Sydney Grammar.

There were 200 other boys in the assembly hall, and because of a conspiracy of factors that must surely deny the existence of a benevolent God, my ballet shoes were sticking out of my school bag. My mother had wanted me to study dance outside of school and that afternoon I would be going to my second class.

I remember the moment with fierce clarity—the sick-making recognition of approaching doom as the boy next to me pulled the shoes from my bag and then held them aloft to the assembly like he'd just found two little black turds. 'Look,' he said at the top of his voice, his nose scrunched up, 'LESER DOES BALLET.'

Certainly there have been worse humiliations for a five-year-old at an all-boys private school, but I couldn't think of one at the time. All that was in my head was how to torture and maim this devil child while disappearing through a hole in the earth.

Having told the yoga group about this aborted dance career of mine, I'd then found myself dubbed 'Baryshnikov' for the entire week, in mock sympathy.

When it had come time, therefore, for each of us to perform, I'd made up a little story about Baryshnikov and I'd assigned the reading of this to Caroline Farrell, an Australian actress and fellow retreat participant. Her job was to read my words loudly in a Russian accent over the top of the music while I . . . danced.

No one knew what I was going to do beforehand so there was an audible gasp as I proceeded to take my shirt and pants off before turning to face the room in my underpants. The gasp turned to shrieks as I scrunched up three tissues and put them inside my underpants to give my balls some Baryshnikovian heft. I then stepped into the middle of the pavilion and began to dance as Caroline began:

I am the Great Baryshnikov, Mikhail Fyodor Romanov Baryshnikov, and I have danced for the descendants of the tsars on the great stages of the world. I have been feted by kings and queens, princes, princesses, acolytes and quislings. Plus I have fucked Jessica Lange. Many times. 'Give it to me like a Muscovite, Micky, give it to me,' she said one night. And so, just like in *The Postman Always Rings Twice*, I threw her down on the kitchen table among the carrots and diced cucumbers and shtooped her. I shtooped her until she came, crying, 'Baryshnikov. The Great Babushka. I'm coming, Babushka, I'm coming.'

While Caroline read I began with little steps across the stage, some light treads, some strides, then three pirouettes around the pavilion, a high kick, a leap into the air—and as I did so the audience began to fall about with laughter. Naturally, their laughter spurred me on to new feats of lumpen-footed agility and, once started, I couldn't stop—one pirouette followed by another, another leap into the air—and by the time I ended my performance five minutes later my audience was stamping its feet, roaring its approval, wiping its collective eye and here I was bowing towards them, cheeks flushed with adrenalin and pleasure. I had been waiting for this moment all my life.

∽

Not long after we arrived in Byron Bay at the beginning of 2000, an old friend living up in the hills had said to me: 'You know people don't move up here to further their careers. They come to access different sides of their personality.'

I liked that idea. I liked the fact that after years of earning a living writing about other people, I could, thanks to the *Women's Weekly*, earn a living writing about other people while at the same time exploring 'the foul rag and bone shop' of my sometimes troubled heart.

I don't think it's a bad idea for a man to do this—to dream, contemplate, reflect and allow himself the time to unlearn and rediscover whatever it is he thinks he might have learnt and discovered, to give over to the exploration of the inner life of his feelings, to the language of his own soul. My guess is most men fear this. Being swallowed up by the swirling contradictions of the heart. Not being in control of one's emotions. Losing one's sense of manhood because that manhood depends on knowing and being right and building systems and being able to rely on powers of reasoning and logic, especially in a world where occupation remains the cornerstone of one's identity.

I can't prove this but I suspect that much of the rage of men, much of the murders, rapes, domestic violence, suicide, alcoholism, sexist language, reckless driving or just plain sullen withdrawal from the world that we hear about every day, is, in part, a flight from the terror of whatever it is we men feel—and that perhaps true courage is to be found in taking the *via regia*, the royal road, inside ourselves. At least that was to become one of my rationalisations during my years in Byron Bay.

During the same period that the *Women's Weekly* was flying me around the world, I was also taking time out to search for meaning in other places. And if that meant occasionally dancing like Baryshnikov in Bali and attending a seven-day retreat run by a group called Path of Love, then so much the better.

Before I attended the Path of Love retreat in March 2007 I'd thought that being in Southern Lebanon during the 1982 Israeli invasion or running the gauntlet of Palestinian stone-throwers during the 1987 intifada was as hair-raising as things could get in this charmed life of mine. I'd thought that the incident in the mid-1990s, when media tycoon Theo Skalkos had snapped my cassette in half, smashed my tape recorder on the floor, then lifted me out of my seat and frogmarched me to the lift, throwing me against the back of the lift wall, had required a fair bit of nerve-steeling. (Yes, alright, I shouldn't have asked him in the first fifteen minutes whether he'd tried to bump off a colleague in a hit-and-run, or whether he'd deliberately set fire to his offices so he could claim the insurance, but how do you put those kinds of questions delicately?)

Well, let me tell you, those experiences were as nothing compared to the terror I faced during the Path of Love retreat in the hills behind the Gold Coast, where I found myself dancing and screaming and jumping up and down and yelling 'Hoo! Hoo! Hoo!' with people called Rafia, Turiya, Alima, Samved, Satyarthi, Shivamurti, Samopan, Satya and Samovar, and listening to meditations and prayers from Bhagwan Shree Rajneesh (aka Osho), a man once branded 'the most controversial guru in the world'.

Rajneesh had fled India in the early 1980s and set up a commune in Oregon called Rajneeshpuram, where some in his group—although not the ones I was with on the Gold Coast—would later be accused of waging the largest ever bioterror attack on American citizens. In 1984, in an attempt to gain control of the local Wasco County in Oregon, these followers had allegedly tried to incapacitate the voting population by poisoning it with salmonella bacteria. As many as 750 people were contaminated.

Some of Rajneesh's top aides had been charged with conspiracy to murder, wiretapping and the poisoning of public officials. Rajneesh himself denied any involvement, but such was his notoriety—he owned ninety-three Rolls Royces and preached open sexuality—that this son of an Indian cloth merchant was deported from America in 1985 on immigration violations. Five years later he died in Pune, India, hopelessly addicted to Valium and nitrous oxide, still revered by hundreds of thousands of his disciples, or sanyasins, worldwide.

In 1985 Rajneesh's spokeswoman, the viper-tongued Ma Anand Sheela, had given an interview to *60 Minutes* in Australia during which reporter Ian Leslie had raised concerns with her about the organisation's expansion into Western Australia. Ma Sheela, a leading conspirator in the Wasco County poisoning scandal, had responded with this immortal phrase: 'Tough titties.'

So I grant you, this was not a positive starting point to my Path of Love retreat, and it wasn't about to get any better when I realised I was going to have to stand in a room—photos of Bhagwan Shree Rajneesh staring down at me from the wall—and expose myself to a group of strangers.

By expose, I don't mean shedding my clothes once again. I mean shedding the mask of my personality and revealing everything—all the sorrow, shame, guilt, regret, anger, vulnerability and aching and craving I could lay my hands on.

'You must be bloody joking,' I said to no one in particular after the retreat had started. 'There's no way in the world I'm doing that.' And certainly not in front of people I had absolutely nothing in common with, nor any interest in ever getting to know. Why would I do this after some of the negative things they'd said about me when we first started?

I'd been standing in the middle of a horseshoe of twelve people and one guy had accused me of being an actor. He'd said he had no idea if anything I was saying was true. He'd said this unblinkingly, as if he actually knew me. *Fuck him*. The woman next to him had said she couldn't even look at me because, when she did, all she felt was fear. FEAR? OF ME? *Fuck her too*. Another woman had said she loved listening to me speak, but after I'd spoken she wasn't really sure what any of the words meant. *Learn to speak English, bitch.* Then the facilitator, a big German guy with glasses and a Kevin Rudd-like nerdish quality, had told me he thought there was a great sadness inside me. *What would you know, you big burping Kraut?* Another woman had piped up that I was like a guy in a bunny suit desperately wanting to unzip the whole thing and jump out. You know, be the person I really was. The guy next to her had said I was a court jester and then the woman alongside him had offered this pearl of an insight: that my intellect got in the way of who I really was. *Screw her and screw the lot of them.*

Things had gone from bad to worse. In the late afternoon all of us, some sixty people in all, were led into a large room with mattresses spread across the floor. And, yes, now I'm thinking exactly what you're thinking: group sex, just like in Pune, India, in the 1970s when Rajneesh was at his height and people fornicated in the ashram in experimental group encounters.

No wonder no one would tell me before I came here what I was in for. All they said was bring a water bottle, comfy clothes, a pair of house shoes, ear plugs, deodorant, mints, vitamins and plenty of courage. What a ruse . . .

So now they are drawing the curtains and turning the music up full blast and closing the doors. We are in a lock-up in the bush and they are putting a blindfold on me. 'No looking at others,' someone with a microphone says, 'just move to the music and feel into your own pain.'

What pain? You're the one with the pain, dickhead, not me. My life is fine. No abuse. No ill health. Parents who love me, a wife and two children whom I adore, friends aplenty, a good job, beautiful home. Lucky Leser.

Now I'm hearing people crying and shouting. I'm peering under the blindfold. Someone slides it back on my face. 'Just feel into your pain, uncover your wounds,' a man says over the loudspeaker. I think his name is Rafia. 'Feel the urgency. We don't know how long we've got. We're all carrying wounds deep inside us. Exposing one's weaknesses and vulnerabilities creates great fear. Will people still love and respect you if you do?'

What a load of shit.

Now the person next to me is sobbing. I think it might be that really cute woman. 'Oh my love, oh my love,' she's saying over and over, and I have no idea whether her love is the child or the husband or the mother she might have lost, but the music is pumping and I'm thinking I should try and fake it till I make it because everybody else seems to be wailing and moving to the music, so I start moving but not wailing and trying to peep under my blindfold but all I can hear beyond the deafening noise of Guns N' Roses is the moaning of the woman next to me. 'Oh my love, oh my love,' and in her plaintive cry something starts to happen. I begin hearing the cry of every person who has ever lost someone dear to them, and now I'm starting to think about my daughters and Merran and our friend Neil Roberts who died under a train in Queanbeyan, and my mother, who lost her own father when she was four, and all those relatives who were shot in the Latvian forest after digging their own graves . . . Why didn't they take the visas when they could? 'Oh my love, oh my love,' and now my eyes are beginning to smart and there's a band of tightness around my chest and I'm finding it hard to breathe and I think I'm starting to shake and now I'm crying. Fuck these people, they're making me cry. 'Are you happy now?' I scream at the top of my lungs, and my goodness that feels good, so I give it another shot. 'Aghhhhhhhhhhhhhh.' And I'm crying now. 'Aghhhhhhhhhh.'

I'm really crying, and I'm crying for my father and the loss of his mother and stepmother and country, and I'm yelling at the Nazis and the entire German race and I'm crying for my sister Deborah, and all the judgements she feels I've imposed on her in her lifetime and I'm yelling at myself, 'You arsehole, David, you fucking judgemental prick.' And now I'm crying for my brother Daniel, and my daughter Jordan who is lying in my arms—I can see her as a small baby screaming—just as she did the first nineteen months of her life, when nothing could soothe her, not her mother, not me, not the hush of a lullaby—and I'm crying for all the pain she seems to be carrying still in this hard-boiled world of ours. And I'm crying for Hannah and the sweet, tender, stoic nature of her heart and how it will be broken because in every life a heart has to be broken. And now I can't stop. I really can't stop and I have no idea where the tears are coming from because my throat and nose and eyes are a spillway of tears and mucus and I'm howling into the blackness of my blindfold and I'm crying for my wife and all the pain and confusion and sense of imprisonment she seems to have felt for years as a mother and as a wife, my wife, and now I am sobbing for myself and the uncertainty of my marriage and the terror of being on my own and the terror of losing my children and the terror of not sleeping and the terror of travelling because I might not sleep and the terror of not being able to hold things together enough to write my stories and to earn a living and to prove myself the man I think I need to be. And I am crying for the pain of the homeless and the pain of the refugee and the pain of all the broken-hearted souls, and the pain of that poor child who lost her mother last week and the pain of the Croat and the Serb and the Arab and the Jew, and now I'm on the floor and I'm actually hyperventilating and I have absolutely no idea where this tidal wave has come from and the big German guy who looks like Kevin Rudd is holding me in his arms and I'm thinking, Jesus Christ, I'm being held by a man I don't even know and what's worse he's a fucking German

*whose father might have once loved Hitler's Third Reich and he's
rocking me in his arms. Can you believe this? I'm fifty-one years old
and I'm blubbering and being rocked on the floor in a room in the
hills above the Gold Coast by a German man who may be the son
of a Nazi but who in this moment is a just a warm Hun with strong
arms and soft brown eyes.*

∾

I saw a lot during those seven days I spent with a group of strangers.
I can't tell you now what any of those people did for a living or
where they lived, whether their homes were in the countryside or
in the city, in an apartment block or a house. I can't tell you about
their tastes and hobbies or where they went for their holidays. In
most cases I can't even tell you their names, and certainly not
their family names, not that I would if I could.

But what I can tell you is how much pain and sorrow I came to
see underneath the surface of their personas; how much vulnerability and longing lay just to one side of the face they chose to
present to the world.

In the late afternoon one woman lay on the floor, softly
moaning into her bitter loneliness. She had moved to a distant
city and knew no one there. Her parents were dead and her
brother and sister lived far away. She spent her nights alone and
often thought of suicide. She had never known the love of a man,
and doubted she ever would. She was only thirty-five yet she was
as weary of life as a woman three times her age.

I can tell you, too, about one man, probably the same age as
me, with the handsome, noble bearing of a sultan, who wept in
my arms, neither knowing my name, nor caring to know. I cannot
say for sure why he cried but I suspect it was for the many parts
of himself that had never been able to cry before. I felt him crying
into the dark corners of hurt and anger he had never known

existed until now. I felt him shedding tears for all the mistakes he had made, for all the missed loves and lost loves that had slipped through his elegant hands.

In that improbable embrace it seemed to me like he was crying into a well deep enough for all of us to disappear into, and as I peered into it, I could see my own reflection.

12

LOST ILLUSIONS

As it turns out, the battlelines were drawn right from the start, although it's much easier to say this now, twenty-six years later.

I had no real grasp at the time Merran and I married in 1988 that I was marrying a woman of strong feminist principles and that fifteen months after our marriage, with the birth of our first daughter Jordan, the second wave of feminism was going to wash over us.

Merran had ambitions, dreams, skills and sensibilities I hadn't even begun to fathom.

'I hope you realise,' a friend of hers had told me one night, 'that your wife is a visionary. She's light years ahead of her time.' He was talking not just about her brilliant academic background in urban design and town planning but also her passion for—and commitment to—marrying art with architecture, collaborating with architects, engineers and planners, and enhancing the role of artists in the building of better cities.

I hadn't and I didn't and it took me a long time to fully appreciate the depth of this truth and how my own lack of spatial intelligence, in combination with my male biases (read blindness), prevented me from seeing what I needed to see.

The French have an expression for this. *Tout est au commencement.* Everything is at the beginning, if we care to look. Neither of us had cared to look when we had our first argument in Jerusalem in 1987. From memory it must have been a Sunday afternoon. Church bells pealing. A golden light fading over the Mount of Olives into the Garden of Gethsemane. The cool of the desert whispering through pine needles. It was my favourite time of day in the Holy City. The half-light that contained both the dying flare of midday and the approaching veil of night. Both an exultation and a lament. This was to be our first lament.

'What shall we do for dinner tonight?' Merran asked.

'I was just going to do something easy,' I replied. 'Get a couple of schnitzels from the supermarket, heat them up, a bit of salad, something like that.'

'Why don't we cook something?'

'Look, I'd really like to get this story done tonight. The *South China Morning Post* wants it by tomorrow morning. Can't we just go the schnitzel route?'

'We haven't prepared a meal together since I got here.'

'I know, because I've been working, and normally when I'm working I just get myself something simple and then go back to my desk.'

'Well, don't you think we could be a bit more creative?'

'I'm trying to be creative here and get this story done. Why don't you cook something, seeing as I'm working and you're not?'

'Because I think we should share these tasks.'

'But you want a proper meal and I've been getting by here on my own just doing the simple dinner thing, so seeing as you're not working and I am, wouldn't that be a supportive thing to do?'

'It might be supportive but it's not collaborative and I think we should be collaborative about these things. I don't want to fall into the traditional role of chief cook and bottle washer.'

'Yes, but if I'd joined you in Vancouver when you were living there and I wasn't working and you were I wouldn't have minded cooking for you, even though I can't cook half as well.'

'Well, I don't know that you would have. I think you would have wanted to assert your independence too.'

And so it went, back and forth, for the next hour or so, until we fell into sullen silence. Perhaps we ended up eating schnitzel that night or perhaps Merran capitulated and cooked in the kitchen, I can't remember. What I do remember, though, is the feeling that seized me at the time, but which I chose to shut out as quickly as I could—that some kind of crack had just appeared in our relationship; the portent of something to come.

Did I see that this was the stirring of a gender war, a huge political story played out in the kitchen, living room and bedroom of a late twentieth-century couple's relationship? No. Did I want to see that? Absolutely not. I had other political questions on my mind. My story on the latest American peace plan for the Middle East was lying half-written on my desk with a deadline looming. US Secretary of State George Schultz had just arrived in town, and the Palestinians were growing restless. The future of the Middle East was being framed while the schnitzels were defrosting. Yes, I think we did have schnitzel, but with a beautiful vegetable dish that Merran made. The perfect compromise.

In bed, later that night, we signed our own Camp David Accords with soft kisses and gentle declarations of love before awakening to a crisp dawn and the first rumblings of the Palestinian uprising.

What I can see now, though, is that in the early years of our marriage I had a lot to learn about honouring my wife's work and passion, not to mention understanding the ways in which she would help to create—and hold up—the platform from which I could launch myself at the world. Each morning I woke with that great, biting urge to push forward, to write about big, hemispheric ideas, but failed to see in the smaller, more incremental things how a family, how a couple, held itself together.

Part of the problem was that I'd never been a domesticated man. For most of my life, in fact, I'd grown up in the care of housekeepers—women like 'Aunty' Julie or 'Aunty' Marietta or 'Aunty' Heather: European immigrants who, in return for a new home in a new land, would cook, wash and clean.

In my Jewish mother's fridge, meats, chickens and cheeses would sit on the shelves for weeks at a time, squeezed behind the gherkins, gefilte fish, herrings, eggs, sour cream, bags of salmon patties and wilting lettuce, slowly turning rotten. My mother's storage system often looked like a freshly abandoned village in the heat of battle—cow pens smoking, chicken runs overflowing, dairy bails groaning under the pressure of bursting udders.

By comparison Merran's mother's kitchen was a textbook study in middle-class industrial efficiency, a disciplined, well-oiled operation where everyone had their assigned task and no one could shirk their responsibilities at the expense of the good governance of the family. And in the midst of all this, a buzz of merriment and good-humoured industry.

If you looked into my mother-in-law Jeanne Morrison's deep freeze you would find pre-cooked meals that had been prepared weeks, possibly months, earlier in a whirlwind of culinary adventurism. The deeper you went into the frozen bowels of the freezer, the more you learnt about what had gone on during another time in epicurean history. A chicken curry from the Palaeolithic era. A steak and kidney pie and chocolate mousse covered with Mesolithic ice. Gravies that had once been desserts winking from an interglacial period.

By contrast, unless my mother was cooking alone, or the housekeeper was doing it for us, my family kitchen always seemed mired in bungling discord, although the results were usually a triumph of taste over method. Somehow my sister, mother and grandmother would turn a simple meal into a conference of Versailles, or a Balkan stew, separating into different warring enclaves. Croatia cutting the potatoes; Serbia carving the chicken; Montenegro smouldering beside the sink.

I'm sure to them it was a way of communicating, but to me there was far too much Jewish matriarchal energy in the room for anyone's good. It left me desperate for clear Protestant air where gravies miraculously transformed into desserts, where sisters and mothers came together in a spirit of uncomplicated free enterprise. No terror of not having enough. No ghosts of Jewish ghettos. No meats turning green under the couch, stashed there in case the knock at the door came in the middle of the night.

No one gave me the manual for domestic competence or for love in the post-feminist age. No one warned me about how love and ardour can die on the Cross of Resentment. No one prepared me for the fact that marriage was going to test all Merran and I had by taking us to the barricades and beyond. Germaine Greer once said the real theatre of the sex war was the domestic hearth. I had no experience of this, unless, of course, you count the books you've read as experience.

For my parents there was no war, just the traditional cooperation, or *compliance*, of a woman putting her husband's interests ahead of her own, and suppressing her own talents in the process.

In my parents' apartment, to this day a testament to their neat domestic arrangement is woven into two little cushions placed on their respective pillows. My mother's reads: 'My family tree is full of nuts.' My father's: 'It ain't easy being king.' The truth of the matter, however, was—and is—that it was never difficult for my father to be king, and my mother's family tree was never full of nuts. Quite the contrary.

My mother's mother, Hansey Eizenberg, was a concert pianist. Her English-born grandfather, David Eizenberg, was a violinist taught by Czech maestro Jan Kubelík, and requested by Dame Nellie Melba to play her obbligatos whenever she toured Australia.

My mother's father, Bert Davis Klippel, was the son of Polish-born music publisher David Davis Klippel who, at the turn of the twentieth century, had set up a music-publishing business with the legendary Frank Albert. Together these two inspirational figures in the Australian entertainment industry had purchased the lucrative copyright to the works of some of New York's top Tin Pan Alley songwriters, among them Irving Berlin and George Gershwin. My grandfather took over the running of this business from his father and also set up Brunswick Records, the first company to press a gramophone record in Australia—of Leopold Godowsky playing his own composition 'Alt Wien'—in 1927.

In their capacity as music publishers and record producers, my maternal grandparents had entertained some of the world's greatest artists—among them the Gershwin brothers, Yehudi Menuhin, Sarah Bernhardt, Sergei Rachmaninoff and Leopold Godowsky. They'd employed cooks, maids, chauffeurs, gardeners and laundresses. They'd each owned a speedboat which they raced regularly on Pittwater. They'd thrown elaborate first-night parties on board yachts on Sydney Harbour and at the Basin on the Hawkesbury River, where they had employed a young out-of-work actor by the name of Errol Flynn.

Music coursed and quivered, therefore, through my mother's bones. She played it from the time she was five years old. She read music. She tapped notes and rhythms on her legs in idle moments. She knew almost the entire repertoire of Chopin. She studied at the Sydney Conservatorium of Music for five years under Frank

Hutchens and even, for a short time, wrote about it as a budding music critic for the *Jewish News* before marrying my father in 1952.

My father's family name, Leser, was German for reader, but my mother was equally bookish, and for every biography of Churchill, Hitler and Roosevelt, or every history of World War II that my father had devoured—and there were literally hundreds—my mother matched with the works of Proust, Flaubert, Virginia Woolf, Anthony Trollope and dozens of other great writers of fiction.

When I was a child, my mother worked for Davis Publications, the wholesale book company my grandmother ran after the music-publishing business was sold to Allens in the late 1940s. She would haul books around the city in the back of her Holden station wagon. Golden books, Sunset books, books on travel, books too numerous and too heavy for a woman to be carting around the city, bookstore to bookstore.

She would return home in the late afternoon, take to her bed, draw the curtains and then lie there for hours, a cold compress folded across her forehead, her neck and back aching, before my father would return from work to rouse her with his demands.

'Where are my shirts? Why hasn't my suit been pressed? Can't you be on time for once? Don't you know how important this is to me? We simply cannot be late.'

'Not those people again, Bern,' my mother would say. 'Who'll be there? Can't I stay home? I don't feel well. Bern, I don't feel well.'

My father, however, never for a moment seemed to consider my mother's aims and ambitions equal to his own, probably because my mother had few ambitions of her own that she could recognise. My father was a man of his generation and my mother a woman of hers, and over the course of sixty-two years (at the time of writing)—through six decades of real and unreal expectations, exasperation, communication, miscommunication, exhilaration and intense, heartfelt collaboration—they have managed to sustain a life together, so they found it just about impossible to understand their daughter-in-law's position, not just because their son was born of their blood and bones but also because they found the political contest that Merran and I became engaged in so foreign to them.

'Do you think you'd be able to shop and prepare a meal tonight?' Merran asked me one day when I was working from home.

'I'm not sure. I've got to finish this story.'

'You haven't cooked a meal in weeks.'

'I know. I've been snowed under.'

'So have I.'

'I know.'

'So when are you going to cook a meal?'

'When I've finished the story.'

'When will that be?'

'Soon.'

'How soon?'

'Possibly tomorrow.'

'Or the day after?'

'Could be. Not sure.'

Neither Merran nor I anticipated the turf war of marriage. Competing careers, colliding ambitions, children who needed love and attention. We didn't bargain on the exhaustion, the ill feeling, the loss of self. And it didn't help, either, that we had few, if any, role models to help guide us through these treacherous waters.

In my own case, even though my father had been honoured in New York by the American Jewish Committee for his promotion of human relations, even though he had constantly promoted and supported women coming up through the ranks of Condé Nast, even though he believed women had as much right to work as men did, he was still a man of his generation, deaf to the howl of feminist unrest at home, and possessed of a relentless, driving ambition beyond the home. That's how self-made men made themselves.

~

No one warns you when you come to Paris just what the northern skies might do to a marriage, how the bitter winds from across the Seine can snap-freeze the love or, at the very least, put it on ice. That's not at all what the travel brochures suggest.

It was February 2008 and this was meant to be the trip of a lifetime. Jordan had just completed her last year of school in triumph—dux of Byron Bay High—and was travelling through Europe for six months while her younger sister, Hannah, was enrolled for a term at the International School of Paris.

We'd been living in Byron for eight years. Merran was in between jobs, although with two strong job prospects beckoning; I still had my well-paid job with the *Weekly* and it felt like time for a change, time to create something new, time to give ourselves a dose of not just any city in the world, but the crème de la crème of cities.

Jordan was by now launched on a career path as a singer-song-writer. She'd begun playing piano at the age of five and had written her first song at thirteen, a sweet aching tune called 'Curiosity', which she'd come to hate and which I was always badgering her to play. At the age of fifteen she'd come to the attention of Murray Burns, keyboardist with New Zealand rock band Mi-Sex, who lived and worked in the hills above Byron Bay, and who loved to foster young talent.

Jordan became one of Murray's musical projects—and

friends—until she moved to Sydney and was taken up by Rob Hirst and Jim Moginie, two men whom she'd first heard as a babe in my arms, dancing in our living room to the sounds of Midnight Oil's 'Blue Sky Mining'. They would become the producers of her first EP.

Jordan's wisdom and empathy had always astounded me, and they came out through her words and music—songs of such depth it was hard to know where her grace notes rose from; almost certainly from her matriarchal line, but also from wherever the great mystery of song lurks.

Jordan might have cried for the first nineteen months of her life but she could practically talk under water. By the time she was two years old she possessed a vocabulary of more than 300 words, many of them orders that she would issue from her crib, like, 'Use two hands,' when I once had the temerity to cover her with a blanket using just one hand.

By contrast, her sister Hannah had been born with the most adoring—and adorable—disposition, a shock of blonde curls and a smile to melt the icecaps. Her first words were 'thank you' and from the very beginning she was an angel at our table and in our arms. From the age of two she addressed adults by their first name and smiled at strangers in the street. 'Hello, Sue,' she would cry out to one of our friends whenever she saw her. Fancy that. A two-year-old addressing an adult with that kind of self-possession.

After the difficult birth of her elder sister, after nineteen months of her sister's continual wailing, this younger daughter of ours had ushered into our lives something sweet and magical. She was a warm bundle of love who nestled in the crook of our necks to coo and gurgle with contented delight.

For her mother this had been nothing short of a miracle: this beautiful blue-eyed creature who found peace and refuge in her arms, who didn't push and pull from her embrace as her sister had done, but responded with all the ardour of a cub to her lioness. As she'd grown into a teenager, she'd become more of everything to all who knew her: more beautiful, more authentic, more accepting; more talented as an actress, designer and photographer; more composed, more consoling to those in trouble, more like her mother and more like a messenger, in fact, from a divine corner of the universe than merely our own flesh and blood.

You watch your daughters swell in their mother's belly, and you take soundings of them in utero, the first flutterings, stretches and wiggles. You rock them through their restless nights in the fog of your own exhaustion. You wake, not to the crack of thunder outside, but to the barely audible stirrings of your child in the room next door. You steel yourself through the endless soiled nappies, sweet odours at first, before they turn into something more threatening. You watch them take their first faltering steps with the same fascination with which you might have once followed your favourite football team. Every step a giant leap for womankind.

You watch them walk through the school gates for the first time, wearing their newly pressed tunics and shiny shoes, clutching their little school bags, and you watch with heart in mouth behind a tree, out of sight, to see if another child might come and talk to them. You bring them home when they're sick, tuck them into bed, make them soup, read them stories, stroke their backs, sing them soft lullabies in the late afternoon.

You watch your older daughter learning to dance, parallel knee bends, combination kicks and swivels, jazz runs and pivot steps; and your younger daughter turning up at the tennis court, all dressed in pink, barely as high as the net, then cracking two-handed backhands down the line to become the little tennis queen of her town.

You come home to find 'to the moon and back' love letters and poems from your daughters and lists like this one from Hannah who, even at age ten, knew the joys of ticking off her accomplishments:

1 Eat.

2 Finish my book.

3 Have a bite to eat.

4 Watch a movie (it's the weekend!).

5 Try and have a sleep.

5(a) Talk to Dad.

6 Download songs.

6(a) Talk to Mum.

7 Say hi to Jordan.

8 Have dinner.

9 Watch *Home and Away*.

10 Maybe watch *The Simpsons*.

11 Read more.

12 Go to bed.

P.S. To myself. Always have a drink of water with me.

You know—because you've played the horror tape in your head since they first emerged, head or bottom first, into the world—what it would do to your own life if anything were to happen to them. You know what you would do to anyone who harmed them. You know the joy that comes from seeing them happy in their skins, their homes, their schools, among their friends, discovering their passions, fulfilling their promise.

You hear of men who have walked away from their children when their marriages have broken down and you want to shake them from their apathy, indifference or fear—I'm not sure which—to remind them of the gift of their own children.

I'm not certain when things began to unravel. I think it was about four weeks after we arrived in Paris. I saw, just in the space of those few weeks, the seasons shift in our bedroom. Winter thawed into spring and the cherry blossoms began to bloom. The lemons in our garden were growing fatter by the day and the lifeless swarm of twisted vines covering the giant wall of our courtyard were now a mass of red and green. This was good, this turning of the weather, I thought. It might save our marriage yet.

Not long before this Merran and I had sat in bed together in the gathering gloom of late winter. It was the eve of our twentieth wedding anniversary—31 March—and the bells of the city were reverberating softly on the cobbled streets and flagstones. It was not far-fetched to wonder whether they were crying for us, although we'd done a fair bit of that ourselves on that very day, and in the frigid weeks leading up to it. One melancholy chime after another, easing us from winter into spring.

One morning I saw an army of handicapped people wheeling towards that great confluence of boulevards in the east of the city known as the Place de la République. From six different directions they came in their thousands, the greatest assemblage of twisted limbs and rolling chairs I'd ever seen. It was bitterly cold and as I stood on that avenue of bare plane trees leading towards the famed square—with all those gleaming statues and dates marking the glories of the French Republic—I felt ashamed for my own creeping sadness, especially when measured against the great well of suffering: the beggars with their hands raised in supplication in the piss- and spit-stained metros; all the lonely, dark-eyed women who bought their tins of tuna and their bottles of cheap Côte de Nuits wine before returning to their bedsits to pass the night alone.

Love, I suppose, is constantly shifting. One day everything looks possible, the next day it feels like the end of the line. You notice all the things that divide you rather than all the things that might keep you on track. You notice—because you can see the stark evidence etched into your wife's face—that she never really wanted to be here in this city, that it was you carrying the dream of Paris all along, foisting it, unwittingly, on your family. You realise that she would have preferred Spain or, better still, somewhere new, and how you are always hankering—interminably, so it would appear—for the same old places.

You notice, too, that she is always looking at art and architecture while you are still banging on about people and all their curious ways. She hates the cold. You prefer it now to the cloying heat of the subtropics. She likes Balzac. You prefer Hugo. She wants to cross the road where and when it suits her—in this case as you're still getting your bearings on Boulevard du Palais. You'd rather she wait till you've sized up where it is you're actually going, so that you can cross the road together.

At the time of our Paris sojourn Merran was a fifty-one-year-old woman going through menopause. I was a fifty-two-year-old man most probably having another mid-life crisis. She wanted to work. I wanted to put my brain in a jar. She had ambitions that had never been fulfilled. I had ambitions that were probably best shelved. She felt invisible. I sometimes felt too visible for my own good. She slept like a log. I still lay awake for hours. She slept in one bed. I slept in another.

Is that what happens to marriage after twenty years? Different beds and a preference for Balzac or Hugo?

All through our time in Paris I thought she would leave. Leave this life we'd dreamt about—*I'd dreamt about*—for many years, ever since I'd first arrived in Paris as a twenty-one-year-old backpacker. Perhaps she'd go to Barcelona and study Spanish for a few weeks, or take a side trip to a sculpture park in Germany, en route back to Australia to spend some time alone, to see what it truly felt like to be without the family she adored but who weighed her down. No, let me rephrase that. I think she just needed to get away from me.

'Do you want to go home?' I said to her one day.

'Maybe,' she replied.

'You can.'

'I know.'

'So go.'

'I might.'

All the things that Merran no longer loved in me. All that vaulting ambition, that thrusting forward, that certitude. All the prerogatives of being a male, of being born to affluence, of being the firstborn Jewish son, of being imbued with a sense that the world was going to look after me because I had a special place in it.

That was something girls from Hunters Hill were never made to feel about themselves, certainly not in a family of five daughters. And then, of course, there was the fact of my being a journalist in the age of media. It was a recipe for self-absorption, for walking around night and day with stories and profiles and the conflicting claims of ideas and people rattling around in your head.

'There's only room in this marriage for one of us to work full-time,' she'd said to me one evening in Sydney shortly before we moved to Byron Bay. She'd come home early from work to find our daughter in hysterics in the arms of a new au pair, the house in a mess, me still in my home office, and nothing ready for dinner. I think it was a champagne glass, although it could have been a tumbler of vodka, that she threw across the living room as she said it.

I didn't take all that in properly, just what kind of a death knell she was sounding on her own professional ambitions, although the bull's-eye shot from the couch should have told me. I was too full of my own stress and fatigue to notice, not to mention my own deeply held—but unstated—view that this was part of the natural order of things: for me to be the breadwinner, the provider, the protector of the hearth. Besides, by the time we were married, I was being paid more to do what I believed—again secretly—was a more important job. And a full-time one at that, because what newsroom would ever have viewed favourably a request to work part-time in order to establish equality at home?

And, of course, according to an old, primitive tape playing in my head, her work was not as important as informing the public and challenging authority and asking important questions and setting agendas and PROVING TO MYSELF AND MY FATHER AND THE WORLD AT LARGE THAT I HAD NOT SQUANDERED MY BIRTHRIGHT TO BECOME A HOUSE HUSBAND!

For years I didn't see how my ambitions—and the relative success that flowed from them—overwhelmed the woman I loved, and how these resentments began to collect like grains of sand in a shoe, barely noticeable at first, easily emptied, but over time accumulating in such a way as to make walking a little problematic.

Merran and I never managed to disengage from this battle, perhaps because it was written into our script from the very start. Merran had so many strings to her bow that at times it was impossible to say what she did—and where her target was—because she did everything so well.

What she didn't do so well was adjust to the idea that she would have to forsake many of her passions and skills for the hard grind of motherhood. That makes it sound like she didn't love our daughters with a fierce devotion. She did, and does. But she didn't accept being a mother as the full realisation of who she was, and what she was meant to be or do. It was a good part of it, but by no means all.

At our best I made Merran feel more beautiful than she'd

ever felt before—her words, not mine—and she made me feel tall and handsome, even though I was short and increasingly bald. I also made her feel more intelligent than she'd ever felt before—a surprise to me given that I always thought her way more intelligent than me, and certainly way more accomplished.

We loved the same people, mostly, and the same books, until Balzac and Hugo began asserting themselves. We enjoyed the same movies and celebrated the same music. She could sing Leonard Cohen's songs long before most people had even heard of the Canadian poet, let alone turned him into the cult figure he is today. She knew the fugitive touch of Keith Jarrett's piano-playing and the chameleon charms and voice of the Thin White Duke, David Bowie.

There was so much we shared. We were good for each other, until we weren't, until it became apparent that I would never be domesticated enough, that I would never cook enough or clean enough, or have eyes enough to see what needed doing around the house; that according to her own mother's code of keeping house, it could never be enough because a day's work was never done until the kitchen was cleaned and the light bulbs changed and the garden weeded and the laundry washed and folded and the children's homework supervised. And that beyond all this there was my ambition still bubbling away, still dimming her light while mine shone—in her eyes—way too brightly for my own good, let alone hers.

In the months of our Paris deep freeze I went to interview Germaine Greer for the *Weekly* in her lair in the English countryside. When I arrived there were white doves fluttering above the stone cottage and Germaine was picking sweet peas in her garden—a posy of soft, fragrant colours arranged in her weathered hands. It was a good omen, gentle and benign, but as I soon discovered, a cunning deception on the part of Nature and Woman.

Once inside her house, she'd slouched against her rustic kitchen island like a gunslinger at rest, legs spread, one foot up on a bench and a look on her face that alternated between good-natured tolerance and shoot-'em-dead disdain. The freshly picked sweet peas floated beside us in a bowl of water.

I'd been in training for this moment for thirty years—primed by the hundreds of interviews that had come before it, but, more importantly, by twenty years of marriage to Merran.

How could a man from the post-war baby boomer generation contemplate marriage and not consider some of the propositions first raised by Greer in *The Female Eunuch*—that marriage was slavery, that a full bosom was a 'millstone' around a woman's neck, that most men hated women at least some of the time, and that a woman's essential quality was one of 'castratedness'.

I didn't agree with all of it, but there was enough in Greer's excoriating prose to force me to examine some of the ways in which women had been oppressed over centuries. And I believed I'd taken up the challenge and retrained myself. I'd learnt to cook (a limited repertoire, I grant you) and to vacuum the living room (sometimes naked for that va-va-voom feeling); I kept the kitchen clean (in fact, I think I got a little obsessive about bench-wiping); I washed up after dinner; I tried to remember to shop more; and I worked from home for the better part of twenty years so that I could be with my daughters before and after school.

But the balance was still lopsided. Sometimes I would be away on assignment for two to three weeks at a time, leaving Merran to juggle the unending demands of home life—shopping, cooking, the girls' homework, bills, house maintenance, the garden—while still managing her own career, and sometimes necessary travel—as a public-art consultant, curator and project manager. Even when I was home the lion's share of those tasks would invariably fall to her because for me to think and to write in the way I needed to meant not thinking about the other things I needed to think about—the things Merran wanted me to think about, the things many women want men to think about.

Albert Einstein once said—and Merran was fond of quoting this—that 'men marry women with the hope they will never change (while) women marry men with the hope they will change. Invariably they are both disappointed'.

Many of my best friends were women. My editors, after those dark Murdoch days, were all women. The stories I wrote were increasingly about strong, brave, redoubtable, often unsung women who worked in the arts, politics, medicine, psychology, fashion and business.

I'd worked for Dr Anne Summers, one of the country's leading feminist authors, during her days as editor of *Good Weekend*, as well as Shona Martyn and Summers' successor at the magazine, Fenella Souter—all three of them large-brained and sharp-tongued, and as disinclined to tolerate conventional male thinking as Germaine Greer was ever likely to shy away from a scrap.

With Germaine Greer the challenge was just to survive. Even before I made the trip across the English Channel from Paris to interview her in the middle of 2008, I knew that no amount of research was going to equip me for an intellectual joust with the most outspoken feminist of her generation. She knew too much, thought too deeply (most of the time) and, for over four decades, had been speaking and writing on too many subjects—sex, politics, menopause, women painters, teenage boys, Aboriginal Australia, Shakespeare's wife, even the merits of football and Posh Spice—for me to imagine that I could ever properly do her justice.

So for three and a half hours in her country home we'd talked about her biographer, Christine Wallace, whom she described as a 'flesh-eating bacterium rolling around in her own excrement'; Richard Neville and his claims—false, she said—that she'd had a hysterectomy ('Who did it? A vet?'); her three-week marriage to Australian journalist Paul du Feu in 1968, during which time she'd managed to enjoy at least seven trysts ('I was not allowed to sleep in the bed with him on my wedding night. He made me sleep in the armchair. He was drunk and he was a nasty drunk.').

We talked about her alleged promiscuity—false again, she said—and the fact that she'd been proposed to by the same man a number of times over the previous decade. (Was she considering it? 'Absolutely not. I'd be more likely to marry my dog.')

We discussed motherhood and whether there were regrets over not being able to have children. ('I gave it my best shot. It didn't work. End of story. I don't know why Australians pretend [having a child] is a one-way ticket to fulfilment, because it isn't. I've watched my friends have children and I've never seen them suffer more than through their children. Either their children were ill or in trouble. Nightmare. Just endless agony.')

The closest Greer came to verging on the vulnerable was when she talked about her father, whom she'd written about in her book, *Daddy, We Hardly Knew You*. She'd gone in search of this man because, as she wrote: 'Daddy never once hugged me. If I put my arms around him, he would grimace. I clung to the faith that he did not really find me repulsive . . . If he had let me under his guard, I should have crept into his heart and found the wound there.'

As she'd delved deeper into her father's story she'd discovered, to her eternal relief, that she was not 'congenitally unlovable'; that, in fact, her father adored her. It was just that the war and his generation of men had left him incapable of showing it.

'That's why I started to write *Daddy, We Hardly Knew You*,' she told me. 'Because I was one of a generation of children whose fathers were literally speechless, who thought if they allowed anyone in closer, all the horror and fear and self-doubt that the war had engendered in them would just overwhelm them. So they were a silent generation.'

Greer's face softened during this exchange and the gunslinger glower melted away. At the end of our meeting I gave her a small gift of two jars of French jam which I'd bought in Paris before leaving. The vulnerability vanished and she said sniffily, 'Jam? I've got plum trees all over the place.' She then read the label on the jam and exclaimed, 'Jam from France? You mean you didn't even make it yourself?'

And this from the woman who hadn't even offered me a cup of tea.

In the years leading up to our Paris meltdown I interviewed June Newton, Helmut's widow. We talked about her marriage to one of the world's greatest photographers. There'd been many affairs in the Newton marriage—most memorably, in the early days, between Helmut and Maggie Tabberer—but June insisted no affair would ever have split them up.

'We never had an understanding,' June said. 'I would never have lived with a person where you had to have an understanding. If things happen, well . . . this marvellous French philosopher once said: "For the perfect harmony and happiness, learn how to let the wind blow freely between the cypress and the oak."' (The quote actually came from Kahlil Gibran.)

Unfortunately, by the time Merran and I arrived in Paris in 2008 the winds had stopped blowing freely.

One afternoon we carried the awful weight of our undoing

into Joël Robuchon's famed eatery off Rue du Bac. No sooner did we sit down than we started arguing and then crying into our foie gras and scallop carpaccio. We stared forlornly at the chestnut cream soup that followed, sat in funereal silence through the *assiettes* of *ris de veau* and *agneau de lait*, and then wept some more as the passionfruit soufflé arrived, before finally stumbling out into the gloaming and back to our apartment. As I lay in bed that night I realised for the first time that our marriage might well and truly be over.

The international economy looked finished as well. By the time Hannah was completing her school term at the end of June 2008, Bear Stearns, the New York-based global investment bank, had just collapsed and the US government was only a few months away from bailing out the government-sponsored enterprises Fannie Mae and Freddie Mac. Lehman Brothers, the once venerable institution, was about to file for bankruptcy. The financial world was falling off a cliff and, with it, went my contract with the *Australian Women's Weekly,* not to mention tens of millions of other jobs around the world.

At the beginning of July, Hannah and Merran returned to Australia while Jordan went on to Belgium, Holland and Hungary for a series of music festivals.

I'm not sure how much of their parents' distress our daughters saw, let alone understood. Jordan was travelling with old friends from Byron, free from school worries for the first time in her life. Hannah had been making new friends from around the world, travelling all over Paris by metro, speaking a little French, shopping at Le Bon Marché and Galeries Lafayette, going to alcohol-free nightclubs in the first arrondissement.

I saw them all off on the same day and then returned to the emptiness of our apartment and the knowledge that Merran and I were no longer the couple we'd been when we arrived. We no longer laughed together. We no longer imagined the same future. Those five months in the fourth arrondissement had been the beginning of the end, although it would take another sixteen months for that end to arrive.

'I know her so well,' Gabriel García Márquez once said of his wife, 'that she is completely unknown to me.'

13

THE SILENCE OF
AN UNBORN LIFE

There were times as a little boy when I used to pray—small supplications to keep my father safe as he travelled, to stop him heaving each morning before work, for my mother's migraines to disappear, for Margot Adams to kiss me after Sunday school, for Bradley Pollack to stop beating me up at school. Some of these prayers had been answered—Margot Adams kissed me more than once, and Bradley Pollack and I became friends—but my father never stopped being sick before work and my mother's headaches and viruses never left her.

On Friday nights I used to sing the Jewish prayers at our family Sabbath dinner and while I knew these were prayers of gratitude for the bread of the earth and the fruit of the vine, I knew that any all-seeing, all-knowing God could see the impostor at our table. My prayers were perfunctory, and never ever did the curiosity about, or wonder of, something bigger or deeper stir inside me.

Even in Jerusalem, where I had spent so much time over two decades, the devotions and entreaties of the faithful spoke less to me about whatever God might mean, and more about the pain of the world and the pain of separation: the Jewish children of Abraham keening on one side of the Temple Mount, while on the other side their cousins, the Muslim children of Abraham, supplicating before the same God but bowing towards a distant holy city. Not just separate but implacably opposed to each other, calling at various times for each other's expulsion and destruction. And then a few hundred metres away, in the Church of the Holy Sepulchre, the various Christian faiths and sects—Greek Orthodox, Armenian Apostolic, Roman Catholic, Coptic, Ethiopian and Syriac Orthodox alike—waging their own bitter, centuries-old struggle for the right to control access to the place where Jesus was crucified.

What was prayer time if not a mighty battle of the sounds? The call from the minarets, the chanting of rabbis, the ringing of church bells, and all of them competing with one another for supremacy.

In the twelve months after our return from Paris I began to do a lot of praying. I prayed that my wife would feel the burden of our marriage lifting and that for what remained of my parents' lives they would find peace of mind. I prayed for my daughters' happiness and good health and sense of purpose and that I, their father, would always be part of their lives; that I, too, might grow old enough—just as my parents had—to know my children as adults.

But I'd learnt something at the Path of Love retreat in 2007 that had nothing to do with prayer being about reaching an accord with a deity, or petitioning an invisible God for favours. It had more to do with the idea of gratitude. Gratitude for the gift and preciousness of this life; gratitude for our good health, and the fragile contingency on which this has always been based; for the music you might hear because you have ears to hear it; for the wild invitation of nature because you have eyes to see it. Gratitude for the harvest of this ordinary day, this house, this food, these friends, these children, this conversation. Gratitude for the happiness that resides in the commonplace and the humdrum—in the *tableau vivant*—in the boil of a kettle, in the ferrying of children back and forth from school, in the preparation of a meal, in the ticking of the grandfather clock, in the prize of your own vigour and strength. Such is the terrible beauty of life that from one moment to the next, everything can alter, anything can happen to you or your loved ones, and this might bring with it the greatest blessing or the greatest devastation. William Butler Yeats knew this from the deepest depths of his melancholy Irish bones.

> Come away, O human child!
> To the waters and the wild
> With a faery, hand in hand,
> For the world's more full of weeping than you can understand.

In August 2009, a year after our return from Paris, Hannah's fifteen-year-old friend Jai Morcom was killed in a schoolyard brawl at Mullumbimby High after suffering massive head injuries. The community reeled with shock and grief, and my daughter entered Yeats' weeping world, as did all who knew Jai. 'He was a beautiful boy,' his father, Steve Drummond, said after the inquest found that his son had *not* been bashed to death. 'He just walked into school one day and never walked out.'

A month later, my oldest friend, David Ashley Wilson, passed away at the age of eighty-four. I had met him when I was five and he was thirty-five. He had become my best friend, although he had started out—and remained until his death—my father's best friend too.

I had loved David Ashley Wilson from the moment we'd met, from the moment I'd first sat on his knee and he'd given me the gift of his curiosity and interest. Did I like my school? What was

I good at? What did I want to be when I grew up? Did I like girls? (Ooooh, yuk, I said. Give it time, he replied with a gleam in his eye.)

We'd had a lifetime of conversations, in person and on the telephone, across deserts and oceans and through swamps and bayous, from Sydney, Melbourne, New Orleans, Washington, Jerusalem and Byron Bay, discussing the state of the world and the state of our hearts—mine much more than his—exploring all the intellectual and emotional regions that were surprisingly available to two men of such contrasting ages.

I'm not quite sure how to describe the love we ended up feeling for each other because the English language doesn't seem to do this kind of love much justice. Perhaps the Greeks express it better with words like *agapi* or *philia*. Words that describe the love a young boy might come to feel for an older man, one that continued right up to when the young boy was fifty-three and the old man was eighty-four, shrunken and soured by the great crossing he was about to take.

I adored this man. He was an ex-boxer, gardener and tradesman, but he was also a historian and teacher, well versed in the affairs of Europe, the Middle East and China, enthralled by nature and animals, full of wild and wonderful contradictions, so utterly human in his contradictions that he showed me how it was possible to be complete not because of one's strengths, but because of one's weaknesses.

I knew his weaknesses because he confided them to me. I knew how deeply insecure he had been all his life, how shy and mistrustful of people he was, how his father had beaten him and never, ever let the word 'love' pass from his lips—especially in relation to his son—and this despite his father having been a priest with a sizeable congregation in rural Australia.

David hated religion and scorned the idea of a deity or higher power, but would always sign off his phone conversations: 'God bless you.'

And here I was flying to Sydney for one last communion with my oldest friend.

'You know what today is, don't you?' he said feebly as I entered his bedroom in the nursing home.

'No—what day is that?' I asked.

'It's the day I die.'

'Are you ready for this?' I said, taking his hand and stroking his forehead.

'Yes, I am,' he replied.

'Is there anything you wish for? Is there anything I can get you?'

'You've done that,' he said, the light in his eyes almost out. 'My last wish was to see you.'

I couldn't—nor did I try to—control my tears.

'You know how much I've always loved you,' I said.

'You have been one of the great blessings of my life,' he replied. 'Do you know that?'

I nodded.

'I have to say goodbye now,' he said. 'I want you to promise me you will look after yourself.'

'Yes, yes I will. I promise I will,' I said, standing up to leave. 'Goodbye, David.'

He died the next evening.

A year later Jordan telephoned me one morning and before she could say anything, I knew something dreadful had happened. 'Dad,' she eventually wailed down the phone line, 'Ben is dead. He died last night in a car accident.'

Ben Donohoe, her boyfriend Nick's closest friend, had been hitchhiking home the previous night with a friend after a late work shift. He didn't even have time to secure his seatbelt before the driver pressed his foot to the pedal and said, 'Strap yourselves in, guys. You're in for the ride of your life.'

'Slow down, slow down!' they'd screamed as the Volvo station wagon hit 150 kilometres an hour in a 50 zone before jumping the kerb and slamming into a tree. Ben was thrown through the windscreen, and his body found later in a flowerbed.

Heartbreaking deaths; shocking deaths; angry deaths; reckless deaths; ugly, confronting deaths; chance deaths; accidental deaths; high speed, out-of-control deaths; defiant deaths; premature deaths; long-overdue deaths; surrendering, gracious, accepting, sublime, fearless deaths.

Marcel Proust put it well when he wrote in *Remembrance of Things Past*:

> We may indeed say that the hour of death is uncertain, but when we say this we think of that hour as situated in a vague and remote expanse of time; it does not occur to us that it can have any connection with the day that has already dawned and can mean that death may occur this very afternoon, so far from uncertain, this afternoon whose timetable, hour by hour, has been settled in advance.
>
> One insists on one's daily outings, so that in a month's time one will have had the necessary ration of fresh air; one has hesitated over which coat to take, which cabman to call; one is in the cab, the whole day lies before one, short because one must be back home early, as a friend is coming to see one; one hopes it will be as fine again tomorrow; and one has no suspicion that death, which has been advancing within one on another plane, has chosen precisely this particular day to make its appearance!

It seems to me we are surrounded by heartbreak and sorrow, and the more the years accrue, the more space we need inside ourselves for the black tide that is flowing our way—at its potential worst the loss of our children, but also the loss of parents and friends, the loss of memory, the loss of health, the loss of opportunity, the loss of time. Just a series of losses and farewells writing their signatures of grief and sorrow onto our faces.

~

In early November 2009, Merran and I separated after nearly twenty-two years of marriage. During the previous few months we had floated the idea of 'living apart together'—being together on weekends but spending time apart during the week. It made more sense to Merran than to me. Jordan was living in Sydney, Hannah was possibly going to boarding school the following year. (She did and she hated it and we pulled her out after less than one term.) We could be social pioneers, marital pacesetters, acknowledging the travails and challenges of modern life by changing our living arrangements while still being in the relationship.

Counselling—with two different therapists—had failed spectacularly. Reading Esther Perel's *Mating in Captivity* hadn't helped much either. 'Today, we turn to one person to provide what an entire village once did: a sense of grounding, meaning, and continuity. At the same time, we expect our committed relationships to be romantic as well as emotionally and sexually fulfilling. Is it any wonder that so many relationships crumble under the weight of it all?'

Ours did. I think Merran saw in me all the hallmarks of my father, a man whose drive and self-absorption, she believed, had blinded him to the needs of his own wife, my mother. My mother had never seen her life quite like that. In many ways she'd relished the opportunities my father had given her, but I think it's true to say that she saw the greatest part of her happiness as being in the home, not in the workplace.

Merran didn't want to suffer the same fate. The struggle to have the career she wanted—and deserved—and to still be the mother she needed to be was a source of daily conflict to her and she blamed me for this. Had I been a lot more, or a lot less, of all the things I was and wasn't, her life would have been easier. Her career would have flourished, her burden been lightened. This had been the background noise to our relationship right from the beginning, and in a moment of clarity I had seen this for what it was: a view of me that I didn't think would ever change, perhaps because it was true.

So one evening in early November I told the woman I loved that I was leaving, and that I was going to go and live in my mother's cottage in Federal, twenty-five minutes' drive up into the hills from Byron. My mother had bought this beautiful weatherboard home eight years earlier but rarely used it, mainly because my father never much liked it. I didn't know whether this time apart would last for weeks, months or forever, only that something had to change.

A few days later I told Jordan and we cried together on the phone. She said: 'Dad, I just want you and Mum to be happy and I will love you no matter what.'

Jordan was twenty years of age and was crying not only for herself—and for us, her parents—but also for Hannah, who was going to hear the news later that afternoon. 'I feel so bad for Hannah that she won't have what I had,' she sobbed into the phone. 'She won't have the love I have known.'

I told her that perhaps she was right, but also that Hannah has an older sister—one who could wrap her in her arms when the world felt too much for her, when things no longer made sense.

I dreaded that afternoon with Hannah. I shrank from seeing my younger daughter's face crumble as I told her I was leaving. I dreaded the thought of causing her this anguish, of vacating the space in her life I had always filled and cherished, and that I knew she assumed was one of life's immutable laws. No more lying on her bed in the early evenings and talking to her about her day at school. The boring teacher. The boys that wouldn't grow up. The dreams of Christmas holidays and shopping sprees. No more going to our corner coffee house, the Top Shop, in the morning for raspberry and banana smoothies. No more afternoons helping her with her French lessons and English assignments. No more weekends talking to her before she went out with her friends, her asking me whether the dress looked good, whether the black shoes matched, whether the gold or silver chain worked better. All those daily rituals would end.

That afternoon, I asked Hannah to sit with us in the living room.

'Darling, we have some bad news,' I began. 'I have decided to move out. Mum and I still love each other very much and this has nothing to do with our love for you, but Mum and I have some problems and I feel we need to have some time apart so that we can try to resolve them.'

Hannah was sitting on the couch next to her mother, the tears raining silently down her cheeks as she stared at the floor.

'Darling,' I said, 'I still love your mum. We're still going to see each other. We're going to have dinner next week for her birthday, just on our own. We'll have dates. You won't stop seeing me. You can come and stay with me up in the hills.'

'Yes,' Merran said. 'This won't look like anything you've ever seen or heard before. It won't be like other families. You wait and see . . .'

Our daughter refused to look at us.

'Darling, is there anything you want to ask us or anything you'd like to say?' I ventured, after the longest silence of my life.

'No,' she said, standing up. And she walked out of the room. 'Nothing.'

◠

It's raining today in the subtropics, after another long, dry spell, and there is this divine melody playing once again on the edge of the Australian continent.

I have begun to listen more closely to the riotous sound of birds at dawn, the piping of magpies, the squawking of the scarlet honeyeater and that wonderful cracking duet of the whipbirds—first the long note from the male, then the whip crack and those semi-tones of seduction from the female. These are sounds you only hear in the eastern forests of Australia and it has taken me fifty-three years to tune my city ears to it.

I have also come to understand better why it is that so many people stay together. They don't want to find themselves sitting in a cottage alone in the hills, drinking whisky long into the night. They don't want to face the terror of their own solitude, a solitude that, in my case, I brought upon myself.

For the first week in my mother's cottage in Federal I felt as if I was recovering from a car crash. I sat for hours on the verandah staring at the trees, sipping cups of tea, then slowly getting up to wander around the house.

I looked at old photographs of my parents, my siblings and me taken in London thirty years earlier by Lord Tony Snowdon, husband to the Queen of England's sister, Princess Margaret.

I had always disliked those photos, hating the way Snowdon had tried to make us look like imitation Bloomsburys, with my father sitting in the foreground in an armchair smoking a cigar, my sister plucking at a classical guitar, my brother holding a recorder that he hardly ever played, and me looking like a Carnaby Street dandy in flared pants and an army jacket, also strumming a guitar. Only my mother looked comfortable, sitting at the piano; she was the only member of the family who could actually play the instrument our royal photographer had assigned her.

There are other photos too—of my father as a boy, taken shortly before he escaped from Germany; of my sister Deborah at the age of twelve, lying on her tummy in the long grass with her best friend Alice, their faces turned to the sun. My brother Danny is here too, with his oldest friend, Tom, and between them our faithful collie dog Twinks, the dog we were forced to give away when my parents moved to London in 1976.

Unlike the millions of separated men who find themselves in a cheerless suburban bedsit, without furniture, without family photographs, without access to their children, I realise I have arrived in a warm place. A family place. And when my brother comes to stay—which is often now—he cooks thick vegetable soups and tends the garden and orders a tonne of wood which I stack on the verandah to keep the pot-belly stove crackling all winter.

Often my sister calls to see how I am. My beautiful, flamboyant, creative sister, who was with me for a few days in Paris when everything began to collapse. For much of our lives she'd often felt as though I got there first. I'd smoked before her. I'd lost my virginity before her. I'd learnt to drive before her. I'd married before her. I'd had children while she'd had none. I'd made a good living while she had often struggled. And I must have assumed that I-know-better role too, because she often felt judged by me.

In Paris, when things were bad with Merran, we corrected this. She held my hand as I cried into another glass of wine, and, God bless her, she actually cried with me.

In these halting, tentative days now, together with the books, paintings and rugs my parents owned, together with my music and these jottings, together with my walks along the ridge of a deep green valley, I am beginning to speak to parts of myself I'd long since forgotten.

Perhaps this is what happens in exile. You come back to what poet David Whyte describes as a central conversation with yourself, some invisible foundation you never knew existed.

❧

and nobody came
to see me.
Only the slow
growing of the garden
in the summer heat

and the silence of that
unborn life
making itself
known at my desk,

Excerpt from David Whyte,
'It Happens to Those Who Live Alone'

For fifteen months I lived in my mother's cottage and, at some point, I began to enjoy my own life again. There was never a day that I didn't ache for my daughters or dwell on the mistakes I'd made and the pain I'd inflicted on the woman I loved and still love.

But I began to look into the mirror with fresh eyes. I began cooking soups and curries, and chopping wood for winter, and lighting candles at dusk and playing guitar on the verandah and singing love songs in pale imitation of Leonard Cohen and Paul Kelly, and even writing a couple myself.

I spent days on my own, not speaking to a soul, and in the 'winter of my listening', as David Whyte once put it, I slowly started coming back to myself and began the process of writing this book. One evening I sat through the worst storm of my life. White gums fell behind the outhouse as gale-force winds and torrential rain wrought havoc up and down the coast. For four days the power was out and I kept the fire crackling and, at night, the candles burning.

I don't know why but I thought about the first time my parents might have danced together, and the song I imagined was Roberta Flack's 'If Ever I Could See Your Face'. I could see both their faces in the soft light of their swooning, the sadness that had visited both their lives, and the comfort they seemed to offer one another. I stood on the verandah listening to that song, and as I imagined the two of them dancing, a flock of geese flew past me, swooping through the valley. 'Look at the sky, Dave,' my mother used to tell me when I was growing up.

Occasionally friends would come to stay, people like Petrea King and her partner, Wendie Batho, and I would bring them tea in bed in the morning and Wendie would make a roast in the evening and we would sit on the verandah looking at the dusky light and talk animatedly, or sometimes just sit together in a blanket of silence.

It had been a lifetime since I'd thought of angels and how, if they were to exist, they might appear to us on this earth. On these visits from two of my dearest friends I came to see that angels were not the supernatural beings of our childhood imaginings; they were here among us, willing to visit us in our dark places.

Jordan was in Sydney developing her career and I saw her as often as I could. Hannah seldom came to visit. I was, after all, in the middle of nowhere. The house groaned at night. The roof crawled with possums and rats. The shower needed fixing and the floorboards had gaping cracks in them through which the air blew cold in winter. It was no place for a fifteen-year-old.

She also had her considerable anger to deal with. She was angry that I thought it only fair and proper she spend half her time with me and half with her mother. She was angry that I was hurt when she didn't come, and that I let her know this, and angry that I made her feel guilty. Most of all, she was angry that I had left, and she told me so one night, although this was two years later, not long before I decided to move back to Sydney.

'Dad, I've got a few things to say and I just want you to listen to me,' she said as she walked into my bedroom and stood facing me as I lay on the bed. She'd been building up to this moment for a long time.

'Sure, darling, I'm listening.'

'Good. I just want to say that I'm sick of you making me feel guilty for not coming and staying with you. I know it upsets you but I just can't handle it anymore. I love my home. It's close to school, it's close to the beach and all my friends live nearby and maybe I'm too attached to our family home, but that's the way it is. I just don't want you to keep making me feel guilty about not coming to see you.'

'But . . .'

'Just let me finish. You keep saying that I need to see you and you need to see me and that you don't want to be one of those fathers who is never around—and you're not one of those fathers, but it's always about your needs. Your need to have me close by, your need for things to be fair. What about my needs?'

'I know, darl . . .'

'Let me finish. What about my needs? I needed you not to go, Dad. I needed you not to leave our house. I needed you to be there with me and for me to grow up like Jordan did with both you and Mum in the house. That's what I needed.'

And with that she burst into tears and all I could do, as I too wept, was tell her that I was sorry, that she was right, and that I had been selfish. I told her that she was a courageous girl for telling me, and I was proud of her, and that if she could speak this truth to me then she would be able to speak this kind of truth to any man lucky enough to love and be loved by her.

14

'HAVE YOU GOT A JOB YET, YA POOR PRICK?'

'Have you got a job yet, ya poor prick?' Peter FitzSimons barked at me.

Peter FitzSimons, author, journalist, broadcaster, former Wallaby—a huge man with a huge heart and a sparkling wit, a living testament to Oscar Wilde's adage that 'moderation is a fatal thing, nothing succeeds like excess'—was calling, as he sometimes did, to see how I was.

'G'day, Pete.'

'So have you got a job yet?'

'Well, it depends on how you look at it,' I replied. 'But no, not really.'

'What are you doing?'

'Well, I've been working on this book . . .'

'How long's that going to take you?'

'Probably about as long as five of yours take.'

In 2009, at the time of Fitz's phone call, I was no longer working for the *Women's Weekly*, and German *Vanity Fair*, the magazine I'd been contributing to for a year, had abruptly folded. Italian

Vanity Fair had also stopped calling and suddenly my income had dried up and I was starting to feel like all those 'poor pricks' who, in these times of new technologies, discarded loyalties and financial collapse, no longer had gainful employment.

Fitz was just putting the finishing touches to his twenty-first book in eighteen years. He'd written biographies of Kim Beazley, Les Darcy, Nancy Wake, Nick Farr-Jones, John Eales, Steve Waugh and Nene King, to name a few. He'd penned sweeping histories of Kokoda and Tobruk, and was getting ready for the release of his biography of Charles Kingsford Smith, to be launched by the then Australian prime minister, Kevin Rudd. He had advances for three more books over the next five years, all of which he was to deliver while this book of mine was experiencing its own strangled birth rites. His publishers loved him. He delivered on time and his books, all written in a folksy, readable style, galloped off the stands.

In between writing his various bestsellers he'd produced regular feature articles for the *Sydney Morning Herald* as well as regular sports columns for the *Herald* and its sister Sunday paper, the *Sun Herald*, and juggled numerous radio, TV and speaking commitments.

Pete and I had known each other for about fifteen years and were friends in the same way boardriders were friends with the ocean. On a good day the ride was a sheer delight, a dance on the edge of a wall of glass where you could surf all the way down the face of the wave into shore. On other days the wave demolished you and it was all you could do to save yourself, let alone think of paddling out for more. Pete was a king tide of nature. One day, in the middle of the *Sydney Morning Herald* newsroom, he actually picked me up in one arm and carried me to his desk like a wounded goat he'd just stumbled across. The stated reason for this bone-crushing display of bonhomie was that he wanted me to read his latest story in the *Herald*. Now he was on the other end of the telephone wanting to know if I had a job.

Our conversation lasted no more than thirty seconds before Fitz signed off with: 'Well, good luck. Got to go . . . Love to the kids.'

'What about you, Pete?'

'Yeah, good, busy, racing.'

American author and historian Henry Adams once said: 'A friend in power is a friend lost.' He might have also said: 'A friend out of work is a friend entirely out of play.'

A few months before this phone call, Fitz and his wife Lisa Wilkinson (host of the *Today Show*) had invited me to join them at their table for a lecture that Ray Martin was delivering in honour of Andrew Olle, the late, great radio and television journalist. The night was memorable for a number of reasons, including Ray Martin's fine encapsulation of what a dreadful year 2008 had been for journalists: hundreds of sackings and forced redundancies, newspaper closures and cancelled television programs.

Another reason it was memorable—for me, anyway—was that Peter and Lisa had seated me next to Joe Hockey, still a year away from his grab for the Liberal leadership, and five years away from becoming Federal treasurer in a Tony Abbott-led government.

Hockey had turned to me between the crayfish entrée and the grilled beef main and asked me what I did for a living. I told him I was a writer. He told me he'd never heard of me. That hurt. I found myself telling him about a couple of stories I'd written in the past that he may have read. He had. He nodded. He seemed to approve. I felt validated but I hated every second of the conversation. I hated that I wanted him to know who I was, or who I had once been. I hated that he looked around the table with the gaze of a man who knew he was sitting in the wrong place talking to the wrong person.

There were days when I knew I was part of the conversation. It was a small part, mind you, but a part nonetheless. Then I left the conversation and tried to create a different one, one that involved raising two daughters in Byron Bay, travelling the world for the *Australian Women's Weekly*, becoming a caricature of a man having a mid-life crisis and, finally, trying to make sense of my own life by assembling the pieces of my father's. That's how this began—trying to excavate my father's life.

'It's a wise child who knows his own father,' Telemachus told the goddess Athena in Homer's *Odyssey*, and to me it seemed the noble thing, the right thing, for me to try to do, until I realised that I couldn't try to know him without knowing myself. That's because each of us, father and son, are helplessly and permanently contained in the other; and, in my case, every quest for professional recognition, every attempt at rebellion, every effort to throw off my father's yoke in order to fashion my own life, has taken me closer to him without my realising it. Until now.

The following year dawned with slightly more promise. In 2010 the *Women's Weekly*'s new editor, Helen McCabe, called out of the blue to invite me to return to the magazine. It was two years after the GFC and she was offering me a contract for less than half the amount I'd been earning prior to the economic meltdown. The print media was beginning to feel like the asbestos industry in its phasing-out days. Journalists were finding themselves out of work, or choosing redundancy packages that were never going to come again. News Corporation was about to be mired in a sensational hacking scandal and Gina Rinehart was circling the once-proud Fairfax mother ship, with some of the best journalists in the country eventually deserting en masse.

I took the job with the *Weekly* and although there were some choice assignments—an interview with Ingrid Betancourt after her release from captivity in the Amazon rainforest; a cloak-and-dagger meeting in Sydney with Somalia's pin-up anti-Islamist, Ayaan Hirsi Ali; an audience with Meryl Streep in New York—the pickings were slim and the stories no longer challenging.

I joined a documentary team with director Ian Darling to make *Stories of Me*, a film about Paul Kelly, and began writing features again for *Good Weekend*. In the midst of this I also returned to Israel with the notion of trying to forge some small peace between Israelis and Palestinians. I know that sounds both grandiose and pathetic, but I wanted to introduce some of my Israeli friends to a group of Palestinians.

One of the Palestinians had been a former member of Hamas, another a former armed operative in Yasser Arafat's PLO. Both had spent years in Israeli prisons before deciding, on their release, that instead of trying to kill their enemy, they might try to talk to them. The third Palestinian, a mother and teacher—but a radical in the eyes of the Jewish state—was living in the sealed West Bank town of Ramallah. She, too, wanted to know Israelis better.

We met—four Jews and three Arabs—late one afternoon in a petrol station in Jericho, in Area C of the occupied West Bank. It was Ramadan, and the muezzin's prayer had just announced approaching nightfall. We sat on plastic chairs, away from the petrol bowsers, telling each other about our lives, and at the end we exchanged phone numbers and embraced one another with the promise of continued contact.

What had I, this son of Zionists, been looking for all these years? Some sign that this land of haunting beauty and unbearable sadness and sorrow could also, in the case of Jerusalem, live up to its name as the City of Peace; that it could become the New Jerusalem of our highest ideals, rather than the Old Jerusalem of treachery, suspicion and holy murder. I still cling to the Talmudic idea that 'whoever saves a life saves an entire world'.

After this I enjoyed some light relief on the Greek island of Lesbos, birthplace of Sappho, the most famous of the love poets of ancient Greece, and named by Plato as the 'tenth muse' and goddess who had inspired all the arts. Sappho's poetry sang paeans to the loveliness of women, and this was reason enough for thousands of women, many of them lesbians, to make the pilgrimage each year to the northern Aegean.

I arrived from Tel Aviv a few weeks before the International Women's Festival, but just in time for a workshop in a small community called Afroz, just north of the seaside village of Skala Eressos. I had heard that Afroz was a gorgeous place, surrounded by mountains and set in a valley of olive trees. It had been established by followers of Osho, and you could spend days meditating, learning about nutrition and studying ayurvedic massage, self-hypnosis and 'prana' healing. You could analyse the polarities of your 'inner man' and 'inner woman', learn how to 'die before you die', or you could bypass all this and just enter the 'tantra lifestyle' with Svarap and Premartha. That's what I decided to do.

When I walked into the tantric sex room there were about forty people there, men and women from all over the world, fully clothed and, to my delight, not a single person I knew, nor was ever likely to see again.

Svarap and Premartha were already explaining the wisdom of tantra when I arrived. 'Tantra taps into our sexual energy,' said Premartha, a lithe and fetching beauty. 'It rekindles passion. It lights the long-lost fire. You need to keep it slow. Pay attention to your breath. Learn to trust. Feel into your chakras, your energy channels.'

After these initial briefings Svarap and Premartha asked us to move around the room without speaking, then to stop suddenly and sit cross-legged in front of the person we found ourselves facing.

'Now look into each other's eyes,' Svarap instructed, 'and hold your gaze and breathe slowly and deeply. Feel yourself gazing deep into the other's soul. Trust the process.'

The woman opposite me was pale-skinned, with bright blue eyes, her brown hair falling around her shoulders. She was petite and lovely, and she was staring at me with an ironic smile. I stared back, concentrating on my breathing, and the longer I breathed and gazed, the more beautiful my pale, blue-eyed companion became. We sat like this for five minutes.

'Now stand opposite each other and hold each other's gaze,' said Premartha. 'Harmonise your breathing with your gaze. One of you will become a mountain; the other will bend like a branch in the wind into this mountain. The branch will surrender. The mountain will stand firm.'

My new friend began falling into my arms, sighing heavily as my base chakra starting murmuring from behind its thread-bare fortress (I was wearing drawstring cotton pants). We stood like this for another five minutes, heart to heart, breast to breast, groin to groin, taking in the rhythms of each other's inhalations and exhalations.

Then it was my turn to bend into the arms of this stranger. More breathing. More breast to breast and groin to groin. More rumblings from the lower chakra.

'Now we'd like you to take it in turns sitting with each other like this,' said Svarap, as Premartha straddled Svarap and wrapped her tawny legs around her loin-clothed partner. 'And just keep breathing.'

We still hadn't spoken to each other. I didn't know her name, nor where she was from, but she was now sitting in my lap with her legs wrapped around me, and her yoni—*yes, her yoni*—and my lingam in rather generous and receptive proximity to one another. She began to whimper. I began to think this was possibly the greatest afternoon of my adult life and that Sappho, goddess of all poets, was blessing me from the celestial light.

We ended up at the nudist beach that afternoon. The Aegean looked dead and otherworldly blue. Naked bodies yawned and stretched under a merciless sun. My new friend and I lolled in the shallows talking. I had my Speedos on. She was topless. She said she was an Austrian television journalist, and that she loved to read Turkish and African novels. She travelled a lot, and this was her first tantric sex workshop. Her voice was deep and husky, her English flawless. She laughed, a sound not unlike a Viennese waltz.

We circled each other and then she began swimming away in the direction of Albania. I stayed in the shallows, anchored to the shore by my manhood.

She swam for a long time before slowly turning and beginning her languorous return to Greece. I drifted towards her, longing for the cold waters to shrink my lingam. She drifted into my arms and wrapped her pale slender legs around mine. We trod water and kissed, and then spent much of the next two days together. Just before we said goodbye she told me her name was Sabine.

On 17 November 2012 I left Byron Bay, having stayed twelve years longer than I'd ever intended. The last story I wrote from the region turned out to be a good prompt for my departure. It was a piece for *Good Weekend* on Serge Benhayon, a former tennis coach from Alstonville who'd become an 'energy healer' after realising he was the reincarnation of Leonardo da Vinci, St Peter, Pythagoras and Imhotep, the twenty-seventh-century BC

Egyptian High Priest. (He also came to see that his daughter, Simone, a former swimming teacher, was the reincarnation of Winston Churchill.)

Byron Bay was full of people who talked about 'energy' and, if truth be known, I'd become one of them, but Serge Benhayon's claims to know what food was energetically sound, what music, what books, what works of art were permissible to his followers on the basis of their 'energetic integrity' was a bridge too far—even though, as an old Elvis fan myself, I was intrigued by his assertion that Elvis had returned to earth as 'an esoteric being'.

Where was he now? I asked, barely disguising my incredulity.

'Somewhere,' Benhayon replied.

In the world today?

'Yeah.'

Where do you think?

'I don't disclose things like that.'

Is he in America?

'No.'

Africa?

'No.'

Is he near Alstonville?

'No.'

Is he in Australia?

'He's in Asia somewhere.'

Asia's a big place. Can we narrow it down?

'I don't know that . . . All I'm doing is presenting it esoterically.'

And all I was doing now was heading away from Serge Benhayon as fast as I could. A few weeks later I drove down the coast with my old school friend Rob Hirst, who had rented us his house for those first five years of our 'sea change' and who, over the years, had proved himself to be one of our most faithful friends.

He'd flown up the night before my departure so that he could accompany me on what he knew would be one of the longest drives of my life. A few nights earlier I'd said goodbye to some of the people who had helped make Byron Bay the place it had been, the place that at one stage I'd thought I'd never leave. A dinner party had been held in my honour and everyone had made a speech, including Merran, who'd warmly wished me well.

I was moving back to Sydney to be closer to family and friends, and to enter a new conversation that was to prove a very, very long way from Leonardo da Vinci's esoteric healing, tantric sex work-shops or Path of Love retreats. It was, in fact, a curious path back to my father's door via a global executive search firm called Egon Zehnder, named after its Swiss German founder.

Egon Zehnder, the firm not the man, had asked me to write a history of the organisation to commemorate its fifty-year anni-versary, and although I knew absolutely nothing about executive search and next to nothing about business, I had known of Egon Zehnder since the late 1970s, when my father had taken over as managing director of British Condé Nast. 'This man, Egon Zehnder,' he told me on several occasions, 'is one of the warmest, most charming and intelligent men I've ever met.'

Egon Zehnder was in the business of finding executives for leading corporations around the world. He'd started out with one office in Zurich in 1964 and over the succeeding half-century had spread to sixty-eight offices in forty-one countries. His organisation's client list was a who's who of market leaders and, during his heyday at Condé Nast, my father had been one of them, employing the services of Egon Zehnder to find senior executives for Condé Nast's expanding global operations. This was a new challenge, a point of entry into a world I'd always resisted but that had irrevocably shaped me.

Like my father, Egon Zehnder had been born between the Great War and the rise of Adolf Hitler and, like my father, revered Winston Churchill and great military figures like Montgomery of Alamein, General George Marshall and the legendary General George Patton. Also like my father, Egon Zehnder was a gentleman possessed of Old European values who had started out in business during a time when permanent careers and institutional loyalty had counted for something; when perfectly viable businesses hadn't been gutted or abandoned, their employees set adrift, purely to prove to the market that they were capable of change; when people visited each other in their offices rather than sent emails; when handwritten notes of thanks weren't considered quaint; when men stood up for women as they walked into a room; when mutual commitment bound people together, not just in the family but in the workplace; when organisations were informed by shared principles and beliefs.

Both men came from a rarified time and place in history. Both were trans-Atlantic figures, members of—or with visiting rights to—the best clubs in Europe and the United States; men whose wardrobes were full of the finest Italian or English suits and ties; men who loved to flirt shamelessly—and did so elegantly—with beautiful women; men who drank kirsch and cognac and smoked cigars after lunch; men who knew all the movers and shakers, concierges and maître d's in all the great capitals of the world; men whose networking skills were so sublime that even if they'd ended up somewhere like Phnom Penh they would have been able to call on someone to meet them for dinner, most probably the French or US or Australian ambassador.

All my adult life I had walked past a framed list of my father's 'philosophies and convictions' on the living-room wall without ever paying it any heed. Just before I left for Europe to interview

Egon Zehnder I took a good look at it. Full of simplistic homilies and aphorisms, it spoke nonetheless to a value system—and a fading world—that my father had always stood for and that was now revealing itself to me through the life of an eighty-three-year-old Swiss German.

> Avoid having your ego so close to your position that when your position falls your ego goes with it.
> Get mad, then get over it.
> Don't let adverse facts stand in the way of a good decision.
> Share credit.
> Check small things.
> Have a vision. Be demanding.
> Don't take counsel of your fears or naysayers.
> Perpetual optimism is a force multiplier.
> Remain calm. Be kind.

The night before I flew to Europe I had dinner with my parents and my sister Deborah. It was the first time in thirteen years that, together with my brother Danny, we'd all found ourselves living in the same city.

Ram Dass, the contemporary American spiritual teacher, once observed: 'If you think you're enlightened, go spend a week with your family', and this particular dinner was a reminder of that shining truth.

'It's wheat-free,' my sister says, bringing the vegetarian lasagne, brown and sizzling in its dish, into the living room as my parents and I sit glued to the news and Leigh Sales' latest interrogation on *The 7.30 Report*.

'What's the white stuff?' my mother replies, scraping it away from the eggplant.

'It's ricotta, Mum.'

'I see.'

'What did you say?' my father says.

'I SEE,' my mother says loudly.

'I see what?' my father says.

'I see it's ricotta,' my mother says.

'Don't you like ricotta?' my sister says.

'What did you say?' my father says.

'I SAID, "DON'T YOU LIKE RICOTTA?"' my sister says.

'What's ricotta?' my father says.

'It's the white stuff,' I say.

'Who doesn't like it?' my father says.

'Mum,' my sister says.

'I didn't say I didn't like it,' my mother says.

'Well, why aren't you eating it then?' my sister says.

'Because it's cold,' my mother says.

'How can it be cold?' my sister says. 'It's piping hot. Is yours piping hot, Dad?'

'Sorry?' my father says.

'IS YOURS PIPING HOT, DAD?'

'Yes, it's hot,' my father says.

'Mine's cold,' my mother says.

'Look, it can't be cold, Mum. Is yours cold, Dave?'

'No, mine's not cold, Deb.'

'You see, Mum? Ours isn't cold, so how can yours be cold?'

'I don't know, but it is,' my mother says.

'Do you want me to put it back in the oven, then?' my sister says.

'No, it's fine,' my mother says.

'How can it be fine if it's cold?' my sister says.

'What are you saying, Barb?' my father says.

'I'M SAYING IT'S OKAY,' my mother says.

'What's okay?' my father says.

'THE DINNER,' my mother says.

'I thought you said it was cold,' my father says.

∾

I have been blessed with a loving, caring family. My sister cares enough to spend four hours preparing a wheat-free vegetarian dinner for her family, knowing that her brother—me—has gone on a special cleansing diet and that our mother, if she's not on a special cleansing diet, should be.

She cares enough that after a busy day as a nutritionist and art therapist she is prepared to dash from her house in East Sydney to our parents' apartment in Elizabeth Bay so that our mother won't have to cook, and so that we can have a rare family meal together.

She cares that our mother doesn't like the ricotta and that her meal has gone miraculously cold. She cares, too, that her efforts have gone unremarked—by our mother, at least—and there's a pile of ricotta sitting on her plate.

Our mother doesn't care for ricotta, but cares that her daughter is upset with her. Our father cares as well. He cares that our mother doesn't like the ricotta and that her meal is not hot enough. He cares that he can't hear anything being said unless it's being shouted at him and that because of this he is unable to join in the conversation, not that this is a conversation he'd ever choose to join.

My father can no longer see through his right eye, but you can sense through his left that he's still searching for the glittering palaces he once moved through with confidence and style. Never a particularly fit or good-looking man, he was always warm and stylish, his thick curly grey hair—which he combed back with Fixaline—a distinguished companion to his black spectacles.

When he wakes now in the middle of the night, filled with indecipherable sadness, when by day he shuffles slowly about the house with his walking frame, unable to find things, calling out for help, demanding that people come, it's obvious he's having a mighty time trying to reconcile how far he has come from the lofty heights of Madison Avenue and Times Square.

People no longer seek out his advice because, as Victor Hugo once wrote, 'Those with an eye to the future flutter round the illustrious present', and my father is no longer an illustrious present.

Most days he doesn't surface till midday, although sometimes as late as 5 pm, and even then only by some stupendous act of determination. Who knows when he will leave us (he's booked the Australia Club for his ninetieth birthday next year!), but I can feel his immense sadness, even now, at the prospect of having to say goodbye to those he loves.

When I ask him how he is feeling, he says that growing old is difficult but he is in no pain. He then looks at me with the most loving expression and says, 'Often when I'm depressed I take out the letter you wrote me a few years ago. It makes me feel better.'

Do you remember, Dad, the first time we went to Germany? The Wall was still up and we had to go through Checkpoint Charlie. We ate a hotdog somewhere in the West and had a photograph taken of us doing so. We both ate simultaneously from either end and I think you got there first, mustard and ketchup all over your chin. We drove from Berlin down to Sondershausen, via Potsdam and Leipzig, to the town where you grew up, and from where you fled in April 1939.

You introduced me to Gerhard, your childhood friend. You showed me the house you grew up in on Von Hindenburg Avenue. You shared with me the stories of your youth—sad, broken stories that I took deep into my soul and that I carry to this day. Thank you for sharing your history, my history, with me. Thank you for explaining to me where I came from.

That was in 1985, four years before the Wall had come down, hammered, beaten, almost psychically commanded into extinction by a people desperate to realise their freedom. We had driven through Checkpoint Charlie, still a forbidding crossing point as opposed to the tourist mecca it is today, and into the cellar-dark coldness of the East German communist state.

From East Berlin we drove down through the north German plains into Leipzig, then west along the banks of the Wipper River into Sondershausen, in north Thuringia, where my father had spent his desperately lonely childhood.

We were inside the giant prison of the German Democratic Republic, a walled-in nation of seventeen million—one Stasi agent, or informer, for every sixty-three people—to spend a few days with Gerhard Braun, my father's oldest friend. It was Gerhard who, as a little boy, had been brave enough to play with my father when it was no longer safe to do so.

Three years after my father had fled Germany in 1939, Gerhard Braun had been drafted into the German armed forces to fight the Allies in Normandy. He was only seventeen years old. Two years later, in August 1944, he'd been injured and taken prisoner by the Canadians at the famous Battle of the Hedgerows at St Lô in north-western France. He'd been imprisoned first in London, then Glasgow, then sent by ship to a military hospital in New York before returning to Sondershausen a year after the war ended.

By this time a third of Sondershausen had been destroyed and the town was well inside the Russian Zone of occupation. Gerhard was arrested for failing to produce the correct documents and imprisoned in a small cell. He then escaped and ran forty kilometres through the night to his grandparents' house in the British Zone, where he stayed for the next nine months.

After this he moved to the university town of Jena in central Germany, where he studied optometry and met Helga, the fellow student who would three years later become his wife. It was not until 1959 that he returned to Sondershausen, now inside the new socialist-run German Democratic Republic. That was the same year my father had started Australian *Vogue*.

In 1969 these two men had found each other again through my grandfather's former secretary. Gerhard had sent a letter to my father in Sydney and two years later, after an absence of thirty-two years, they'd been reunited in this old Prussian garrison town.

This was where my father, Bernd Leser, had grown up and where my grandfather, Kurt Leser, was born, and my great-grandfather, Arthur Leser, a butcher to the counts and princes of Thuringia; and my great-great-grandfather, Moses Leser; and so, too, my great-great-great-grandfather, David Leser. This is where I came to bear witness to my father's early life, to get a glimpse of the boy he'd once been, to listen to him speak German, to stand in his shadow and the shadow of all the Leser men who had come before us.

15

THE NIGHT HAS A
THOUSAND EYES

In December 2012, I took a twin propeller plane from Vienna to Leipzig in a snow storm, hoping that the winds blowing in from Siberia wouldn't stop me from arriving in the land of my forefathers. I actually had no idea why I was returning, only that after meeting Egon Zehnder in Zurich and visiting Sabine in Vienna, I felt drawn once again to the Germany of my father's childhood.

In Zurich, Egon Zehnder and I had talked about his life and career and growing up on the eve of war, as well as his father's efforts to save desperate Hungarian Jews by concealing forged passports in his suitcase. As the bells from Zurich's Fluntern church tolled in the background, I'd thought momentarily about my grandfather, here in 1916, a sergeant in the German Imperial Regime injured in the trenches with shrapnel and mustard gas, being repatriated by his French captors back to Germany via Switzerland.

In Vienna, Sabine and I had combined our journalistic skills to try to find any living relatives of the SA officer who had saved my grandfather and father's lives. I had learnt his name—Erhard Greifzu—from my father but Sabine and I had been unable to find any of Greifzu's descendants. We'd talked long into the night about the fact that for hundreds of years, stretching back into the Middle Ages, there'd been a symbiosis between German and Jewish cultures, one that had represented the best of the German enlightenment with writers like Heinrich Heine, composers such as Gustav Mahler, and latter-day Hollywood film directors such as Otto Preminger and Billy Wilder. Until Hitler's ascent to power in 1933, these two cultures had been interdependent, almost inseparable, but by attempting to exterminate the Jewish people the Nazis had ended up severing the Jewish and German souls from one another. In the process, German culture had amputated a pivotal part of itself from which it had never recovered. It was just a theory, but it was one that resonated.

In 1995, when my father and I had visited Berlin for a second time, a local sculptor had invited us for dinner in his large ware-house on the edge of the old border crossing that had miraculously opened up six years earlier. Throughout the dinner the sculptor had peppered my father with questions about his early years in Germany and the views he now held of the German people. At the end of the night, this bearish man had taken my father in his arms and said to him tearfully, 'Bernd, thank you. Thank you for coming back.'

Perhaps this was why Germany now had the only growing Jewish population in all of Europe—some 200,000 and counting—because in some part of the German and Jewish souls, we were looking for one another again. And perhaps that was why I was back in Germany too—a son still carrying the body and soul of his father.

It was the first night of winter 2012 and the streets were frozen white when I arrived in Sondershausen. Gerhard Braun was waiting for me in the car park outside my hotel the following morning, wearing a beige parka, his grey hair combed back from his beaming, youthful face.

We greeted each other warmly, before lapsing into silence. Neither of us spoke the other's language, but we had an interpreter with us, Antje Weida, Gerhard's delightful great-niece who had travelled from Gottingen, 100 kilometres away, in order to translate for us while Gerhard took me on the Grand Tour of my father's childhood home.

Here was where my grandfather's textile factory had stood, before being destroyed during the Allied bombings of 1945; over there was the synagogue on Bebra Strasse—today a shopping mall—with its simple but beautiful onyx plaque honouring the Jews of Sondershausen: *Nicht Vergassen*, not forgotten. On up into the hills with their sweeping views over a snow-laden town, and the monument at the top to the fallen from both world wars. The wind biting, even my pockets frozen.

Back into town and there was my father and grandfather's thatch-roofed house, painted yellow now, with rosehips growing at the front fence and the hedgerows offering protection from the wind and ice.

Just two blocks away was the house of Erhard Greifzu, the SA chief, and the road leading down to the park where he'd come to meet my grandfather just days before Kristallnacht. Virtually a clearing today, seventy-four years ago it was full of oaks and bushes in front of a World War I memorial. Gone, too, was the park bench behind the bushes where couples once canoodled, or speculated on the fate of millions, or perhaps issued warnings in secret.

'This was a good place to meet,' Gerhard told me, 'because you could see if anyone was coming, and if they were, one person could go one way and the second the other way, and you could just say, if asked, "We are visiting the monument." Everyone knew the night had a thousand eyes.'

And then over to the three-hundred-year-old Jewish cemetery accompanied now by the curator of the local museum, Bettina Bernienghausen, who has spent years studying Sonderhsausen's Jewish community, even though not a single Jew lives in the town today.

'Here is your great-great-grandmother's grave,' she said, and there was the headstone of Seraphine Leser (nee Goldschmidt), the grand matriarch of the Leser clan who between 1858 and 1879 had managed to produce fifteen children before—so the story went—throwing herself out of the window on realising she was pregnant with her sixteenth. But on closer inspection of her grave, this seemed an improbable story, given that Seraphine died in 1889 at the age of fifty-two, and her last child, Harry Leser, was born ten years earlier. It was unlikely that Seraphine Leser could have fallen pregnant in her early fifties.

The snow was tumbling across the cemetery now and the chill was lodging itself deep in my bones. Gerhard followed me with his umbrella through this Narnia land of snow and gravestones, taking photos of me alongside my ancestors. He came here often, he told me, sometimes to inspect the plots, at other times just to sit in the adjoining garden and read.

'Your great-grandfather, Arthur Leser, is buried here,' he said, 'but there is no headstone. And this is Hermann Braun's grave and an empty one next to it for your great-great-aunt Sophie.'

How did he know this? Why had he made it his business to know? What meaning could he have derived from being the keeper of my family's history?

Later, over lunch with his son Harald and daughter-in-law Martina, I began to fathom the depths of Gerhard Braun, this giant figure burnished into the Leser mythology. The table was laden with homemade sausages and salamis, strudels and cakes, an assortment of chocolates, coloured balls and Christmas ivy, and four gold candles. In between bites of sausage and strudel, Gerhard recalled the period leading up to Kristallnacht, three years after Hitler's ascent to power.

'It only started becoming difficult in 1936–37. People began talking about my friendship with your father and my parents had confrontations with people who said things like, "Why are they still playing together? Why doesn't Gerhard have other friends?"

'But my father was 100 per cent anti-Nazi and everyone knew that. He later took an oath refusing to join the Volkssturm [the national militia comprising sixteen-to sixty-year-olds that Hitler set up in 1944] and was lucky they didn't shoot him.'

Gerhard and my father had become friends at the Goethe Primary School in 1931. The two boys loved to play with my father's little train set after school. At other times they would run in the garden and pick apples from the trees.

By the time they entered secondary school, my father was the only Jew in a class of twenty-seven. 'Nobody is alive from that class anymore,' Gerhard said. 'Just me and Bernd.'

In 1938 my father was sent to his Jewish boarding school in Coburg, and the next time Gerhard saw his friend was just after Kristallnacht, when my father returned to Sondershausen. 'Ernie was with him in the street and my mother saw them and said, "Look, Gerhard, Bernd is here," and I said to Bernd, "How are you?" And Ernie said, "Gerhard, we have no time, we have to leave."

'We only spoke for ten minutes in front of my parents' shop because Ernie kept saying, "We can't stay, we have to go." Your father was wearing a Star of David on his chest, just like the other Jews in town had started to do.'

'Bernd was lucky he left. There was another very nice family, the Simons, who had a ten-year-old boy. One night in 1942 they were picked up and then they were gone.'

The liverwurst, knackwurst and thuringer rotwurst are piling up on my plate and there are still five different cakes that I know the family wants me to sample. Martina is crying and all I can think about is how the cruel, miraculous fortunes of fate saw one boy fleeing to the other side of the world, to end up publishing glossy magazines, while the other boy remained at home to live under, first the Nazis, then the Communists.

Where were they, I asked, when the Wall finally came down?

'It was absolutely great. Absolutely great,' Harald beamed. 'We were living in a little flat in Sondershausen and it was night-time and I was asleep on the sofa and Martina's grandmother was visiting from Hamburg.

'Martina used to be a hairdresser and they had dryers on their heads and they couldn't hear what was going on, even though they could see the television. Martina woke me and I looked at the screen and said, "This is not normal. It can't be true. We are free to travel. It can't be true." And when we realised it *was* true, that we were free, my father and I drove to West Germany and bought a lawnmower.'

Twenty years after the Wall came down my father sent Gerhard the 732-page special edition of German *Vogue* produced to mark the thirty-year anniversary of its launch in 1979. It included a story I had written about my father's early days in Germany, his departure five months before the outbreak of World War II, and his return forty years later to establish *Vogue*'s presence in his former homeland.

The story surprised many who had not known of my father's origins, and he seemed relieved to finally have that part of his history laid bare. He wanted Gerhard to read the story, so he arranged for Condé Nast's Munich office to send what must have been the largest magazine ever delivered by the German postal system to Sondershausen.

Gerhard wrote to my father shortly afterwards.

My dear old friend,

Many times I have had your *Vogue* in my hands—and read through it again and again, thinking and reflecting, letting a long life pass by. For sure, my dear friend, I cannot simply read those lines because while I'm reading I see everything clearly before my face, pictures of that time, the surroundings. I live again through a time passed by long ago.

David has summarised your long life in only a few pages and . . . the reader can feel from every line how exceptional your life has been with all its ups and downs, with happiness and agony—and with your indomitable will to live and work.

When you were young, your home country was not friendly towards you (or the people at this time). Only a few continued your friendship, something you needed so much then. I know this too well.

Against all odds and through difficulty, we have established a friendship that has survived and proven of value for more than a lifetime. I would like to thank you for including me in your lines. I am deeply moved!

My dear Bernd . . . I hope that we will have the possibility in both our lives to see each other one more time.

Your old friend Gerhard

❧

There are many people who have absolutely no idea where they come from, nor do they much care. Perhaps they are less sentimental or curious about these things than I am, or perhaps they just feel freer to imagine their lives shaped by invisible forces, or shaped by no one in particular, least of all long-forgotten ancestors.

I don't know when it was I began to care. Perhaps I always did, although never enough, until now, to try to wrap my arms around this history of mine.

Perhaps my surge of curiosity was awakened on that trip in 1985, when my father and I visited Gerhard Braun in Sondershausen for the first time and he took us to the park where my grandfather and the SA officer had held their fateful meeting forty-seven years earlier.

What I remember most about that first visit was how Gerhard had guided us to a meadow with a long, sloping view to the lake and a park bench, almost hidden in the long grass; and how my father had taken my hand in his to describe the historic rendez-vous between his own father and the SA chief; how his voice had then caught with the emotion of its dramatic implications—a Nazi official daring to risk his own life for a Jew.

I have thought often of the peace and tranquillity of that park, and my father remarking on how curious it was that such a meeting, such a moment of menace and redemption, had occurred in a place such as this—all those concerts in the nearby amphi-theatre, and then boating on the lake nearby.

Perhaps this is when I was first struck by the thought that I was only alive and free because of a miraculous exchange that had taken place in 1938. And, in turn, that this exchange had only become possible because of an act of valour twenty-two years before that, during World War I.

❧

There is hardly a man I know who can speak easily or lovingly about his father. Some have been handicapped from the start because they lost theirs early, through death or abandonment.

Others tried for years, but encountered only confrontation and heartbreak. The majority were caught somewhere in between these two cold fronts, as if one wrong move by either side might suddenly bring the whole house down.

My father and I have had our stand-offs, our fierce clashes, but there has never been a second's doubt that he loved me, that there wasn't anything in the world he wouldn't do for me. Except, perhaps, give me the time that any child yearns for from their parents.

For years while I was growing up, I could never really understand his absences. I could never understand how dinners and cocktail parties and first nights could be more important than spending time with me, his son. I couldn't articulate this, of course, but I can see now how it fuelled my ambition, my underlying anger and rebellion, and my search for meaning in so many places—synagogues, temples, yoga retreats, tantric workshops, old Jerusalems, new Jerusalems, Paths of Love, paths away from my family's door.

I can see also how it fuelled a huge desire to do him proud. All my life—even in his presence—I have missed him and wanted him and carried an image of him deep inside me as a way of trying to bring him closer to me. I have, as a little boy—but also as a grown man—listened to his story, taken on his history, assumed his pain and ambitions, struggled with his multitude of ghosts, all in the name of a love and identification I could never quite name.

'What was silent in the father speaks in the son,' Friedrich Nietzsche wrote in *Thus Spoke Zarathustra*, 'and often I found in the son the unveiled secret of the father.'

Perhaps I knew from the time I was small the traumas my father had borne as a boy himself—small compared to what many endured, but considerable enough and beyond anything I was ever to experience. I'm sure he told me about how his mother had left the family home and his stepmother had died and how his second stepmother had helped him escape from the country that no longer wanted him.

In my mind's eye I could always see him travelling on a train by himself from Sondershausen to Berlin to visit his mother, dressed in lederhosen, with his name, 'Bernd Leser', on a small sign hanging around his neck, as he stared forlornly out the window at all the empty fields and grey tenement blocks festooned with swastikas. A little boy, mostly friendless, motherless and stateless, travelling on a big train through a terrifying fatherland.

Paul Auster wrote in *The Invention of Solitude*: 'You do not stop hungering for your father's love even after you are grown up.' One moves in the shadows of one's parents and, as a son, particularly in the shadows of one's father. If we all have, as Richard Freadman says, 'a core story to tell, a story that lies at the heart of all the stories', then maybe, along with the story of my grandfather and his Nazi friend, the story of my father has always been my core story. Because like Paul Auster, I have carried around my father's solitude all my life, and like Auster's example of Pinocchio's creator, Geppetto, in the belly of the whale, I have always had the desire to save him from this solitude.

I can see the weight my father has carried more clearly now than at any time in my life, and even though it was always his to carry, it has felt heavy on my shoulders too.

My father was—and is—a good man, in some ways a great man, with great flaws, great attributes and great contradictions. He was humble but at times impossibly lofty. He was deeply insecure but tightly wound and, therefore, seemingly invulnerable. He was an honest man, a loving man, and he had lived such a lonely childhood, without a mother, without a sibling, without friends for the most part, and he'd been mocked and bullied and banished at school, and forced to flee his country, and then he'd launched himself on a near miraculous path of reinvention, such that no one would ever have guessed he was once a little German Jewish boy exiled from his homeland.

But the truth is also that all my life I have loved this man and missed him in equal measure. Even when I was with him I missed him. Missed the times we'd not shared when I was young. Missed the words that might have filled the silences that often seemed to creep over our conversations. Missed the times together that could have occurred when I was in Australia and he was living in England and America, rising further and further to the top of an impossibly glamorous profession, and further and further away from me.

I know that when he is gone, I will miss him even more—for the times we will never share again, and for the times we could have shared but didn't when he was still alive.

My father gave me a gift that I don't often see other men being handed. The gift of feeling 'beloved on this earth', as Raymond Carver once put it, of being able 'to call myself beloved', which—as it so happens—is the meaning of the Hebrew name, David. *Beloved*.

In growing up with this love, my father—and my mother too—enabled me to love myself and to be able to pass this love on to my own children. To this day my father still sends my various articles to friends around the world with the naïve pleasure and pride of someone who thinks his friends might be interested. He still writes me letters telling me how proud he is of me—as a son, a father, a friend, a writer. Remarkably, he still calls me 'darling' and tells me he loves me whenever I speak to him on the phone, or whenever I come to visit.

That's something I like to think might be the crux of everything, and that no amount of therapy, or love from a woman, or friend-ship circle, or professional success can ever replace. That's because nothing can ever fill the great well of longing that comes from the absence of a father's love for his child.

As my father moves further into the evening shadows of his own life, I can see that he is still trying to hand me the torch so that my way might be clearer and lighter than his ever was.

Actually, he passed me this torch a long time ago. I just needed to have eyes to see it.

ACKNOWLEDGEMENTS

Like all books, this beast had many shepherds to help guide, urge, prod and cajole it up the mountainside, often in the face of considerable prevarication and self-doubt.

It began ten years ago with my father agreeing to being interviewed and, ultimately, with his recent acceptance of my prerogative to write this book as I saw fit, despite his preference that certain passages be given the red line. In this he was not just my father but also very much the publisher and champion of free speech.

To Alan Close and Sarah Armstrong, a huge thanks for helping reignite this project in the foothills of Bali during a writing retreat in 2005. To Shelley Kenigsberg, my thanks for following suit two years later from another remote corner of the island.

As fellow members of our exclusive writing club in Byron Bay, Vanessa Gorman and Alan Close constantly reassured me of the value of writing boldly and honestly. Their early readings of this manuscript—and their laughter in all the right places—did wonders for my self-belief. To Vanessa go extra special thanks for your constant love and friendship.

Thank you, too, to Craig McGregor, veteran author, journalistic hero and friend, who continually encouraged me back to the blank screen; and to my oldest friend Anna Fienberg, author and 'queen of the metaphor', for your belief in this book from the beginning, for reading an early draft of the manuscript and for providing me with a lifetime of writerly conversations.

To Amanda Ressom, Rafia Morgan, Turiya Hanover, Alima Cameron, Nyck Jeanes, Volker Krohn, Jutka Freiman, Greg McHale, Michael Shaw and Jane Enter, my profound thanks for helping facilitate and encourage the investigation of difficult psychological terrain and, in so doing, reminding me that a journalist's voyage of discovery often begins with himself.

To Cameron O'Reilly, Ian Darling, Paul Collings, Rob Hirst, Andrew Lee and Monica Masero, many thanks for your unstinting support. Cameron, as you rightly said to me whenever my confidence wavered: 'You're already very pregnant with this book. You may as well give birth.'

To Sue Joseph, my supervisor at University of Technology Sydney and—at times—my one-woman cheer squad, we both know this book would never have seen the light of day had you not proposed it as part of a doctoral program. Thank you for your constant support and feedback. I promise you the exegesis is coming!

To my friend and former assistant, Carla Versitano, who read an early draft, *grazie* for helping me continue in the face of our many obstacles, large and small.

To my first literary agent, Mary Cunnane, who closed up shop at the very time she was reading this book—*purely a coincidence, she tells me*—my thanks to you for giving this project your imprimatur and for recommending Gaby Naher as the person to pick up where you left off.

To Ali Lavau, and Sarah Baker at Allen & Unwin, my thanks

to you too. This book is infinitely better for your many suggestions and scrupulous editing. To my publisher, Jane Palfreyman, thank you for putting me in their safe hands and for believing in this book from the outset.

To Merran Morrison go arguably my biggest thanks of all—not only for always believing in the value of this memoir, and for urging me to rescue it from the bottom drawer, but also for allowing yourself to be written about when so much was at stake. I don't know many spouses who would have shown such grace under pressure.

To my parents, Bernard and Barbara, and my sister Deborah and brother Daniel, my love and gratitude for your trust in allowing me to write about our family from my own perspective. As we all know, it is no small thing to invite so many potential strangers to our table.

Finally, to my daughters Jordan and Hannah, who chose not to read this book before its publication, thank you for your huge leap of faith, and for allowing me to write about some of the matters closest to our hearts. I hope your love and trust will be vindicated.

'Card Game' by A.D. Hope is reproduced on page 147 by arrangement with the Licensor, The AD Hope Estate, c/- Curtis Brown (Aust) Pty Ltd.

The excerpt on page 263 is from William Butler Yeats' 'The Stolen Child'.

The excerpt on page 272 from 'It Happens to Those Who Live Alone' by David Whyte is reproduced with permission.